CITIES FIT TO LIVE IN

CITIES

URBAN ENVIRONMENT NO. 1

FIT TO LIVE IN

and how we can make them happen

Recent Articles on the Urban Environment
edited and with a Foreword by

Walter McQuade

THE MACMILLAN COMPANY, NEW YORK, NEW YORK

COLLIER-MACMILLAN LIMITED, LONDON

The Macmillan Company
866 Third Avenue, New York, N.Y. 10022
Collier-Macmillan Canada Ltd.
Toronto, Ontario

Library of Congress Catalog Card Number: 76–158069
First Printing
Printed in the United States of America

Contents

Foreword

THIS book is about thinking about cities. The thoughts come from a group of professionals generally called city planners, although some of them would contest the designation, for city planning today is a somewhat uncomfortable profession, at least in the United States.

A leading British planner, Arthur Ling, recently asked Carl Feiss, an equally eminent American: "What is happening to the planning profession as such?" [1] He got a typically Feissty answer: "I would like to be a psychiatrist and put the American Institute of Planners on a couch because it would be a very remunerative and long treatment." Feiss went on to describe a three-way split that divides the planners in the United States today—the professors of city planning at the universities, the planning officials at various levels of government, and the independent consultant planners. These groups disagree vehemently on the very dimension of their profession.

It is obvious that the large cities are fallen on evil days, also that we all feel implicated in the downturn. What the planners disagree about among themselves is the extent of their negligence—or, to put it more accurately, their professional capability to provide political leaders with solutions that will really solve anything. The poverty, the squalor, the human-against-human violence of the cities—are these troubles as amenable to planning solutions as the physical complaints such as traffic congestion?

The easy answer is No. But city planners are people who spend most of their working hours trying to affect the form, texture, and feeling of cities. They must take all urban disorders personally.

The book you hold in your hand could easily have concentrated on certain of the newer directions in city planning, such as the growing involvement of communities in the planning act or the whole issue of "new cities." Or the book could have been focused on those psychological studies regarding the territorial imperative of humans in cities and the effects of various kinds of overcrowding; or on the visual culture of the cities; or on specific conundrums such as the location of jetports. A very fat volume could have been put together on the subject of urban housing alone.

Or the book could have been split into two sections, one about the rich in cities, one about the poor. What does Thamesmead have to do with Resurrection City, LeRoi Jones with the developers of the Astor Hotel site in Manhattan? It is in the hope that they do in fact have to do with one another that the book is organized less categorically. The material was chosen simply for its interest and pertinency. Where articles are grouped, the grouping was indicated by the content; for example, a section of pieces on advocacy planning, a development with a controversial past and an unsure future.

Is it evasive to suggest that the hope of the planning profession—and of the cities too—lies in a broadening of sights? I hope it is not evasive, because it is a conclusion that seems to me to be unavoidable. The danger, of course, is

[1] As reported in the *Journal of the Town Planning Institute* in England, March, 1969.

that large treatments tend to get very abstract. In the past this has been an abiding sin of city planning and of planners—broadness has meant vagueness. Although the many planners I've known and worked with have been among the pleasantest, most decent, wittiest, and warmest of people, and almost all of them have been winning speakers, when they wrote it down, they disappeared. After you had read a few thousand words of their writing you began to forget what they looked like. They were gone, leaving you alone in a tent of paper decorated with statistics.

This is not so true as it used to be, certainly not of the authors included in this book, and perhaps we can take it as a hopeful sign about planning in general.

The single other prefatory point to be made is that this book is not particularly directed to planners themselves, although I hope it will be useful to the profession as a kind of mirror. My thanks are due to the authors and the original publishers of their manuscripts; to Clement Alexandre of The Macmillan Company, whose idea the anthology is; to Miss Jacquelyn Menefee, also of Macmillan, for her vital assistance; to Mrs. Sophie Mitrisin and Miss Evelyn Leasher of the New York City Planning Department library for helping generously to satisfy my own appetite for reading in the planning field.

There is also a group thank you due an assortment of people headed by the Mayor of New York, John V. Lindsay, the Chairman of the New York City Planning Commission, Donald H. Elliott, and the other commissioners as well—Gerald R. Coleman, Martin Gallent, Ivan A. Michael, Chester Rapkin, and John E. Zuccotti. I have learned from them all. Also, these words are being put down on paper in the New York City Hall. There is a tradition called "night mayor" here in which various lesser officials are tapped to spend the dark hours as duty officer prowling City Hall, retiring in the morning. As a member of the Planning Commission, tonight is my turn. My tour is almost over now. There is a lightness in the sky beyond Brooklyn Bridge. The telephone has stopped ringing (I hope). Out there is the city, with almost nobody in the streets yet to distract one from its final reality.

As dawn comes on a winter morning you get the impression of New York as an enormous object, as a monument of substance not impulses, of stone not events. The streets are quiet except for a taxi or two bleakly stalking, or an early garbage truck lumbering along like a jungle beast. There are some neon tubes which someone forgot to turn off during the night, and the neon is looking tired as the dawn seeps in. The inanimate city is somber, huge, complex, and in a way reassuring. The people who live behind the millions of dirty windows are just beginning to stretch and wake up, and at this hour you know they are just like anyone else, staggering sleepily toward their coffee cups before their mammoth collective shrewdness and ambition and ruthlessness and obstinacy get warmed up and going.

Then, after breakfast, the people hit the streets, and the city takes its rightful place as their background—a background for hard work, for hope, for tough and breezy humor, but also for outrage, for misunderstanding, for self-seeking, for fear, for innocent oversimplification, for human confusion and congestion of all kinds. When this happens, suddenly it is much harder to make physical planning decisions.

And it will not get any easier. Perhaps, in the end, like the lost Mayas, all of us New Yorkers will abruptly move out, all at once retreat from our city into the sea or up into the mountains. Maybe that will happen, but I doubt it. Toward the end of his most recent campaign for re-election, John Lindsay was asked, in a weary moment, if he thought New York would endure as a city. He said yes, that man would prevail, he thought, and New York, too.

The sky is much lighter now. The people, the real city, not the Mayan city, have had their coffee and are about to submit to the subway. The Mayor is having his coffee too, most probably, and will be coming down here to try to deal with all of those human problems that are stretching the city planning profession, to get us all through another dangerous New York day. My thanks to him for the use of the office.

—*Walter McQuade*

section one PROBLEMS

Introduction

VIOLENT crime; rioting; open hostility between community and police
force; the alienation and loneliness of life in large apartment developments; drugs; garbage: these are the problems discussed in the following
articles, and none of them is new to the urban scene. Certainly crime, as
Robert Gold indicates, was at least equally widespread during periods of
the past, as in Paris of the 1600s, when whole neighborhoods made their
living off it for generations. Perhaps cities are not really any sicker now.
Perhaps they only seem so, because it is *our* illness, and the remedy is not
in sight.

Perhaps. But, in fact, all the specific difficulties, as these pages repeatedly
demonstrate, are charged and darkened in the U.S. today by an overriding
general problem that *is* new: racial polarization. It is this which renders the
difficult so close to impossible, and threatens to reduce our cities to armed
fortresses. Drug addiction in a unified population is one problem; it becomes another, and far harder to solve, when the Reverend Andrew Young
can call it, with reason, "a kind of suicide for people who don't have the
strength to live or the courage to die, and the white man is always there
to help him kill himself."

—W. McQ.

1

Urban Violence and Contemporary Defensive Cities

Robert Gold

VIOLENT crime has been increasing at an alarming pace in large metropolitan areas of the United States [1] at a time when efforts are being made to renew entire neighborhoods in central cities and new suburban communities and new towns are being built to accommodate our growing national population. Some of the causes of violent behavior may stem from the physical environment. For these reasons, it is timely to inquire whether the design and form of our cities are related to urban violence, and whether violence can be controlled or prevented by planning the physical environment. Whatever the causes of violence, it is now a hard fact of American life that violence has consequences of its own and is causing changes in the urban environment. Therefore, it is important to determine what these changes are,

Robert Gold, AIP, is Assistant Director for Social and Economic Research of the National Capital Planning Commission in Washington, D.C. During 1968 and 1969, he was on part-time loan to the National Commission on the Causes and Prevention of Violence and has participated in other research on urban problems. This article is an abridged version of "Urban Violence and the Design and form of the Urban Environment," Chapter 16 of Volume 12, *Crimes of Violence,* Task Force on Individual Acts of Violence, Report to the National Commission on the Causes and Prevention of Violence (Washington: Government Printing Office, 1969). Robert Gold is the principal author of the chapter. E. Brendon Murphy and James McGregor of Princeton University wrote some of the preliminary materials. The chapter is also based on the proceedings of a Seminar on Architectural and Urban Design and the Prevention of Violence, convened on November 16, 1968, under the auspices of the Task Force on Individual Acts of Violence. Reprinted by permission of the *Journal of the American Institute of Planners,* Vol. 36, No. 3 (May 1970).

why and how they are occurring, and what they portend for the future of urban society in America. Historical precedents and the warning of the Kerner Commission that America "is moving toward two societies, one black, one white—separate and unequal" [2] compel us to consider the dangers of violence in our cities.

Few definite relationships between the design and form of the urban environment and violent behavior have been defined in the past. The purpose of this article is to summarize available knowledge, report different ideas, and describe some conclusions about these relationships.

URBAN ENVIRONMENT AND VIOLENT BEHAVIOR

Three possible relationships between the design and form of the urban environment and violent behavior can be suggested:

1. Design and form of the urban environment may directly *control* violence. Residential areas, for example, may be selected by a criterion of distance from populations with real or assumed tendencies to commit violence, or individual buildings or entire communities may be "fortified" by crime-control features with social and aesthetic values subordinated or entirely eliminated.

2. Design and form of the urban environment may encourage positive forms of behavior by such means as participation in the process of planning, building, and managing the environment. To the extent positive behavior is promoted, negative behavior—including violence—is *prevented.*

3. Design and form of the urban environment may *invite* violence. Because people may consider buildings or open spaces as negative symbols or may attribute sufficiently neutral or negative values to certain places, they are willing to destroy or deface buildings or to commit violent acts in these areas.

If violent crime continues to increase, the very character of our cities may depend on which of the relationships between design and behavior are emphasized by urban designers, public officials, and to an even greater extent, urban consumers. If all three relationships are valid and if urban design or consumer choices are primarily oriented toward crime control, our cities will be caught in a cycle of increasing violence in which crime control features of the urban environment will generate more violence and create other economically and socially undesirable conditions.

The following environmental variables are factors in the three relationships mentioned above:

1. *Space* and *location* can permit or limit behavior.

2. *Distance* and *access to space* can separate potential victims from potential offenders.

3. *Visibility* can enable observation, a deterrent to violence.

4. *Scale* can control types and amounts of violence. The absolute size of a design feature can impede entry, while overall size relative to the population groups who may commit or act to control violence can constrain their participation. A garden wall and a city wall are similar means of restricting access to space, differing only in scale; yet the protection afforded by setting a house apart from others and setting a city apart from its surroundings is quite different.

5. *Mastery, control, and ownership of property* may influence the values people impute to the urban environment and thereby affect behavior.

6. *High residential densities, poor physical condition, and low general quality of the urban environment,* usually associated with other features of poverty and deprivation, may be causally related to violent behavior.

It is important to ask: What role has the urban environment played in the past in preventing or controlling violence, what present trends can be observed, and what are the consequences likely to be if urban violence continues to increase?

HISTORICAL PERSPECTIVE

During many periods in history, urban populations were exposed to violence committed by individuals or small groups against other persons and property: civil rebellion, riots, and commotions in opposition to political leadership or conditions in society; and military attack from outside the society. We are mainly concerned with the first type of violence, although civil rebellion is indirectly of interest because, at times, individual violence became so widespread in cities that it had the characteristics of riots. Although fortifications built to prevent invasion had secondary uses in maintaining public order, military attack is wholly outside our scope. A few selected examples illustrate historical responses to violence in cities.[3]

Building Types

The history of cities from the Middle Ages to the present can be described as a sequence of changing defense perimeters. The comparatively small, walled city, with sentries and gatekeepers, protected everyone inside. General descriptions of life in medieval Europe suggest that criminals were driven out of cities whenever possible. They retired to forests and preyed on unprotected travelers. Cities were fortified by walls as much for protection from these domestic "enemies" as from foreign ones. In later years, the larger city contained its own criminal quarters and demanded new forms of protection. The primary environmental units of defense against violence were individual buildings. Apart from larger structures designed for military or civil defense, there are numerous individual buildings for which safety was obviously the paramount design consideration—medieval towers, for example.[4] Many family-owned, slender, prismatic towers—some over 300 feet high—were built in Italian cities during the twelfth century. The ground floors were used only for access to the floor above, which could be reached by retractable ladders. Towers of similar nature, built before the twelfth century, are found in villages in Svanetia in the western Caucasus, where blood feuds and vendettas were common until the nineteenth century. Other examples are the Round Towers of Ireland, built as both belfries and sanctuaries by monastic communities between the tenth and twelfth centuries.[5] These towers were between 70 and 120 feet high with entrances about 15 feet above the ground, which were also reached by retractable ladders.

Whether intentional or not, residential buildings providing good defense against violent entry can be cited throughout history. Safety was provided through architectural forms, such as iron grills and safety chains on doors, and by such management procedures as posting doormen or guards at entrances. Houses of wealthy Greeks and Romans were arranged around interior courtyards so that most of the door and window openings of each house faced inward.[6] Living quarters in the urban palaces of the Italian Renaissance were on the second floor or above. Palaces were arranged around interior courtyards reached by archways from the street while gateways and other entrances were guarded by heavy doors. First-floor windows were relatively small, often placed high up in the walls, and were protected by iron grills. Even the heavily rusticated stonework of the first-floor walls suggests an obstacle to attack or violent entry. Many older apartment houses in French cities had similar arrangements, with one large gateway leading from the street to an interior courtyard. The front façade of many Georgian townhouses was separated from the sidewalk by an open area about 6 feet wide and 6 feet deep. This area was enclosed by iron railings and bridged by steps leading to the front door. Basement windows were fitted with iron grills, and front doors were heavily constructed and bolted with massive locks.

Early Civilizations

Many early civilizations created organizations to maintain public order and prevent crime in cities.[7] Jerusalem under the Hebrews was one of the first cities to deploy a police force organized to protect different quarters of the city. In early Chinese cities, policemen were posted on important streets and kept registers of all in-

habitants. Each had several assistants, with each assistant responsible for ten houses to which he had permanent rights of entry. In ancient Incan cities, each policeman maintained a night-and-day watch over a group of ten households. He had permanent rights of entry to these houses, and people were not allowed to lock their doors at any time.

Both Greek and Roman police forces were organized to protect different quarters of each city. Roman police controlled an area extending a number of miles outside Rome. They were assisted by citizens who patrolled their own streets. The organization of French police was strongly influenced by Roman examples. Citizen night watches began in French towns during the sixth century.

The evidence suggests that from early times municipal administrations were aware that violence and the urban environment were ecologically related, and that the primary environmental unit of defense against violence for the private citizen was the individual dwelling.

Medieval Cities

By the thirteenth century, most medieval towns had been granted charters of self-government and were in effect city-states under the political control of their citizens—mainly merchants, craftsmen, and artisans. A high degree of social organization existed, and municipal institutions were developed to handle every aspect of community life.[8] The size of these towns facilitated communications and enabled every town to have a defensive wall around its perimeter. These walls were up to thirty feet in height and normally had two to four gates. Within the walls, all citizens and visitors were subject to municipal laws, which offered considerable protection to persons and property. The Catholic Church also contributed to public safety by offering sanctuary on its properties. Penalties for crime were harsh, and anyone found guilty was banished from the town. The citizens of each town provided for its defense. The gates were closed at night, and the walls and streets were patrolled. The sense of community in these towns, the degree to which citizens protected each other, and the citizen's view of his town as an island of peace in a hostile world were remarkable. Violent crime does not appear to have been a major problem in these communities.

These peaceful conditions did not endure indefinitely. By the fifteenth century, security problems had become serious in many towns.[9] Large numbers of undesirables were attracted to urban centers. Murder, rape, and robbery were widespread, and many persons abused the right of sanctuary in churches because ecclesiastical courts were less severe than civil courts.

Paris

The city of Paris is worth examining because its problems of public order developed earlier, were more severe, and are better documented than for most cities. Paris was one of the largest medieval cities, and its physical form—a pattern of narrow irregular streets, few open spaces, and tightly packed houses—is typical of this era.

In 1032, Henri I instituted a city police force, consisting of a chief and twelve armed men.[10] At night, the force was supplemented by citizen guards who patrolled the streets at regular intervals. In the reign of Louis IX, a cavalry force of sixty men was added. Apparently these measures were not effective. A report in 1258 states there were fires, murders, rapes, and robberies all over Paris every night, even under the walls of the Palace of the Louvre.[11] Louis IX was particularly concerned about crime and made a serious attempt to purge vice from the city, but failed.

In 1306, new police reforms, introduced by Philip IV, assigned policemen to a dozen quarters of the city rather than to the traditional central location. Extra policemen were assigned to the suburbs outside the city walls about 1450. In 1559, the civilian night watch was abolished, and again the number of professional police was increased. However, in the sixteenth century, the police system fell into disrepute because of corruption. Repeated attempts to banish criminals from Paris and to control their movement through the city gates failed and lawlessness increased.

During the late sixteenth and early seventeenth centuries, the state of public order and safety in Paris continued to deteriorate.[12] There was no street lighting, because householders

Kilmacduagh Round Tower, County Galway, Ireland
(PHOTO COURTESY IRISH TOURIST BOARD)

did not put lights in their front windows though this was required by law. The citizen guard no longer patrolled the streets at night. There were whole districts in the city where criminals were so numerous that armed police refused to enter after nightfall. Some criminals even formed guilds, and police were suspected of being in league with criminals. Ambushes were common in the center of the city. House-holders barricaded their doors at night and kept weapons beside them.

In the reign of Louis XIII, the police were again ordered to clear the streets, but failed to do so. Medieval slum districts, known as *cours des miracles*, were completely under the control of criminals and destitutes. The authorities were powerless in these sections of the city. Because the streets were so dangerous, decrees forbidding citizens to carry arms were largely ignored.

After 1667, Louis XIV reversed the trend of increasing lawlessness through rigid new legislation, police reforms, and appointment of the very able Gabriel-Nicolas de la Reynie as the new Lieutenant-General of Police who extended the responsibility of the Paris police beyond the prevention of crime and apprehension of criminals to include, among other things, the authority to carry out public works. La Reynie restored order during the next decade. By the end of the century, he had illuminated the streets with more than 6,000 lanterns and driven out the inhabitants of the most notorious *cour des miracles*, near the Port Saint-Denis, by razing the entire district. La Reynie was also responsible for planting trees on the Champs Elysees and building the Pont-Royal. He had a city plan prepared for Paris. There is no indication from the information available, however, that he saw any connection between his activities as an urbanist and his efforts to control crime.

The lieutenant-generals who succeeded La Reynie in the eighteenth century extended his work and made remarkable improvements in the urban environment. Under their direction, the remaining *cours des miracles* were razed, street signs were placed on corner buildings, the house numbering system was devised, the Corn and Leather markets were built, street lighting was extended to all the streets of Paris, four whole districts of Paris were paved, the

rue Feydeau was constructed, and the Paris Bourse was founded.[13]

By the eighteenth century, public order had generally been restored to Paris. The city was much safer than London, and one writer claimed that a person could walk the streets day or night with purse in hand, without the slightest fear.[14] These developments occurred during the period of the absolute monarchy in France. During the seventeenth and eighteenth centuries, France was the acknowledged leader in European architecture and urban design.[15] Great palaces, gardens, public buildings, parks, and royal squares were constructed. The typically medieval urban form of the center of Paris was radically changed. The glorification of the monarchy was a major influence and motive in creating this architecture. However, it is notable that the literature of the period contains no discussions of any relationships between the mainstream of urban design and concerns for the problems of public order.

London

The prevalence of crime in early eighteenth-century London was much higher than in any other part of England.[16] Conditions of crime and public disorder during this period were similar to those in late sixteenth-century Paris. Criminals and destitutes occupied whole districts which were completely outside the control of public authorities. To protect themselves and their property, citizens armed themselves, barricaded their doors, and kept off the streets at night. Severe penalties were adopted for even minor crimes, but deterrence was negligible because of insufficient law enforcement. The severity of the law can be judged by the fact that there were 223 crimes which were solely punishable by the death penalty.

Similar to the Parisian *cours des miracles*, there were entire populations living in densely settled slum districts of London whose sole means of subsistence was crime.[17] Blocks of dwellings were built over alleys, in courts, or on other open spaces, creating labyrinths of interior passageways which connected whole districts. Rooms were filled with people living under appalling conditions. There was little if any security for law-abiding citizens, who armed themselves and their servants and fortified their houses. Many people kept pistols within reach while they slept. Similar conditions existed in other English cities in the late eighteenth century as towns grew quickly in size and environmental conditions deteriorated during the Industrial Revolution.

Crime in London began to decrease slowly in the late eighteenth century. After 1829, new police forces were very successful, and within thirty years violent crime ceased to be a national problem.

Conclusions from History

Although there is little uniform historical evidence about relationships between design and form of the urban environment and violent crime, some generalizations can be made to obtain a perspective on problems in contemporary American cities.

1. The *level* of urban violence has not been the same throughout the history of Western civilization. During some periods, urban violence was so widespread that protection was exceptionally important in the design and form of the urban environment. When medieval cities were established, urban violence was exceptionally low. During other periods, safety in cities was imposed by repressive police tactics. Urban violence was so uncontrolled in some cases that it was the single most important fact of city life.

2. The actual or potential *targets* of crime are not apparent from historical evidence. The information available implies that a man who could afford to arm himself and fortify his house had something to defend, and hence was the actual or potential victim.

3. There is some historical evidence about

Castello Estense, Ferrara, Italy
(PHOTO COURTESY ITALIAN STATE
TOURIST OFFICE)

violent *offenders*, but the portraits are strangely depersonalized. The clearest picture is suggested by the *cours des miracles* in Paris, where pools of criminals lived in the same districts and victimized city residents for more than a century. These areas may have been entirely criminal districts in which all or most of the inhabitants made a living through illegal activities. However, there is no evidence that all Parisian criminals of the time lived in the *cours des miracles,* and many residents of these districts may have simply been impoverished.

4. Historically, three environmental approaches to crime control can be distinguished:

A. *Arrangement of urban form and activity.* Most people in most societies have opposed violence. The arrangement of urban form and activity suggests that when enough people who disapproved of crime were brought together, their presence *generally* deterred crime.

B. *Use of protective devices.* These have included all physical devices for the safety or protection of people and property, such as walls, moats, doors, and particularly door locks and entryway designs. They were widely used to control access to space, that is, to seal off or insulate particular areas from trespass.

C. *Management of the environment.* Control of the environment to prevent crime has been the principal objective of law enforcers throughout history. The razing of the *cours des miracles,* the Chinese block surveillance systems, and the Incan police organization are only a few of many examples of environmental management.

CURRENT TRENDS OF URBAN VIOLENCE

Although many questions are unanswered and many refinements are needed in reporting crime and violence, particularly by types of geographic areas, it is important to summarize available findings on violence in America that are pertinent to the design and form of the urban environment.[18]

Rates of arrest vary considerably by economic status, race, and age of offenders. It is necessary to conclude from the admittedly imperfect data that the true rates of the four major violent crimes—criminal homicide, forcible rape, robbery, and aggravated assault—are many times higher for poor than for affluent population, for Negroes than for whites and for younger age groups (especially those eighteen to twenty-four years old) than for older age groups. The racial difference is particularly relevant to the urban environment. In 1967, the reported Negro arrest rate was about seventeen times the white rate for homicide, eleven times the white rate for forcible rape, and ten times the white arrest rate for robbery and aggravated assault. Socioeconomic differences and numerous biases in arrest data—for example, poor Negroes may be disproportionately arrested on suspicion—cannot be overlooked, but neither can Negro-white differences in arrest rates be fully explained by these features.

To a considerable extent, the characteristics of persons who most frequently commit violent crimes are the same as those of the population group residing in central cities of large metropolitan areas. Consequently, the combined reported arrest rate for the major violent offenses in 1967 was about eight times greater in cities with populations of 250,000 or more than in those with populations between 10,000 and 25,000 and ten times greater than in rural areas. Six cities of more than one million population, representing about 12 percent of the population of all reporting areas, contributed about 33 percent of all major violent crimes reported in the United States. Twenty-six cities of 500,000 or more population, whose residents totaled about one-fifth of those in the reporting areas, contributed nearly half of all major violent crimes reported. Suburbs have generally reported lower crime rates, except for forcible rape, than all but the smaller cities. The same relationships are generally true for nonviolent property crimes.[19]

The true offense rates for homicide, robbery, and aggravated assault have probably increased significantly during recent years in the nation as a whole and particularly in large cities.[20] In cities with populations of more than 250,000 persons, the reported offense rate for robbery per 100,000 population increased 90 percent between 1963 and 1967. In the same four years, the reported homicide rate increased 46 percent. It must also be concluded that the true rates and volumes for the same violent crimes have increased rapidly in suburban areas during recent years, although they started from a much lower level. Thus, while the reported rates for all four violent crimes increased significantly in both central cities and suburban areas, the gaps between the two sets of rates and volumes widened considerably, making even greater geographic differences.

The statistical portrait of victims resembles that of offenders. The National Opinion Research Center Study for the President's Crime Commission showed the probability of being a victim of forcible rape, robbery, and aggravated assault is many times greater for central city residents than for suburban residents, for people twenty to twenty-nine years of age than for people of older ages, for males than for females, for Negroes than for whites, and for poor than for affluent populations. A recent survey in Chicago concluded that the chances of physical assault for a Negro ghetto dweller were 1 in 77, while the odds were 1 in 10,000 for an upper-middle-class suburbanite.[21]

When victims were related to offenders, homicide, forcible rape, and aggravated assault were found to be principally intraracial crimes, committed mainly by Negroes against Negroes and whites against whites. The only exception was robbery, where over 40 percent of all interactions involved Negro offenders and white victims.[22]

Thus, while the middle-class, white taxpayer often bears a disproportionate share of the cost of crime control and perhaps of robbery, the low-income Negro living in the central city pays disproportionately in the pain caused by other types of violence. Although the rate and volume of crime is increasing in suburban areas, much more violence today is committed in central cities.

CURRENT PRACTICES IN ENVIRONMENTAL PROTECTION

Urban environments have already been designed to some extent for protection. Yet, despite historical precedent, professional planners, urban designers, and architects in America have paid little attention to violence. There are some fragmentary references in the professional literature, and there have been practical applications in a few cities. However, there is no well-founded body of information on protection in the design professions today.

There are a number of reasons for this apparent neglect. Comparatively little empirical study has been undertaken to relate physical design to the behavioral sciences. Theories of violent behavior have presented few, if any, practical guidelines for urban design.[23] The philosophy and proposal of the Utopian Socialists who called for and attempted reform during the nineteenth century had a profound influence on the work of important twentieth-century urban design thinkers, such as Le Corbusier and Ebenezer Howard. Much of our physical planning even today is based on the behavioral assumption that if the quality of the urban environment were good enough, crime and violence would disappear. This implies that, since the goal of the design professions is to improve the urban environment, violence per se need not be considered. This tradition explains, in part, why few contemporary design proposals specifically acknowledge or consider crime or other social pathologies as major problems.

Yet some writers have considered relationships between design and crime. Also, increasing numbers of urban consumers have illustrated design possibilities in seeking to control crime by "hardening targets," and some neighborhood groups have adopted techniques of environmental management to make their communities safer.

Modern architectural features, such as elevators, enclosed stairways, pedestrian underpasses, and underground parking garages, offer seclusion and screening from public view and are often settings for violent behavior. This problem can be overcome. For example, the stairways of one public housing project were built on the exterior of buildings, enclosed in glass, and lighted well. Crime in these stairways virtually ceased. Visibility has also been improved by selection, placement, and trimming of trees and shrubbery, better street lighting, use of closed-circuit television systems, and elimination of places of concealment.

Improved safety devices, including locks, safety chains, and inexpensive alarms have recently been developed and are being utilized more and more. A simple alarm buzzer that can be easily carried or attached to handbags, doors, or windows is now available. Electrified fences are being used in suburban neighborhoods to protect residential properties. Increasing numbers of people are purchasing sophisticated intruder alarm systems, clock devices that turn lights and radios on and off in unoccupied dwellings at set hours, firearms, chemical weapons for personal protection, and watchdogs. Neighbors are more watchful of each other's dwellings, and guards, doormen, attendants, and closed-circuit television systems are becoming increasingly common.

One new subdivision under construction outside Washington, D.C., offers maximum security for all residents.[24] The sixty-seven high-cost residences in this 167-acre project will be individually guarded by electronic alarms and closed-circuit television units. The entire development will be surrounded by two fences, broken for entry at only two points, both with guardhouses. Residents will be telephoned to approve visitors. The two miles of fencing will be surveyed by a closed-circuit television system and fortified by hidden electronic sensors. All residents will carry special credentials for identification.

Bricked-in, boarded-up, barred, and shielded windows are observed with increasing frequency in some cities. In some cases, no windows or evidence of occupancy at all has been observed on ground floors of buildings. In the future, retail establishments and perhaps residences may find it desirable to use new kinds of glass that take ten to twenty-five minutes to break. The cost is at least four times that of conventional glass, but insurance premiums are reduced on the contents of display windows and other merchandise.[25] Other features of building construction can also affect protection. "Soft" interior walls and unpartitioned ceilings allow burglars to move easily between adjoining establishments. Floors, roofs, skylights, and elevators can be designed to reduce vulnerability.[26]

Address numbers are frequently obscured, especially in suburban areas. It has been shown in one city that police response time can be short-ened, with increased apprehension of criminals, simply by uniform placement of address numbers so they are plainly visible to police day and night.

Since 1965, South San Francisco has had a municipal ordinance for crime control requiring the police to submit recommendations on zoning and other land-use applications. Local standards for lighting and other features have shown positive results in crime reduction. Because design and relatively inexpensive equipment can contribute to crime control, it has been suggested that every local police department should consult with architects and property owners on protective features, particularly at the early stages of building design and construction.

Examples of environmental management by citizen groups in the New York City area have been reported recently. Residents of the Castlehill Complex on Seward Avenue formed a volunteer Tenants' Patrol. Members are on duty in the evenings and carry no guns or night sticks. Their duties include escorting women and children to apartments, discouraging excessive noise, and keeping the public areas of the buildings free of drug addicts who tended to congregate there. Women representing about 480 families in Marian Gardens (Jersey City) formed a Mothers' Patrol. Members patrol the neighborhood in cars to control vandalism and delinquency among children and adolescents.

More than 3,000 citizen volunteers with limited powers assist the police in New York City, especially during evening hours. One such group, the Electchester Auxiliary Police in Flushing, Queens, patrols its own neighborhood. Each member works three or four evenings a week. Members check the security of buildings and perform services such as escorting people from bus stops to their homes. Since the auxiliary began its work last year, the crime rate in Electchester has fallen 35 percent.

Several writers concerned with environmental relationships of crime have pointed out that places where large numbers of people congregate and spaces that are well lighted and visible from the interiors of surrounding buildings tend to have less crime because of the criminal's fear of apprehension. Concentrations of people in particular places depend on activities people engage in during different times of the day or

night, land-use patterns, and modes of transportation. Jane Jacobs believes that mixtures of
land uses are needed to achieve greater safety
and that safe streets are those frequented at all
times of the day and night. Such streets have
commercial and other activities at the ground
level, some of which go on during evening
hours, with residences on upper floors.[27] The
difficulty in this idea for planning contemporary
cities has been illustrated by a study of Oakland, California. Establishments open during
evening hours occupy only four miles of the
city's 2,400 total miles of street frontage.[28]

Another author believes that three kinds of
urban areas should be distinguished to explain
relationships between personal safety and activity patterns during evening hours when most
crimes are committed: (a) areas of solely daytime activity that are safe in the evening because they are virtually deserted and therefore
unattractive to criminals; (b) areas that are safe
because the intensity of evening activity makes
the risk of being seen committing a crime too
great; and (c) areas between the extremes that
are unsafe.[29] To discourage crime, the author
proposes that theaters, bars, restaurants, and
other establishments open during the evening
hours be grouped together in a small number of
"evening squares" which would be safe because
of the number of people present and because
good design would eliminate poorly lit places
and those screened from the view of many people. Parking lots, for example, where crimes
often take place, should be near the center of
these safe areas, not at the periphery. Industrial, commercial, and other daytime activities
should be located in areas where there would
be no need to enter or pass through them during nighttime hours. Low-density suburban residential areas, which are relatively free of violent crime, would be linked to other safe areas
by automobile corridors that would be comparatively safe, because people driving on expressways or arterial streets are rarely the victims of crime.

CONTEMPORARY DEFENSIVE CITIES

There is little doubt that large American
cities are currently being fortified against crime.
Historically, when political institutions have

failed to protect the public, individuals have
taken steps to safeguard themselves, their families, and their property. The present period is
no different in this respect. The urban environment is being fortified today, not primarily by
public decisions, but mainly through the multiplicity of private choices and decisions individuals make in our decentralized society. The
private market is responding to growing demand for an increasing range of crime-control
devices and other means of safety. In some
cases, safety has already become a commodity
that is explicitly sold or rented with real estate.

It is important to consider how Americans
will live in our large cities in the future, because if urban crime continues to increase, it is
likely that the urban environment will increasingly reflect this condition. Five geographic elements of a modern defensive urban environment based on safety can be suggested:

1. An economically declining central business
district in the inner city would primarily serve
central city residents and be protected by comparatively large numbers of people shopping
or working in buildings during daytime hours.
During evening and nighttime hours, the central area would be largely deserted and "sealed
off" to protect properties and tax base. Anyone
on the streets would attract police attention.
Modern technology would enable surveillance
of downtown streets by closed-circuit television
units mounted on building roofs. A variety of
other crime control devices, combined with
methods of environmental management, would
protect the interiors of individual buildings.

2. High-rise apartment buildings and residential "compounds" of other types would be
fortified "cells" for upper-middle- and high-
income populations living at prime locations in
the inner city, their residents protected by various expensive methods.

3. Suburban neighborhoods, geographically
removed from the central city, would be "safe
areas," protected mainly by racial and economic
homogeneity and by distance from population
groups with the greatest propensities to commit crimes.

4. Expressways would be "sanitized corridors" connecting other safe areas and would be
safe themselves because they permit movement
by comparatively high-speed automobile transportation. Other modes of transportation would

be safe or unsafe in different degrees during day and nighttime hours.

5. Other residential neighborhoods in the central city would be unsafe in differing degrees during day and nighttime hours. At the extreme, some residential neighborhoods would be human jungles. Crime in these areas would be frequent, widespread, and perhaps entirely out of police control, even during the daytime. These neighborhoods would be modern counterparts of seventeenth-century Parisian *cours des miracles* and various districts of London during the eighteenth century. Subcultures of violence would be localized in these areas of even more homogeneous lower-class populations than today.

This model assumes that if violence in our large cities continues to increase, the future urban environment would not be abandoned, but would be lived in defensively as during the violent times in the past. Individual structures and groups of buildings would be the basic units of environmental defense, constructed or altered to resist unauthorized entry. More efforts would be made to increase visibility and eliminate "blind spots" in the environment. People would avoid areas known or believed to be dangerous. A basic strategy, again as in the past, would be to exclude those regarded as potential criminals from certain areas of the city. Other areas would be perceived as "no-man's land" to be avoided by all outsiders except the police.

The model is based on defensive features found today to some extent in almost every large American city. These rudiments can be vastly intensified, enlarged, or extended. It is also based on historical considerations. The urban environment has always been designed in part for protection, and it is noteworthy that many environmental responses to urban violence have not differed greatly under different political systems.

Although current uses of the urban environment to obtain safety are not fundamentally different from those used in the past, the underlying social factors along with the economic and social consequences that defensive cities portend for the future—especially in light of the values of our democratic society—are very different today.

Race and Physical Distance

However sensitive we are to present inequalities and historical injustice, our findings show that: *(a)* Negro crime rates are higher and in some types of crimes are rising more than white rates; *(b)* increasingly more Negroes are living in central cities of our large metropolitan areas; *(c)* the volume of crime committed in central cities is greater and is increasing more than in suburban areas; *(d)* victimization risks for both whites and Negroes are far greater for central city than suburban residents; *(e)* violent crime generally diminishes proportionately with physical distance from the inner core of central cities; and *(f)* physical distance of residential neighborhoods from low-income Negro populations in central cities is a variable in obtaining greater safety.

The historical trends of suburbanization, involving residential movements of whites from central cities to suburbs of large U.S. metropolitan areas, began even before World War II. These trends are likely to continue in the future for many reasons unrelated to crime. Nevertheless, it must be concluded that crime during recent years has been an important factor in suburbanization and a cause of white population losses in central cities. As a consequence, central city populations have recently diminished in total size.[30] In this sense, Negro crime has not changed the direction but simply accelerated the trends of white suburbanization.

The physical distance of suburban neighborhoods from central cities is the principal way that suburban residents are protected against crime. Distance substitutes for and is more effective than other deterrent features in central cities. Single-family houses, typical of most suburban communities today, are more vulnerable structures from the viewpoint of design than multifamily apartment buildings and urban row houses. An apartment building or urban row house has more residents and fewer doors and windows at ground level to use for forcible entry. The view from upper floors overlooking fewer entrances allows less concealment and makes it much less practical for criminals to attempt entry.

The purchase of guns by large numbers of

white suburbanites during and following Negro riots of the last few years may be explained by a number of factors, including the greater vulnerability of suburban areas. However, this behavior also suggests two additional features. First, many whites overreact to Negro crime and violence, even when not threatened, although the degree of reaction does not change the conclusion that white population movements from central cities to suburban areas have a rational basis. Second, many Negroes perceive urban violence differently from many whites, and this difference has other significant implications.

Subcultures of Violence and the "Valve" Theory

Urban subcultures of violence in America [31] have major implications for contemporary defensive cities. These subcultures consist of particular population groups that favor and accept violence as normal behavior, not as an illicit activity. The values and attitudes of the subcultures need not be shared by everyone living in particular neighborhoods, but they are most prevalent among lower-class Negro males, ranging in age from late adolescence to late middle age, living in central cities. Failure to commit violence, "to prove oneself a man," for example, is most likely to result in social ostracism, although all persons belonging to the subcultures do not commit violence in all situations.

Few studies distinguish significant differences among poor Negro and white populations living in large American cities. Nevertheless, there are reasons to believe that both the Negro and the white poor are heterogeneous populations in many ways. Evidence suggests that only a small proportion of all Negroes living in large cities and only some of the Negro poor belong to subcultures of violence. These populations have other attitudes and features differentiating them from the larger white and Negro urban society and from the other poor.

It is likely that Negro in-migrants to northern cities from southern rural areas did not bring the values and attitudes characteristic of the subcultures with them. Instead, the subcultures are an urban phenomenon that has emerged indigenously among those born and raised in large American cities. Bringing together large numbers of Negro poor for a substantial time in racially segregated and economically deprived neighborhoods has bred a modern counterpart of the violent subcultures of past centuries.

Members of the subcultures are not "professional" criminals who minimize risks, but angry young men who have no stake in society. They have "heroes" only in their own neighborhoods to imitate, and they commit crimes haphazardly and dangerously, victimizing Negroes more than whites. It is likely that criminal activity does pay off for these subcultures. They have the same material aspirations as the larger Negro and white society, but they have a separate economy of livelihoods and monetary profit made possible by urban living. For these people, the subcultures offer substitute incentives and values for those of the larger society. Once established, attitudes toward violence are learned from life in the subcultures. In this way, as during past centuries, the subcultures of violence can be self-perpetuating for long periods.

Although there are no statistical measurements, the violent subcultures probably account for most crimes committed in central cities today, and contemporary defensive cities may result, in large part, from their existence and growth. In turn, the increasing fragmentation of the urban environment and the specialization of geographic "cells" of defensive cities would institutionalize and perpetuate the subcultures of violence even more. The traditional "value" theory of crime shifts asserts that the volume of crime is not reduced by "hardening targets." If one type of crime, such as robbing buses, is "shut off," crime will shift to other targets, such as robbing taxicabs or stores. Applying this theory to defensive cities, those population groups who flee from the central city to suburban areas or who can afford housing in the fortified "cells" within the central city would obtain protection. Crime would be shifted to unprotected neighborhoods inhabited by the poor, who even now are usually the victims of crime. Crime would be intensified in the neighborhoods where the subcultures of violence are localized, accentuating the values and attitudes distinguishing them.

Economic Effects

Crime is likely to have far-reaching consequences for the future economic health and tax base of central cities. It is axiomatic in economic development programs in the United States that private enterprise avoid or move away from areas of crime or violence. For many reasons, commercial and industrial development does not flourish in areas where public safety is not assured. If crime continues to increase, central cities are likely to become economically depressed—the holes in the doughnuts of prosperous metropolitan economies. The economies of many cities are likely to function at lower levels of development than today—in volumes and types of economic activity, levels of productivity, and types of occupations and earning levels of central city residents. Tax rates are likely to be high, with lower levels of services. Growth of employment opportunities and tax bases as well as investment of private capital to improve the urban environment of central cities are likely to be impaired.

Fragmentation of the Urban Environment

As metropolitan cities in America have exploded horizontally and as metropolitan populations have increased in size, larger geographic areas have come to serve increasingly specialized residential functions. From the beginning of this century, large northern cities functioned as specialized residential places for ethnic minorities in American society. There are two main differences between the present day and the first half of the twentieth century: (a) Negroes now comprise the dominant unassimilated minority in American society; and (b) Negro populations in central cities are much larger now than any other single ethnic minority was in most large northern cities during past decades. As a consequence, the relative scale of specialization now applies to much larger neighborhoods in central cities. Similarly, the economic and social homogeneity of white populations residing in suburban communities and in some central city neighborhoods are features of geographic specialization.

In this way, the urban environment of large American cities has been increasingly socially fragmented since the end of World War II. A concern for protection has probably always been associated to some extent with other more obvious features of increasingly specialized residential functions. However, contemporary defensive cities would create even more fragmentation with even greater social consequences within comparatively limited geographic areas.

The Kerner Commission warned America of the danger of being split into two separate and unequal societies. It is important to describe one of the ways this can happen in the urban environment of large American cities—as a response to crime.

Using *distance* and *access to space* to separate groups of potential victims from potential offenders requires an implicit recognition that some social groups have members who are likely to commit criminal acts. Denying access to space usually involves a more explicit recognition of social groups associated with crime on the basis of such obvious or visible human features as race. In both cases, there must be social expectations about what groups are likely to contain criminals and where crimes are likely to be committed.

Except for fugitives from justice, there are no criminals at large, by legal definition, in contemporary American society. We do not condone the medieval method of banishment or outlawry. The concept of the criminal has changed as legal rights have been expanded. Consequently, it is not possible now to recognize formally or informally potential offenders as individuals, but only as members of social groups.

Greater safety would be obtained by using distance and denying access to space. Yet, as we have seen, the other consequences of contemporary defensive cities are socially distructive: further fragmentation of the urban environment, formation of excessively parochial communities, greater segregation of racial groups and economic classes, imposition of presumptive definitions of criminality on the poor and on racial minorities, increasing chances of vigilantism, and polarization of attitudes on many issues. The use of space in this manner would inevitably limit the freedom of law-abiding citizens of all races and economic classes to move safely through large sections of the urban environment, to enjoy the diversity of urban life, to choose living accommodations among many safe residential neighborhoods, and to understand and communicate directly with other social groups in our pluralistic society.

OTHER BEHAVIORAL RELATIONSHIPS

Not all crime is committed by strangers. A significant proportion of all murders, assaults, and rapes are committed against friends or intimates.[32] In these cases, the physical environment is irrelevant, except perhaps in individual psychological ways.

Nor does historical evidence support the premise of environmental determination that there are simple or direct causal relationships between the physical environment and positive or negative forms of behavior, including crime. Cities have differed during past centuries in amounts of violence, but not because some had particular designs or urban forms conducive to violence and others did not. Indeed, it is likely that the physical environment is more a result than a cause of human behavior. This is consistent with the traditional view prevalent among humanists that the architecture and urban design of any era are the products of the total social and technological milieu in which they were created so they reflect the paramount values of a particular society or culture. This view emphasizes the physical environment as a cultural achievement and a reflection of society, but does not admit that the environment may have a hand in causing human behavior.

Controlling Violence Directly

The discussion of contemporary defensive cities supports the conclusion that the design and form of the urban environment can control violence through use of distance and by protecting parts of the urban environment. In this relationship, the urban environment operates directly to control crime. However, this does not say that the urban environment can operate directly to create positive forms of behavior. The "valve" theory suggests that defensive cities would not eliminate or attack the roots of crime, but simply determine its types and locations. Theoretically, people might be shifted out of crime by creating a totally fortified environment to "shut off" all types of crime in all areas.

In this case, people would shift to positive forms of behavior. This possibility calls for an extremely repressive closed system of the urban environment, one that would be very difficult or impossible to create.

The "valve" theory, of course, implies that there is a given quantity of criminal behavior or a propensity to commit crime in particular populations. This view is consistent with the existence of violent subcultures, but raises strong objections from some behavioral scientists who believe it creates a totally false perspective of human behavior.

Encouraging Positive Behavior

The idea that design and form of the urban environment can be used to encourage positive behavior has historical roots in the philosophy of the Utopian Socialists during the eighteenth and nineteenth centuries in England and America and is accepted today in many ways. The legal powers of local governments to regulate or redevelop the physical environment by zoning or urban renewal, for example, rest on court interpretations of the Fourteenth Amendment, which specify the ". . . reasonable tendency to protect the public health, safety, morality or general welfare. . . ." Yet, whatever other purposes have been served, public programs in our large cities during the past two decades have failed to enhance public safety by controlling or reducing crime. There are few, if any, documented cases where urban environments have been consciously designed for low-income populations who have responded favorably by changing from negative to positive forms of behavior. To be sure, crime and other social pathologies are associated to a considerable extent with poverty, high residential densities, and deteriorated physical conditions, but all the poor living in deteriorated neighborhoods are not criminals. Even our slum environments in major cities are vastly improved from what they were at the beginning of this century. Many examples can be cited to show how our affluent society has raised its standards of what poverty is at the same time that we have made vast improvements. Poverty in the physical environment today is a matter of absolute standards, but according to some views it has also become a matter of the relative difference between the levels at which the poor and the affluent live.

Some recent experience holds promise for the future, but much more evidence seems to indicate that violence can continue independently of whatever changes are made in the design, form, density, or quality of the urban environment. Increasing crime in white, middle-class, suburban areas refutes the hypothesis that the quality of the urban environment associated with affluence is sufficient to prevent crime in all population groups. Indeed, in many instances, the physical environment may simply be a stage on which individuals and social groups act out their lives. The actors and the play, not the stage, may actually create positive or negative forms of behavior.

Although every major explanation of violence suggests that the urban environment plays some role in creating or preventing crime, social science theories do not suggest that the urban environment directly creates positive forms of behavior.[33] Instead, various theories assert that there are intervening variables between the environment and behavior, that people impute values to the environment that are essentially independent of any particular environmental design or form, that human behavior can be a response to the environment in terms of an individual's psychological needs, or that social variables, rather than operating directly, operate in consonance with the physical environment to encourage positive or negative forms of behavior.

Two possibilities are especially worth considering from this perspective. The first is that some means of controlling crime may have other desirable effects on human behavior. For instance, increasing visibility on comparatively small scales of architectural design may not only control crime but also further social contacts among residents of a building. Concentrating activities to improve visibility may also encourage social contacts when numbers of people congregate in "evening squares" or along streets with mixtures of land uses. Concern about crime may bring members of a community closer together and increase social cohesion.

The second possibility is that people may be motivated to endow the urban environment with social values, and in this process change behavior patterns. "Homelike" and "community-like" qualities are general terms lacking precise meaning in the physical environment. Instead, they are little more than metaphors for values that people subjectively attribute to what they like or identify with in the environment. The present emphasis on different forms of community participation is based on the premise that the entire process of planning, building, and managing the urban environment can be used to create identity between people and physical features so that individuals and social groups will contribute constructively and attribute positive values to the homes and communities in which they live. The idea that the urban environment should be designed more to facilitate repair rather than to resist breakage suggests that the particular design of a building or other physical feature may be less important in shaping human behavior than the process by which it is designed and built.

Some professionals believe that mastery, control, and ownership of property are critical features in using the urban environment to create positive forms of behavior. The example of a playground designed and built by children in one American city some years ago can be cited. Although no statistics were kept, there appeared to be a decrease in vandalism in the neighborhood as work on the playground progressed and the children increased their mastery over a small part of the environment. The children asked the city to build a chain link fence around the playground to keep balls from going into the streets or nearby buildings. The city constructed the fence, but did not like the crude equipment the children had built and removed it. The next day the fence was completely destroyed by the children, and it appeared that other vandalism in the neighborhood was resumed.

Various cases of environmental management have also been observed in which gangs of hostile youths who had vandalized a neighborhood and victimized its residents changed their behavior when given the responsibility for protecting the neighborhood. Some members became increasingly eager to help and did more than simply chase rival gang members from their "turf." Public programs enabling the poor to own their own homes are based on a similar premise of endowing the urban environment with positive values.

At present, there are few, if any, behavioral studies and only limited observations that suggest but do not test these principles. Much larger experiments in community participation have been started in various cities, some of which may ultimately show whether or not the process of building the urban environment, rather than the particular design or end result of the urban environment, can influence social behavior. But it is too early to tell whether these experiments will be successful, and, even if they are successful in other ways, whether they will reduce crime.

CONCLUSIONS

If urban crime continues to increase and is not abated by other means, defensive cities are likely to become a reality in America, even though they would be a retreat to earlier periods in history. The consequences are foreboding and would be economically and socially destructive. Unquestionably, our major cities are being fortified now, and defensive cities may become a reality, not necessarily by public decisions, but through mass choices of urban consumers in our decentralized society. Distance and the ways the urban environment can be changed to control crime are means that individuals will understandably use to protect themselves, their families, and their property. Such defensive use of the urban environment will not attack the causes or roots of crime, and may add to them, but it is unclear whether the environment can be used positively to reduce the overall volume of crime. Even if positive uses of the urban environment are found, they are likely to require time, public decisions, large public investments, and the consensus of many people. Decisions by individuals to obtain protection can be made more rapidly. Moreover, criminal behavior, once established, can be expected to change slowly, however the urban environment is changed. Consequently, there is an urgent need to find other ways to reduce urban violence.

NOTES

1. This article is mainly concerned with violence committed by individuals and small groups of persons against other persons in large American cities. Major violent crimes are criminal homicide, forcible rape, robbery, and aggravated assault. Major nonviolent property crimes—larceny, burglary, and auto theft—are incidentally of interest.

2. *Report of the National Advisory Commission on Civil Disorders* (New York: Bantam Books, 1968), p. 1.

3. Chapter 16 in Volume 12, *Crimes of Violence*, Task Force on Individual Acts of Violence, Report to the National Commission on the Causes and Prevention of Violence (Washington: Government Printing Office, 1969), contains a more comprehensive summary of historical responses to violence in cities and more amply supports the conclusion that urban environments have always been designed in part for protection.

4. Bernard Rudofsky, *Architecture Without Architects* (New York: The Museum of Modern Art, 1965).

5. Marcel Le Clere, *Histoire de la Police* (Paris: Presses Universitaires de France, 1947).

6. Vitruvius. *The Ten Books of Architecture* (New York: Dover Publications, 1960).

7. Le Clere, *Histoire de la Police.*

8. Henri Pirenne, *Medieval Cities* (New York: Doubleday Anchor Books, 1956).

9. La Clere, *Histoire de la Police.*

10. *Ibid.*

11. *Ibid.*

12. Philip J. Stead, *The Police of Paris* (London: Staples Press, 1957).

13. It is believed the Paris Bourse was developed as a financial district so police protection could be provided more readily.

14. Stead, *The Police of Paris.*

15. Nikolaus Pevsner, *An Outline of European Architecture* (Baltimore: Penguin Books, 1966); Siegfried Giedion, *Space, Time and Architecture* (Cambridge, Mass.: Harvard University Press, 1962); and Paul Zucker, *Town and Square from the Agora to the Village Green* (New York: Columbia University Press, 1959).

16. Charles Reith, *The Police Idea* (London: Oxford University Press, 1938).

17. *Ibid.*

18. Chapters 3 and 5 in Volume 11, *Crimes of Violence*, describe the characteristics and trends of violent crimes in America. This section summarizes the findings which are most pertinent to the urban environment.

19. See, Federal Bureau of Investigation, U.S. Department of Justice, *Uniform Crime Reports—1967* (Washington, D.C.: Government Printing Office, 1967), Appendix 5, Table 1E.

20. Although the reported rate of forcible rape also increased greatly, studies for the Violence Commission were unable to reach conclusions about the true rate because of many reporting problems.

21. Norval Morris and Gordon Hawkins, *The Honest Politician's Guide to Crime Control* (Chicago: University of Chicago Press, 1970).

22. The percentage of Negroes who robbed other Negroes was almost as great.

23. Chapter 16, Volume 12, *Crimes of Violence,* contains a summary of psychological, anthropological, ethological, and sociological explanations of violence related to the urban environment, which is omitted entirely in this article but supports the conclusion stated in the text. The summary in the original chapter is based on Chapters 7 through 11 in Volume 12, *Crimes of Violence.*

24. *Washington Post,* March 16, 1969, p. A8, and *The Wall Street Journal,* June 19, 1969, p. 1.

25. Small Business Administration Report on Crime Against Small Business, Appendix D, Architectural Task Force.

26. *Ibid.*

27. Jane Jacobs, *The Death and Life of Great American Cities* (New York: Random House, 1961).

28. Shlomo Angel, "Discouraging Crime Through City Planning" (Working Paper No. 75, Center for Planning and Development Research, University of California at Berkeley, 1968), p. 2.

29. *Ibid.,* pp. 15-19.

30. Recent population changes in central cities are described in: "Statement by Conrad Taeuber, Associate Director, Bureau of the Census, Before the House Committee on Banking and Currency, June 3, 1969."

31. Chapter 5 in Volume 11 and Chapters 11 and 14 in Volume 12, *Crimes of Violence,* discuss the subcultures of violence in America in detail. This section defines and describes the relevance of the subcultures to the urban environment.

32. Chapter 5, *ibid.*

33. See n. 23.

2

The Trial of LeRoi Jones

Louise Campbell

"THE purpose of this trial," the judge tells a prospective juror, "is to see which of the witnesses will be truthful. Is there any chance that you can look at the police and not believe them? Are you willing to accept the fact that policemen are people like other people? That some are truthful and some are not?"

The possible juror is a gray-haired retiree who lives in a middle-income white suburb. He has already said he doesn't believe in riots and the judge has told him that the three defendants in this courtroom are not charged with rioting but with being on the streets with guns at a given time. The given time is two days after the start of the 1967 riot (July 14) and the place is Newark, New Jersey.

It is hard to assemble a jury. A wide sampling of the white middle class of Essex County has passed through the courtroom. So has a sampling of Newark's black community, whose class is not always determinable by a white reporter. Members of both groups are easily ruled out by self-confessed attitudes about the 1967 riot.

It is fairly easy for defense counsel to elicit statements from white suburbanites who extend a general aversion to riots to specific prejudice against the three defendants before the court. It is almost impossible to find a black person whom the prosecutor cannot lead to admission of prejudice formed by witnessing police action during the riot or by personal experience with the police at some other time. Both defense

This article is reprinted from *City*, Vol. 3, No. 4 (July 1969) which is published by The National Urban Coalition, Washington, D.C.

and prosecution try to draw out statements that will cause the judge to excuse persons they do not want on the jury, thus reserving their own rights of challenging prospective jurors as long as possible.

The judge begins the questioning of each prospective juror by introducing the three defendants. One of them is famous: LeRoi Jones, playwright and poet, hometown boy who is back from Paris, back from Broadway, Greenwich Village, and even Harlem. ("He's here in this town with us—he's not running around somewhere like these other big names," a one-time high school classmate, who remembers Jones as editor of the high school paper, says later in the anteroom.) The others are Charles McCray, who was top accountant in Newark's anti-poverty agency until he lost his job because of his arrest, and Barry Wynn, actor at Spirit House, a theater organized by Jones.

Jones's best-known play is *The Dutchman*, more aptly titled *Fantasie de Métro* when it is produced in Paris. It is a tale of a white woman's attempt to seduce a Negro on a subway train, his resistance and violent death. Critic Robert Brustein called it a "fantasy of uncontrolled revenge." It seems unlikely that any of the persons examined for jury duty has ever read this play or anything else Jones has written. In an earlier trial, a judge remedied this lack by reading aloud some of the more violent passages from Jones's published works, an impulse that may or may not have influenced the jury's finding of guilty as charged but did persuade an appellate court to disallow this result on grounds of judicial prejudice.

In the front row allotted to the defendants,

Jones, 34, not tall and almost fragile-looking, shows no sign of the incandescent rage that flares here and there in his books. Nor does he look much like a reporter's preconception of the black activist who summoned United Brothers to a national assembly in Newark last summer and is regarded by many whites as a force at whose word young blacks will lay down their lives in the streets of Newark. The pale brown face that shows behind a well-trimmed beard is like that of many writers: the calm face of an intelligent child, a watching and listening face.

Like a badge of office, Jones has a pencil behind his ear and now and then makes a note. Not until the end of the morning when he rises to leave the courtroom is Jones the leader of men visible. His wife, a beautiful brown woman with her infant son in her arms, joins him; several rows of young aides fall in behind in almost military order, and the procession, grave, exotic in beautifully cut and colored African garments of handspun wool, leaves like a pride of princes.

By afternoon the judge's questions are all familiar. "Do you accept the presumption of in-nocence? Unless you are convinced beyond a reasonable doubt, will you acquit the defendants? Do you know of any reason why you cannot be fair and impartial?"

"No," says a middle-aged man in a trim business suit, "except the reason every black man has."

This man survives rapid fire from the prosecuting attorney. He has never been arrested and has had no other contact with the police. He saw nothing of the riot and lost no work because of it. He belongs to no organization that advocates black power; his only membership is in the Baptist church. Then the prosecutor reaches the question that has picked off almost every black person examined for the jury. "Will the trial interfere with your work and cause you to lose income?"

Few blacks have the sort of jobs where the employer pays the difference between a juror's fee and normal salary, and the prosecutor can quickly gain admissions that worry over this hardship may cloud attention to the case. For the first time, this prospective juror hesitates. Then he says firmly: "I can work nights." But

his willingness does not recommend him to the prosecutor, who is obliged to use challenge to excuse him from service.

At recess a half-dozen young law students, sent by their summer employers to observe the famous trial lawyer appointed to defend Jones for his second trial, discuss a rumor. The defense is asking whites for lengthy employment and other personal history; this is to find evidence of personal instability. The students say the defense believes that only unstable whites will line up for these black defendants. Yet in the end the whites selected do not reflect this. If there is a general clue, it seems to be that the defense has liked Jewish members of the white community.

Now the clerk draws another name that turns out to be black. This gray-sweatered man of uncertain age has to be told to keep his voice up; the courtroom has been designed for anything but its purpose—its blank walls swallow words like stones in a pool. "Do you think you can be fair?" the judge asks.

"No," the man says baldly. Why not? "Because these men were arrested here in Newark."

For the first time the defendants break up. They struggle against laughter, hiding their faces behind their papers. The man is lost to the jury.

Next a young Italian-American disqualifies himself. Not only does he believe the defendants had guns in the Volkswagen camper-bus they were driving the night of the riot, but he believes they would have been fools not to have them. It is every man's right to have a gun; he keeps them in his home for protection, takes them in his car for target practice, believes no license is required. The judge calmly excuses him, advising him his mistake may be an expensive one.

Now Miss Frances Murray takes her place for questioning. Miss Murray, a thin black woman in a printed cotton dress, shows the marks of many years of hard work. Her head tilts carefully toward the judge as if she has had much practice in absorbing instructions from white folks. But the legal vocabulary he finds hard to abandon spins off her like pie pans.

"All you know so far," the judge tells her, "is that these men are charged with carrying guns. Do you know of any reason why you could not be impartial in reaching a decision?"

"If you tell me they had guns, then I guess they did," Miss Murray says mildly.

The judge tries again. "I didn't say they had guns. This is what they're charged with. They say they did not have them."

"But if *you* say they are charged . . ."

"It's not what I say," the judge explains. "It's what the witnesses say. That's the purpose of having the jury—to listen to what everybody has to say. Have you sat on a jury before?"

Miss Murray says that she has been a juror in a damage suit resulting from car collision.

"Well," the judge says kindly, "you didn't know before you heard the evidence whether the defendant's car had a light or whether it didn't, did you?"

It now seems to strike Miss Murray that this may be an occasion where a white is actually asking her for answers that he has not already thought up for her. "I didn't know afterward, either," she says candidly.

The judge's moon face rotates impassively around the room. "Did you listen to the other jurors?" he asks. "Were you able to take account of their opinions and discuss yours with them?"

"The other jurors ignored me," Miss Murray says matter-of-factly.

There is a question that gives her no difficulty. "Do you feel that the color of a man's skin has anything to do with his guilt or innocence?"

Finally the ancient claim of Anglo-Saxon justice, however bloodied, rings in the room. "Although these men are charged they are presumed to be innocent. They stand before us innocent of the crime. Do you understand that?"

"Uh-huh," Miss Murray says raptly. It occurs to the listener that this may be the first time persons of such social weight have shown genuine and prolonged interest in Miss Murray. Her own quality has appeared, unbruised through all the years, and even the brisk young prosecuting attorney is subdued by it. Defense waives questions. "Your answers are honest. We are sure you are more than qualified for jury service."

And so it comes about that Miss Frances Murray will have a chance to help answer one of the gravest questions that has faced this nation. Who are the criminals in our streets? For three policemen have sworn in an earlier trial and will swear again that two guns were found when they arrested these defendants. The defendants will testify that they were brutally beaten and then framed with guns which the police supplied as a cover-up when they found out they had seriously injured their prisoners.

Some 23,000 are said to have died at Gettysburg for Miss Murray's chance to share in answering the question. Yet she is one of only four black persons on the fourteen-member jury (two alternates). Prosecutor Andrew Zazzali has used twenty-six of his thirty allowable challenges to remove Negroes. Black youths occupy two rows of spectators' seats. When the white-heavy jury files past them on its way out of the courtroom, they marked the color of justice with muffled snorts of derisive laughter.

Newark is still dismembered by the 1967 riot, one of the worst examples of race strife in the country's history. Deep wounds in the social contract are as unhealed as the riot-damaged streets. Yet no other city has succeeded in so clearly asking a question to which the U.S. majority believes it already has the answer: Who is responsible for civil disorder?

White men at the top of state and city life have joined with black men to put their names to commission and committee reports assembling evidence that, as the Committee of Concern charged, the police may be the "single most continuously lawless element in the community." Now the jury is hearing testimony bearing directly on this charge.

LeRoi Jones's views of the white liberal are well known, and the reporter approaches him diffidently at recess. But Jones is friendly, casual.

"We have become a main police target here because we've been able to rally a great many black people together in different walks of life. I was born in this town, and I know middle-class Negroes, all kinds of Negroes. Our efforts are not only to elect a black mayor in 1970, but to make sure the candidate reflects the people's own will."

The prosecutor moves his case briskly. It depends almost entirely on the testimony of the police. A detective present at the arrest says he found a gun under the dashboard of the camper. Patrolman John F. Delaney testifies that he helped stop the bus-camper at 2:45 A.M. and that a revolver dropped from Jones's tunic as he left the car. Police Director Dominick Spina testifies that he saw the guns when the party arrived at the station house. All the police witnesses say that firing from a camper-bus had been reported earlier and that they were on the lookout for such a vehicle.

In a day-long cross examination, defense counsel Raymond Brown begins to break Delaney's dogged recital. The watching law students refer reverently to Ray Brown as today's Clarence Darrow, and Brown is the defender whom prosecutors in many states most dislike to see enter the courtroom. He is a Negro who looks like a white man. He gives half his time to civil rights cases at no pay, and the rest to criminal law.

As adjutant-general of the state's National Guard, Brown was on the streets of Newark behind white guns during the riot. Later as vice chairman of the state's Select Commission on Civil Disorder, he helped produce a report that said the "fate of a city today is in the hands of a policeman," a report signed by two former governors.

Little by little, Delaney is nettled by inconsistencies that Brown unravels from his testimony. Then Brown gets Delaney to acknowledge that he dragged Jones from his car, that he held a gun at his head, that he failed to fill out a report of the arrest until four hours afterward, when he returned from the hospital where Jones and McCray were treated for injuries they say they received when the police beat them with fists and rifle butts.

Brown brings out that Police Director Spina greeted the defendants facetiously when they were brought to the police station, that he made inquiries as to the reason for their bloodied heads. He establishes that none of the three was told what he was charged with until they had been in jail for seven days. But Delaney sticks to his main story—that a revolver fell out of Jones's tunic, which he picked up and put under his belt. Delaney says the gun stayed in his belt during the entire four hours he guarded the defendants at the hospital and was still there when he returned them to the station for lockup.

When the defendants take the stand, they say they were on the street because they wanted to reach a small book and record store owned by McCray, which they feared had been damaged. They describe the alleged beatings in detail. Jones says Patrolman Delaney pushed his wife to the floor when she tried to get to him. He carries a scar on his forehead visible throughout the courtroom. McCray is still without several front teeth. Jones says his wallet with $60 was taken by the police and never returned, that seats were ripped out of the camper, damaged to the extent of a $1,000 repair bill.

The defense calls hospital personnel who confirm the defendants' injuries and say they saw no gun in Delaney's belt. Witnesses who saw the arrest from windows overlooking the street confirm the defendant's account of what happened and say they saw no guns.

Prosecution and defense (Brown is ably supported by Irvin Booker and John Love, counsel for McCray and Wynn) duel with objections. Brown, whose knowledge of the law is formidably wide and exact, pushes the young prosecutor so hard that he loses his temper. The judge dismisses the jury while he warns Zazzali that another attack on Brown may cause the prosecutor to be dismissed from the case.

Cross-examining, the prosecutor goes over every minute of the defendants' accounts of the hours preceding their arrest and every inch of their route. It is life in interminably slow motion; Zazzali runs everything through six times but fails to shake any defendant and finds only one inconsistency. He produces a photo, which he refuses to show to defense counsel, that apparently contradicts Jones's statement that he had lost his head bandage and was handcuffed when he arrived at the police station after treatment at the hospital.

All of a sudden a Jones aide arrives and elation spreads visibly among defendants and their counsel. One witness had been missing. Now,

in a bit of good theater, defense counsel announces that in the very nick of time the witness has been found. He is an injured man the defendants saw on the street and drove to the hospital before they were arrested.

"We bring him as we found him," Brown says, and it is plain that the witness, of no fixed address, has drawn the usual screen over the nags of life.

Johnny William Walker, spirit unflattened by years of sitting in the gutter, tells the court he "was just sitting there minding my own business when the state police shot me up. They shot me in the leg." Walker airily raises his leg above his head and a gun shot wound is seen on the bare flesh.

"I was sittin' there bleeding when Jones leaned out of the car and said: 'What happened, brother?'" Walker testifies that Jones was in the front seat, and not in the back as the police had testified, that the defendants drove him to the hospital and remained with him until he secured treatment.

When the mysterious photo produced by prosecutor Zazzali is two days later introduced as evidence, defense obtains a blow-up that turns it against the prosecution's case. The photo does contradict Jones's statement that he was unbandaged and handcuffed when he reached the police station. But it shows the jury just how battered Jones was. And the defense uses it to destroy a salient of Patrolman Delaney's testimony: the photo shows no gun in his belt at a time when he says it was there.

The jury is out ninety minutes. Miss Frances Murray, who has become foreman as first to be seated, says quietly: "We find the defendants not guilty."

3

"Welcome to Marina City"— The Shape of the New Style

Roy Blumhorst

AFTER two weeks in Marina City I was still unsure about how to meet its people. One day I found myself an elevator passenger with two young women. I reached for the 45th-floor button, and so did they. Here was my chance. With typical suburban-pastor friendliness I said: "We must live on the same floor."

No answer. They seemed to respond with a "What's with him?" kind of glance. They were not irritated, but they made no effort to reply.

We left the elevator at the 45th floor and headed down the corridor. As I reached for my doorknob, they reached for theirs six inches away. Again my suburban-pastor mind drew a brilliant conclusion, and I exclaimed happily: "We must live right next to each other."

At this there was an audible sigh, a condescending "somebody's going to have to say something" response: "Well, welcome to Marina City."

This experience illustrates one important characteristic of life in the city—distance. People assume a certain distance from persons they have not met, whether in the hall, next door, or in the laundromat. Casual chance meetings do not afford an opportunity to meet people and build friendships. The necessity of keeping a certain distance is a constant barrier.

I met the distance in other contacts. At first people gave me names and phone numbers of Marina residents. "Tell him I said to call" was the usual suggestion. I soon learned to refuse such little requests. Such phone calls did not

respect the distance. The person on the other end of the phone and I had never met. Why should we meet now just because we had a mutual friend? I soon began to appreciate the distance as a useful, acceptable way of living. The distance is partly necessary because of safety. The two girls should certainly be cautious with men in elevators. The abundance of people makes distance necessary too. One who lives among 50,000 people must choose some and forget the rest. The distance is also necessary because of the closeness of apartment living. One knows he will be living six inches away from the next-door neighbor for some time. He will bump into him in the elevator and see him in the hall. Wisdom suggests caution about becoming too friendly. Apartment neighbors cannot avoid seeing one another. The fear of developing an unpleasant relationship keeps one from forming any at all.

Three words most often arise in discussing involvement with other people: independence, privacy, control. One great desire is to preserve individual independence. "I want to be free to develop in the direction I wish to go and to do what I want to do. For this reason I do not care to get too involved with neighbors or other people." Another concern is to preserve privacy. The pressure on many people at work, on the street, and elsewhere causes humans to seal off some small place around themselves and to mark it with a KEEP OUT sign. The desire for control is a third concern. A person wants to control his social relationships as much as possible and personally to choose people for his friends.

The distance is symbolized by the cage-type door that extends across the elevators of Marina

City with a phone system for calling the apartment. One enters only by permission of the resident. Carl Sandburg Village nearby has the same phone but with a less forbidding glass door. At Outer Drive East a visitor goes past a desk and a smiling receptionist while inconspicuous guards eliminate uninvited and unwanted persons. A closer look around these buildings indicates that the building itself either assumes or contributes to the distance. The lobby is not the community gathering place for residents. It is strictly a waiting room. Many buildings have no recreational facilities for tenants. In many of the places tenants could not find a place to gather if they wanted to.

People looking in from the outside seem to see only the distance and consider it all bad. "Those people are isolationists" is a common evaluation. "The reason people move there is to get away from people" is another. The person making the evaluation apparently does not see the usefulness of this distance, nor does he seem to see it as only one dimension of life in the city. Actually the person who feels obligated to be everyone's neighbor may not be a close friend of anyone. As a person "naturalized" to the city apartment I did not find the distance at the elevator a form of hostility. The distance became enjoyable. I did not feel compelled to speak to everyone on the elevator or to strike up a conversation with every person in the laundromat. If I did, life in the city would be burdensome indeed. There are too many people!

The need for distance, however, does not replace the need for people. The person living in an urban apartment not only wants to get to know other people; he *needs* them. The human being is not built to run alone. He has love to give, and he needs to receive it. His happiness and his sorrow must be shared. He needs people to whom he is tied and with whom he counts.

Apparently for most of the world's history the individual has fulfilled this need in a family. All persons have been in some way attached to a basic family unit whether aged grandmother or orphaned teenager. The family is still the primary group for many people in many places. All other groups are optional.

The family is no longer the basic unit of apartment dwellers or of many city residents. Two thirds of Marina City residents are single.

The married couples usually have no children. "Most of us have no relatives very near" is one person's comment. This leaves individuals without an automatic primary community in which to live. I was never aware that my family provided all the community I needed until I began to live in Marina City. The plain work of assisting the wife, rearing children, and living together as a family is quite enough. Other relationships are much more optional. Many of our neighbors at Marina City did not have this task. They needed people.

Theirs was the opposite task—to build meaningful friendships and form some kind of primary relationships. The secondary ones can be developed more easily—at work, at recreation, and in various interest groups. But these are not enough. Can a person tell all his troubles to someone at work? One who does may begin to lose status on the competitive ladder. A basic physics course includes discussion on closed and open substances. Each kind of molecule has a certain number of "hooks." In a closed substance the hooks are all interlocked so that the substance has free hooks ready to combine with another element. This might be a good analogy for the comparison of the family and the single person. The family is a kind of closed element; the single person has hooks ready for others.

The urban dweller must resolve a conflict. On the one hand is a useful need for distance deepened by a desire for independence, privacy, and control. On the other hand is a need for people, greater perhaps than for rural or suburban families. How are the two resolved? That people are working on the problem can be illustrated.

One example is a Marina resident who gives complete privacy as her main reason for living in the towers. If an unauthorized person comes to her corridor, she immediately calls the management to have him removed. Because work often keeps her for long hours in the evening, she doesn't want to feel obligated to anyone about coming or going at a certain time. Independence, privacy, control would aptly fit her desires about her place of residence. How does she handle the need for people? She may be in the lobby late at night talking with the service employees. She knows all about them and is concerned about their personal welfare. She seems to have worked out a healthy ambiguity—

(PHOTO BY ORLANDO R. CABANBAN/BERTRAND GOLDBERG, ARCHITECTS)

maintaining privacy but finding community especially with the service people in the building. She also seems more willing than most to enter into the private concerns of people at work. In addition, she finds community by working in several service organizations.

Another solution to the conflict is provided by the *joiners*. One young couple was active in the Young Republicans and in a local congregation. As friendly, open, enthusiastic people they admitted that they joined Young Republicans to meet some people and soon became interested in the cause behind the organization. Though they knew few people in the building, they were quite happy because they had several significant groups in which they felt a sense of belonging. Numerous groups in the city thrive because of the "joiner" answer to the need to maintain a distance and yet meet people. The task is to find the right places to meet people in order to drop the distance.

A larger group, the *wishers*, offers another possibility. The early widow, the maturing, successful, good-looking but single young man or woman have often come to the city in the realization that suburbs are full of families. They hope that among the thousands like them in the city they will meet and form friendships. The high rise seems a good place because it is filled with their kind of people. The new resident may soon be disappointed. One young widow joined the Trim Club though she was not in need of trimming. An older widower came to some of our groups and asked us not to discuss anything religious (since he by definition was against it) but to talk about drapes, furniture, or anything insignificant as an excuse to get together. Many just continue to express their

wish for contact with people by saying: "My biggest disappointment in this building is that I still don't know anyone."

A young man may say: "Frankly I wish there were some way to meet some of the girls who live here. I'm sure some of them would like to meet fellows too, but there isn't any way. If you go up and introduce yourself, they're suspicious; and if you have a party, you're admitting you need it."

A small group of people handle their distance-yet-need-people ambivalence by openly providing opportunity for others to meet people. We might call them the *catalysts*. Our experience with such a couple began in the laundromat. The wife had the rare quality of using the laundromat without appearing forward. Smoothly and naturally she used a chance meeting there as an invitation to coffee in her apartment. Shortly afterward we became the reason for a party hosted by this couple. We found ourselves introduced to an expanding circle of people. The couple took delight in the number of younger "unique" people they could find and in the kind of stimulation an evening with these people could provide. Their catalytic function seemed very much appreciated in the building, and they themselves found a useful role in fulfilling it. Operating with the need for distance as a framework, they nevertheless were able to find excitement in helping fill the need for people creatively.

The city creates a need for distance; being human creates a need for people. These two desires cause one tension in city life. The resolution of this tension is a factor in shaping the urban-style life.

4

Narcotics: Root of Urban Tension

Gail Miller

WHITE America, middle-class America, suburban America, recently discovered that the nation had a drug problem. The discovery came through the communications media, which were attracted to the joyful hedonism of a turning-on generation, and sometimes through conversations with the police or one's own children.

Black America has known about the problem for some time.

White America's reaction to finding the problem suddenly on its doorstep has been one of shock. Conservatives call for stronger law enforcement and a restoration of parental authority. Liberals call for understanding of the alienation of youth and more rehabilitation centers.

Black America watches the peddlers openly ply their trade on its streets.

There are now two turned-on subsocieties in the nation, quite separate, and, of course, unequal. The white kids pool their allowances for pot and an occasional trip on something harder. The black kids, particularly in the big eastern cities, get hooked earlier on the ghetto staple of heroin, stay hooked, wind up needing more money to support their habit than they have time or health to earn.

Narcotics officers, federal and local, chase the peddlers and users of pot, raid campuses, clean up the hippie havens and send the runaways home. This leaves less time to patrol the ghetto streets or trace the source of heroin supply—or cope with the street crime that feeds the habit.

This article is reprinted from *City*, Vol. 3, No. 3 (June 1969), published by The National Urban Coalition, Washington, D.C.

Narcotics are a prime contributor to the tensions that grip our urban society. Crime, bred by narcotics to a degree that is unmeasured, builds white fears. Whites, with tragic accuracy, associate dope with the black ghettos, and some regard it as an interracial import to their world. Blacks, for their part, seethe at what seems the ultimate corruption of the minority by the majority—who runs the dope trade? They watch the police watch the peddlers; they curse; and respect for white society and its agents dies.

What follows is a summary of the narcotics situation in America—its history, its dual nature, and what is and is not being done about it. The premise is that doing more must be a very early step toward healing our cities and society.

The United States has long been a drug-oriented society. European settlers in the southwest found the original Americans tripping on peyote, a type of cactus with hallucinogenic properties. A religious ritual among numerous Indian tribes still involves the sucking and swallowing of "mescal buttons," slices of the peyote which are rolled and dried in the sun. Early Spanish missionaries tried discouraging the practice, saying it led the user to the pit of hell, to which the Indian replied it really took him several steps closer to heaven.

Opium first came to this country with the English settlers who had learned the habit of opium-eating from the Chinese. Oriental immigrants instituted the first opium dens in America, which became somewhat fashionable in the mid-1800s, chiefly in San Francisco and New York City. The drug first became illegal with the passage of an ordinance in San Francisco in

1875; the New York State Assembly prohibited opium traffic in 1882.

Morphine had been isolated from opium in 1816, but addiction only became a major problem thirty-two years later with the invention of the hypodermic needle. Direct injection greatly magnified morphine's effect, and its use spread throughout this country and Europe.

In 1874, a chemical modification of morphine was developed in England, called heroin, and said to be ten times more potent. There was little interest in the drug until 1898 when German scientists, in a classic miscalculation, put heroin on the market as a remedy for morphine addiction. The cure proved ten times more deadly as well. Another "remedy" for morphine addiction appeared at the same time: cocaine, an alkaloid of coca leaves.

Barbiturates—depressant drugs usually prescribed as sleeping pills—were introduced in 1903, and by 1937 the American Medical Association warned against "Evils from Promiscuous Use of Barbituric Acid and Derivative Drugs." Deaths from barbiturates rose alarmingly in the mid-1940s—about half suicides and half accidental. In 1949, a quarter of all poisoning cases admitted to hospitals were due to acute barbiturate intoxication. Some 1,500 derivatives have been synthesized over the years, and as each new brand was introduced illicit pill poppers gave it a name: Nembutal is known as "yellow jacket," Seconal is called "red bird" or "red devil," and Amytal is bootlegged as "blue heaven."

Amphetamine was synthesized in 1927 and later recommended in its vaporous state for treating colds, hay-fever, and other respiratory infections. The Benzedrine inhaler was first marketed in 1932. In 1936, students at the University of Minnesota, who had been conducting experiments with Benzedrine, sampled the drug and found it helped keep them awake for cramming. Truck drivers and night guards soon became steady consumers. A song entitled "Who put the Benzedrine in Mrs. Murphy's Ovaltine" revolved on many a victrola while bored socialites popped bennies along with their barbiturates for a "bolt and a jolt." Narcotic addicts even found that these "thrill pills" could intensify a heroin high.

Perhaps no other drug has been more shrouded in mystery or encrusted with misconception than marijuana. In Arabia, it is known as "hashish" and still carries with it the lurid tales of Hasan and his assassins who were credited with performing their most revolting atrocities under its influence. Marijuana was introduced to this country by Mexican laborers in the southwestern states, and its use soon spread throughout America. And as it spread, stories began to appear in the press concerning its effect, reporting a variety of incidents where individuals supposedly lost their control and committed unpremeditated acts of violence.

Synthetic hallucinogens make up the most recent addition to the drug scene. In the late 1930s Albert Hofman and his colleagues in a Swiss laboratory were working on chemical modifications of ergot alkaloids when they produced a compound known as LSD. In 1943, Hofman accidentally ingested or inhaled some of the substance and experienced the first LSD trip. It was used in controlled studies for its mind-altering properties, but by the time studies were undertaken in 1960 to determine just how LSD works, illegal production and distribution had mushroomed. Researchers at Harvard are said to have given LSD to students outside of proper research environments. Its use spread further when Timothy Leary and Richard Alpert, the former Harvard psychologists, founded the International Federation for Internal Freedom, which encourages use of hallucinogens.

The lack of scientific knowledge pertaining to drugs for so many years has been reflected in the hit-and-miss history of drug regulations. The first international effort to control opium traffic was in 1909 when the International Opium Commission convened in Shanghai. International narcotics control rested in the hands of the League of Nations from World War I until after World War II, when the United Nations adopted a Narcotic Protocol, giving the authority to the World Health Organization.

The Harrison Narcotic Act was passed in the United States in 1914, but not until 1930 was the Federal Bureau of Narcotics established. Opium dens could still be found in most American cities, and the bureau's first commissioner, Henry J. Anslinger, was under fire from Congress and the public from the time of his appointment until his retirement in 1962.

Anslinger, always outspoken, said this concerning his successful 1937 campaign to include marijuana under the Harrison Act: "As the marijuana situation grew worse, I knew action had to be taken to get proper control legislation passed. . . . On radio and at major forums, such as that presented annually by the *New York Herald Tribune*, I told the story of this evil weed of the fields and river beds and roadsides. I wrote articles for magazines; our agents gave hundreds of lectures to parents, educators, social and civic leaders. In network broadcasts I reported on the growing list of crimes, including murder and rape. I described the nature of marijuana and its close kinship to hashish. I continued to hammer at the facts."

In 1944, New York Mayor LaGuardia empowered a special committee to study the matter in his city. Most of the marijuana smoking was found in Harlem, where about five hundred "tea pads" were operating. The committee reported that there were no visible withdrawal symptoms when "tea heads" or "grasshoppers" discontinued smoking reefers; that there was no significant relationship between marijuana use and crime; nor was there evidence that marijuana was the first step to hard-drug addiction. "The publicity concerning the catastrophic effects of marijuana smoking in New York City is unfounded," the committee concluded.

Evidence today shows that conclusion to be more nearly accurate than that of Commissioner Anslinger. The President's Advisory Commission on Narcotics and Drug Abuse in 1963 spoke of the "relatively trivial" nature of the marijuana evil and suggested that all mandatory sentences be eliminated from crimes involving its consumption alone, and many officials now propose that the law deal with marijuana users along the same lines used with persons who drink alcohol.

The dispute continues. The early laws still prevail, and the number of people who smoke marijuana has grown to an estimated five million.

Use of the more potent hallucinogens began in 1960 and reached a peak in San Francisco's Haight-Ashbury in 1966. Timothy Leary, an early experimenter, wrote: "I think that psychedelic drugs, marijuana, peyote, LSD, STP—are sacraments. I think they are developed by a divine process, the DNA code to help man survive. . . . If it flips you out, turns you on, blows your mind, it's holy."

Encouraged by Leary and others, students flocked to San Francisco in the spring of 1966, where, it was rumored, one might find himself, the meaning of life—and love. Everyone turned on. They smoked pot, dropped acid, shot speed. They saw inside themselves and beyond—in living color. They found new beauty in flowers; in poetry; hard-rock bands, like the Grateful Dead, played high on acid; the music was distorted and the stoned listeners liked what they heard. They lived together in communes, sharing what they had. *Time* magazine reported: ". . . in their independence of material possessions and their emphasis on peacefulness and honesty, hippies lead considerably more virtuous lives than the great majority of their fellow citizens."

Money and dope changed hands openly and without fear, for laws were virtually suspended in the Haight. There was an air of lunacy as the kids tasted the forbidden fruit. "We are the people our parents warned us against!" they scrawled incredulously, exuberantly, on coffeehouse walls.

Nicholas von Hoffman, an over-thirty columnist, glommed onto the catch phrase as a title for his book, a staccato account of their life style. "The Haight offers plenty of elucidating philosophy," he wrote. "These ideas are important, but they don't encompass what the people on the street do. What they do, regardless of philosophy and world-view, is deal dope."

This description was not acceptable to the folks back home who preferred to think of their wandering offspring not as drugged lawbreakers, but as flower children; the love generation. The nation thought the Haight was a festival. Those coming home from the Coast taught those who couldn't go to set up small replicas of the Haight in their own community, and little hippie communes began to spring up in every major city.

As medical evidence began linking LSD with chromosome damage and birth defects, its popularity waned and kids began tripping on amphetamine and methamphetamine—"speed." They found that the pills and capsules that had kept them awake to study, when used in large enough quantity, or dissolved and mainlined (injected), produced a feeling of elation, omnipotence, increased capacity for physical activity, and sometimes hallucinations.

Again, medical facts and witness to bum trips that led to personal destruction or permanent psychosis resulted in an effective "Speed Kills" campaign that has practically eliminated its use in California, and kids there have turned now to barbiturates—"downers"—for a confident, tranquil, euphoric kind of high. Sudden withdrawal from barbiturates is more serious than from heroin. Vomiting, uncontrolled tremors, and grand mal convulsions which may be fatal are common symptoms which increase in intensity in direct ratio to the dose used.

Heroin is scarce and expensive in the West because of the route of the supply, and while unauthorized research continues to find a suitable substitute, one youthful expert says: "There's no smack [heroin] in California; not much acid. Out here it's definitely the year of the downer. But it's not the same. Reds [Seconal] make you mean. There've been twenty murders in the Haight this year."

Despite the efficiency of the underground communications network, eastern kids are still balling on speed, dropping acid when it's available, and taking a generally less sophisticated approach to drug use than their western counterparts. There is one major exception: they have been introduced to the delusive delights of heroin.

Organized crime, unable to control distribution of the hallucinogens, amphetamines, and barbiturates, saw an untapped market among the middle-class kids for the product it held exclusive rights to: heroin. Unlike the impoverished youngsters in the slums who had, in desperation, embraced "H" since the turn of the century despite the high cost of escape, the white kids had seemingly boundless resources with which to indulge their fancies. Pushers were directed to mix small amounts of heroin with the marijuana they sold the white kids, which would produce a stronger high and eliminate the need for overcoming the social stigma against *horse*, *boy*, or *Harry*, as it is variously called. The kids would become hooked before they knew they were using the dread drug of the ghetto.

Heroin use among high school students in eastern cities has grown at an accelerating rate, with estimates ranging as high as 50 percent of the student body in some schools in Washington, Baltimore, and New York City, and 35 per-

cent in Philadelphia and Boston. Many of these are suburban, not inner-city, schools.

Ex-addicts say the kids are getting "garbage" —heroin that has been cut so many times it is incapable of causing more than a psychological addiction. But the pusher tells them they're hooked. They think they are, and continue to use the drug in ever stronger doses as their body develops a tolerance.

As heroin becomes the drug of preference, a role it has long enjoyed in the black community, its ignominy diminishes, along with aversion to the needle. Warnings about "the friendly stranger" may be irrelevant as kids, anxious to share their experiences with friends, become pushers themselves.

The phrase "don't trust anyone over thirty" didn't come about by accident. White youngsters lost respect for mature evaluation of drug dangers during their frolic in San Francisco. The streets of Harlem, however, are considerably less joyous than the streets of the Haight.

Heroin administered intravenously (mainlined) produces a feeling of elation similar to that produced by the amphetamines, and in addition, a brief euphoria, tranquility, and a momentary "thrill" or turning of the stomach— a warm, tingling sensation similar to orgasm. Following the initial effects, the subject "goes on the nod," a state of imperturbability. This pleasant drowsiness lasts, in the beginning, several hours. As one's body develops a tolerance, it requires larger and more frequent doses to produce a high, until finally the addict experiences few or none of the desirable feelings, and continues usage only to prevent withdrawal symptoms which vary in intensity from yawning and perspiration to moderate tremors and insomnia to severe vomiting and muscle cramps and spasms.

To keep from feeling ill, an addict's body may require up to fifteen bags of heroin a day, though most get by on about ten. Prices vary, but average about $5 a bag. The addict cannot work. It is not only a physical impossibility, but he couldn't earn enough to support his $50-a-day habit. So he turns to pushing or other crime. Female addicts are usually prostitutes; males mug pedestrians, hoist taxis, hold up small-business men and steal merchandise. They must steal about five times the amount they need to sell their goods to a "fence" at below-wholesale prices.

Addicts, however, are not the maniacal criminals many fear them to be. They are rather docile individuals, deprived of their sex urge or almost any aggressive emotion, concerned primarily with where they'll get the money for their next fix, and secondarily with the companion fear of overdose.

The black community learned opium-eating around the turn of the century from oriental immigrants who made their way across the country and settled among the Negroes, co-segregated in eastern ghettos. Most of the heroin that comes into the country now originates in Turkey and goes then to Corsica. The Corsicans have efficient contacts with the Mafia in New York City where it goes to receive its first cut before being parceled out around the nation. A Turkish farmer receives about $350 for 10 kilograms (about 25 pounds) of raw opium. That amount produces 1 kilogram of roughly pure heroin, which is cut first with milk sugar and then further diluted by each of seven or eight handlers, with anything from talcum to cleanser, and by the time it reaches the street, it sells for about $225,000.

It is estimated that half the heroin addicts in the country are in New York City, but it is impossible to determine the total number. Official statistics are unreliable owing to varying definitions of drug use and addiction, random reporting methods, and the obvious fact that a very large percentage of drug users do not come to the attention of either law enforcement or medical authorities. Nevertheless, the National Institute of Mental Health estimates 100,000 addicts, and the Federal Bureau of Narcotics and Dangerous Drugs had 67,011 active addicts officially registered as of December 31, 1968. A spokesman for the bureau said that the number "could realistically be multiplied by three."

Using the NIMH estimate of 100,000 addicts, multiplying it by $200—a conservative estimate of the amount each must steal per day to net $50—heroin addicts steal a total of $20 million worth of merchandise a day, or roughly $6 billion per year. The price the nation pays in "involuntary social costs" to combat drug abuse, also by estimates of NIMH, is $541 million annually. This excludes thefts, but includes law enforcement, theft insurance, property crimes, and productivity losses.

Behavioral scientists use certain criteria for determining factors that cause an individual or a group to have a greater than average potential for drug abuse. Among these are one's IQ; his degree of respect for himself; his family's status within the community; his own status within the family; presence or absence of a father in the home; and the economics of his family and the community. Residents of city slums meet all the criteria for being considered a "high risk" population.

A study was done recently in St. Louis by Drs. Lee Robins and George E. Murphy of 235 young men, selected from public elementary school records beginning twenty-six to thirty years ago. The criteria for eligibility for the study were: being male, born in St. Louis between 1930 and 1934, attending a St. Louis Negro public elementary school for six years or more, having an IQ of at least 85 while in elementary school, and parent's or guardian's name and occupation appearing on the school records.

The record showed half with school problems, half without; half with father in the home, half without; half with parents or guardians who were unemployed, domestic servants, or laborers, and half with parents or guardians in better jobs. The study was limited to those men who had lived in St. Louis between 1959 and 1964 to ensure they had exposure to the same drug market and had all had a risk of being known to local law enforcement and health agencies. Drug addiction seldom begins after age thirty-five; age sixteen is considered a critical age for introduction to heroin among disadvantaged youth.

The population studied was expected to have a high rate of drug use, but it was surprisingly high: 14 percent had an official record for selling, use, or possession of narcotics. Of the 86 percent *without* a record, nearly half reported having taken drugs and nearly all had tried marijuana. Seventeen percent had taken amphetamines, and 14 percent barbiturates. Thirteen per cent of the sample reported having tried heroin, and 10 percent had been addicted to heroin.

Based on this and other detailed samplings, many experts believe this to be a fairly accurate pattern of drug use in the ghetto. However, the number of addicts in New York's slums is undoubtedly considerably higher, perhaps double the national average—or 20 percent of the population.

For many years there was official opposition to factual drug education on the ground that knowledge would stimulate more widespread use. The national policy has changed over the past decade, but despite this, in a speech in January, 1969, John Finlater, associate director of the Bureau of Narcotics and Dangerous Drugs, said: "There is evidence that the slum children of New York who are the prime subjects for addiction actually do *not* know the facts. Isidor Chein's study, *The Road to H*, shows that only 17 percent of a group of 133 young users in the New York slums reported learning anything cautionary about drugs before first experimenting with heroin."

Federal statistics are not broken down in such a way as to define how narcotics affect the crime rate, or at least such statistics are not available to the press. Of the 187,613 persons arrested in New York City in 1968, however, 17,039—or 9.1 percent of them—admitted using illegal drugs. Of those arrested for burglary, 11.9 percent admitted drug use; 14.5 percent arrested for possession of burglars' tools, 16 percent arrested for auto theft, 8 percent arrested for robbery admitted they were drug users. Of the 17,039 admitted users, 86 percent used opium derivatives and 5.2 percent smoked marijuana.

There is considerable public pressure on the police department to make narcotics arrests. It is unquestionably easier to bust a pot party than to arrest an elusive heroin pusher in the ghetto, much less to gather enough evidence to convict a member of the Mafia.

The Bureau of Narcotics and Dangerous Drugs reports that federal arrests for hard drugs in 1967 were 1,506, while in 1968 they dropped to 1,225. Yet there is no evidence that the supply was diminished. With more and more federal and local police units assigned to the hippie and student drug-using subculture to protect them from the dread evils of pot, the

Mafia was making its arrangements to take heroin into psychedelia.

Former Attorney General Ramsey Clark said in an interview in January, 1969: "There is no question that organized crime cannot flourish without at least the neutralization, if not the corruption, of segments of local government." *Life* magazine said after the Chicago melee during the Democratic convention: "In Chicago, it's a risky thing for a policeman to take on the Mob. The reason is obvious: the Fix, which links crime with politics, is widespread. A Chicago cop is expected to 'bend' with the political forces of the Fix, not push investigations right into it." The story quoted a young rookie: "There is no way you can be on this police force and not take payoffs. I'm offered money every day. Now I get a payoff from my sergeant."

Rev. Channing Phillips of Washington, D.C., the first black put up for major-party nomination for President, says: "Anyone who's been around the ghetto for ten minutes has seen a policeman turn his head at a dope transaction, or accept a payoff from a pusher. With the sophisticated investigative devices we have, I don't see how anyone could believe for a minute that the law enforcement officials don't know who's behind the dope traffic. It's not a lack of knowledge; it's a lack of will to move against it. Look, if the FBI can bug Martin Luther King's phone right after the day of his death, you can bet they can bug the Mafia's—unless they're saying Martin Luther was a more dangerous guy than the dope peddlers."

Even the Federal Bureau of Narcotics has not been immune to the opportunities for corruption inherent in the drug traffic. John Ingersoll, former Charlotte, N.C., police chief, was appointed head of the bureau in August, 1968. "We haven't prevented enough drug abuse," he said at the time. "We haven't apprehended enough drug peddlers. We haven't rehabilitated enough drug abusers." A few months later, a third of the bureau's New York City agents "resigned" and the Department of Justice said it had found "indications of significant corruption during the past decade."

In California, the Department of Criminal Statistics recently announced that 37,513 arrests were made in connection with various marijuana charges during 1967. (Of these, 10,987

were of youths under eighteen. These "pot busts" represented 60 percent of the total drug-related arrests for the state.

In Washington D.C., there were 460 narcotics arrests between November 1, 1967, and January 25, 1968. Sixty percent of the arrests involved marijuana and the hallucinogens. For similar periods in 1965-66 and 1966-67, 65 percent of the arrests involved heroin and other addictive drugs. Moreover, in 1967, the District of Columbia conducted at least nine separate investigations of several months' duration involving hippies. There was only one similar investigation of heroin traffic during the period.

Individuals turn to drug use for a variety of reasons. Many feel that, no matter what the rationalization, people turn on for fun. Bernard Finch has written: "The pursuit of pleasure, as with animals, was primitive man's goal." Some see the drug scene as evidence that ours is a hedonistic society.

Dr. Stanley F. Yolles, director of the National Institute of Mental Health, contends: "To understand scientifically the problem of drug abuse, one must look beyond the specific problems of some of the underlying causes of widespread drug use and abuse. . . . Behavioral scientists use the term 'alienation' to describe the cross-generational disease epitomized by the youth-coined term 'don't trust anyone over 30.' Alienation has been characterized as a refusal of what is, without a vision of what should be. The current problem of alienation in the United States affects the rich and the poor, the college student and the school dropout, the urban and the rural youngster." A study by Drs. Alfred M. Freedman and Richard Brotman points out: "Some youngsters who feel helpless to accommodate or change an unacceptable world, consciously choose to alter their own. . . . Since you cannot alter the world or determine the direction in which it will go, you must alter your state of consciousness and perception, that is, see the world and experience the world through a 'high.' Drug use and abuse touches our deepest values, hopes, aspirations and fears. As the problem is complex and changing, so must be the strategies designed to understand and cope with it."

The development of such strategies in the United States has been hampered by rigid laws and public attitudes. The laws have prohibited extensive human research on drugs. The findings of much of what research has been done, in federal hospitals at Lexington, Ky., and Ft. Worth, Tex., can be released only to the World Health Organization or the United Nations.

In 1966, the United States launched its first major national program to control addiction and rehabilitate persons already addicted to narcotic drugs, basing its strategy on the premise that an addict is a sick person in need of treatment. But the Narcotics Addict Rehabilitation Act (NARA) demands total abstinence: relapse, a 90 percent factor in former federal rehabilitation programs, is punishable by dismissal from the program and transferral of the patient back into the hands of the law.

The act provides for civil commitment of addicts, both those charged with or convicted of violating a federal criminal law and those who desire to be committed for treatment in lieu of trial on the criminal charge. It provides hospitalization, therapy and aftercare for addicts when they return to their communities. If the patient's improvement is steady, from institution through outpatient care, he may be discharged from treatment at the end of three years and the criminal charges against him dismissed. There is also a provision for addicts not charged with a criminal offense but who apply for treatment. Voluntary patients are admitted infrequently, however, owing to limited space.

Addicts are not admitted, under any circumstances, until they have been examined and the determination is made that they might be successfully rehabilitated. Since the first patient was accepted under the act on June 29, 1967, a total of 1,889 addicts have been examined and 840 committed for treatment.

The feature of NARA expected to produce the most positive results was the provision of contracting with local facilities, either private or government-operated, for aftercare services. It is believed that even when an addict successfully kicks the habit in a hospital, when he returns home and tries to deal with everyday problems, he often resumes contact with his druggie friends—and his habit. This provision, unfortunately, has not yet been widely used. Few communities want to be the site of a drug rehabilitation center. The provision also sets rigid requirements for staff and procedures, which some private agencies resist on the ground

that their success in rehabilitating addicts has been primarily due to avoiding use of professional staff and traditional methods of therapy and surveillance.

Synanon is perhaps the best example of an agency which has had proven success in rehabilitation but is unwilling to qualify for federal funding. Begun in 1958 by ex-alcoholic Chuck Dederich, first in a storefront and later in a converted armory in Santa Monica, Calif., Synanon has been widely criticized for its unorthodox treatment techniques. The organization is made up of and managed entirely by ex-addicts; some return to the community, but many take up permanent residence in the Synanon society. Group pressure, "attack" therapy, and development of confidence and self-control are among the methods used in curtailing addiction. Synanon at first existed almost entirely on handouts of food, clothing, and occasionally cash from addicts' families and a few others who saw merit in its approach. Citizens of Santa Monica tried to bar licensing of the first center on grounds ranging from zoning violations to charges of operating an illicit house of prostitution.

Synanon now operates six centers in and out of California. Applications for federal funds have been turned down because of Dederich's refusal to employ a professional psychiatrist as director and institute urinalysis as a means of detecting an addict's relapse to drug use. "Trust," he says, "is one of the principal reasons for Synanon's success. You can't measure human dignity in percentages." As for the professional staff, he has medical advisers, but feels one reason other programs have such a high failure rate is that psychotherapy does not work with addicts: the therapist and addict don't trust each other and have no common frame of reference. Ex-addicts, on the other hand, professionals in the con game, are as persuasive in rehabilitating others as they were in finding the means to support their own habits. They know when they're being put on; having gone through withdrawal themselves, they know what works best in individual cases. They know, too, according to Dederich, when an addict has had a relapse and how to deal with him "without having him pee in a bottle and have some chemist tell him he's back on dope."

Daytop Lodge, with two locations in New York, patterned itself after Synanon and hired away some of its staff. The major difference is that it does comply with federal regulations, and receives government funds.

Daytop administrators feel that neither punishing the addict by jailing him nor "slobbering over him with sympathy and pity" has shown much rehabilitative value. Their philosophy is to consider the addict an adult acting like a baby—childishly immature, full of demands, and empty of offerings. The addict holds himself blameless for his addiction and is convinced he has been thrown into life not as well equipped as others. Heroin enables him to escape the unfair battle, and in pursuit of heroin he is able to muster extraordinary cunning, shrewdness, and acting ability. He is untouched by psychotherapeutic approaches and is rarely motivated toward any kind of treatment except as the lesser of two evils: rehabilitation or jail.

Before he is admitted, he must telephone for an interview and initially is told to call back the next day at a specified hour. If he forgets and calls late, he is turned down. If he calls promptly, he is told to call again at another specified time. If he makes the second call on time, he's given an appointment for an interview and then kept waiting for as long as four hours before anyone sees him. He is told in the interview that he will be treated like a three-year-old, because that's the way he has acted. He is cautioned about asking questions about things he doesn't understand: "Your brain is not strong enough for that kind of exercise just yet. In time you will understand." He is told to *act as if* he understands; to *act as if* he wants to do the right thing, cares about other people, etc. His withdrawal distress is treated matter-of-factly with no payoff for histrionics.

He is given a very low-status job at first, scrubbing floors or cleaning toilets. He may progress to any job within the organization; all except that of the director are held by ex-addicts. Three times a week, all Daytop residents undergo a group encounter therapy session. This is the only time residents may use profanity and they do so enthusiastically. One member after another assumes the "hot seat" and is attacked and criticized for failing to be 100-percent honest, for being insensitive to others' feelings, for failing to adhere to basic precepts of Daytop.

The director refuses to quote numbers of re-habilitated addicts. In addition to some three hundred who live drug-free in the two Daytop residences, one on Staten Island and the other at Swan Lake in the Catskills, there are at least sixty who have returned to the community to lead normal lives.

A program of drug maintenance, similar to that used in England, is gaining support in this country. Methadone, a synthesized opiate that is itself addictive, has recently been advanced as a promising way to help addicts back into society. Manufactured legally in this country, it costs about 10 cents a dose, and if carefully administered, seems to allow the patient to lead a normal life without a desire for added stimulation. He relies on it much as diabetics depend on insulin.

New York City is the first to approve an extensive methadone maintenance experiment, under the direction of Drs. Vincent Dole and Marie Nyswander. Of the 108 patients admitted prior to February 1, 1966, twenty are still in the program. The first phase of treatment involves hospitalization of the addict and withdrawal from heroin. The patient is then started on small doses of methadone, in gradually increasing proportions until he reaches a plateau of relatively great strength. It is important that methadone be given in doses adequate to block the euphoric effects of heroin. It does not itself produce euphoria, sedation, or distortion of behavior—as long as it is ingested and not mainlined. The patient remains alert, functions normally, and is not psychologically aware of his addiction unless the drug is withdrawn, and then he experiences withdrawal distress similar to withdrawal from heroin—cramps, chills, nausea.

In the maintenance program, the methadone is dissolved in fruit juice and taken orally under supervision. It is always dispensed from a hospital pharmacy; outpatients are given no prescriptions and are required to return each day for their dose and urinalysis to determine whether they're using auxiliary drugs. Methadone only blocks the effects of the opiates. The addict may still get a kick from the amphetamines or barbiturates, and despite rigid precautions, there is already a considerable amount of illicit methadone on the streets.

Many think methadone will revolutionize the handling of heroin and opium throughout the world. Others doubt the morality of a deliberate lifetime commitment to drugs and recall the enthusiasm with which heroin was accepted to treat morphine addiction.

Apart from the disagreement among the experts as to the merits of the methadone maintenance program, it is unknown whether it will be accepted in the black community to any great degree. Militant leaders already are voicing concern that it is another subtle means of control over the black man, whatever its value to society as a whole.

The President is about to introduce his Omnibus Narcotics Bill, which, if sent to Congress as it is now drafted, will seem to some a radical liberalization of the law: it proposes taking marijuana out of the narcotics category and placing it among the hallucinogens.

The bill, as of this writing, provides that "persons who casually use or experiment with controlled dangerous substances should receive special treatment geared toward rehabilitation." And "persons addicted to controlled dangerous substances should, upon conviction, be sentenced in a manner most likely to produce rehabilitation." At the same time, the bill places entire responsibility for its administration in the hands of the Attorney General, and appears to take away whatever meager authority was vested in the Department of Health, Education and Welfare under the 1966 Narcotic Addict Rehabilitation Act.

Changing the classification of marijuana, should the Administration persevere and the Congress assent, would tend to release more official time and attention for the more serious narcotics. The emphasis on rehabilitation cannot be faulted, although there will remain problems of insufficient knowledge, public acceptance, and funding to make rehabilitation work. Rehabilitation efforts now are as neglected as, say, the deficiencies of the criminal justice system in handling not just narcotics but all forms of crime—or, for that matter, as the causal problems of social distress and disorganization.

It is a commonplace to say that narcotics, and crime as well, are linked to the conditions of life for millions in the cities. But the linkage in the case of narcotics is of a special kind: if the behavioral scientists are correct, the use of the dead-end drugs is related directly to the alienation that characterizes slum-ghetto life— that is perhaps the chief by-product of poverty and racial prejudice. Further, the spread of alienation—and of drug use—to this generation of white, middle-class youth relates, at least in part, to their disenchantment with a society that cannot solve its most destructive human problems.

The suspicion grows, in the minds of the young and the blacks, that society doesn't want to solve them, has too many vested interests to maintain—that, in the case of narcotics, there is more than inattention involved in the tolerance of the role of organized crime. It is not enough to dismiss this suspicion as partially paranoid: its existence is sufficient to poison the atmosphere of the cities, and thus of society. It has reached the point where not the Carmichaels or Cleavers or Panthers but Rev. Andrew Young of the Southern Christian Leadership Conference can say: "Flooding the ghetto with drugs is typical of the white establishment's genocidal approach to the black man's problems. There is a constant war being waged in the ghetto between the people and the forces which would enslave them, and narcotics is probably the most deadly of these forces."

Young continues: "There's a legitimate paranoia in the ghetto, brought on by the loan shark on the corner, the door-to-door salesman, the numbers racketeer, the kids peddling hot merchandise—somebody is always offering these people 'a deal.' These are all obstacles—temptations that have to be overcome in order for the black man in the ghetto to live a decent, productive life and get out. But there's always somebody offering the good life *now*. Why wait? Get it on credit. These are things the middle-class white people don't come in contact with. They don't have to make a conscious moral decision every day of their lives.

"Drug addiction is a kind of suicide for people who don't have the strength to live nor the courage to die," Young concludes, "and the white man is always there to help him kill himself."

The spread of addiction could be a kind of suicide for an urban society.

5

Garbage, or Can We
Ever Get Away from It All?

Roger Starr

ON A narrow strip of Jersey marsh, garbage men are building a land bank; it grows day by day, stretching always a little farther from the black, polluted waters of Newark Bay toward its final limit: the edge of a six-lane interstate highway. At any hour, one can watch at least thirty sanitation trucks making their way across the top of the new bank. The covered trucks follow rutted roadways built from loads of broken brick and concrete that have been set aside from the flimsier trash, garbage, and household refuse. The trucks rock slowly up and down over the ruts, like heavy work-boats pitching in an oily sea, as they head for the open face of the bank, the slope on which loads are currently dumped. In fifteen years, more than a thousand acres have been covered with waste twelve feet deep from the cities of northern New Jersey. The speed of covering continually increases, both because the population of north Jersey is growing and because every American discards more waste each year.

New Jersey is one of the few states with strict regulations governing the operation of sanitary landfills. The proprietors of this marshland site must cover the dumped material with clean soil six inches deep, leaving only one day's working surface open and uncovered, to a limit of 15,-000 square feet. Following the trucks out to the working face, one meets the smell of refuse only

Part of Roger Starr's garbage underlies an enlarged Longshore Country Club near his home in Westport, Connecticut. And he is now helping to fill an unsightly mud-flat area near the Saugatuck River.

Reprinted from the Winter 1969 issue of *Horizon* by permission of the American Heritage Publishing Co., Inc.

when one approaches that uncovered space, where five Caterpillars rumble back and forth over recent dumping, compacting the fill and spreading the dirt that lies in piles on the already completed surface. When the smell comes, it is not the heart-stopping stench of sewage and animal decay but the stale, dusty odor of trash and chemicals, sweetened by only an intermittent whiff of the sickly scent of wet garbage. Papers that have blown loose from the heavier material before the dirt can be pushed over it dart fitfully across the landscape. They provide the only sign of life: the papers and the birds. Small bands of starlings, stubby creatures, peck at scraps of food caught in the soil cover; they are ignored by the great crowd of seagulls. A few of the gulls work their way up into the sky on heavy wingbeats, to glide there, high above the emptying trucks; thousands squat near the trucks on a layer of fill already discovered, waiting for news of sudden riches from the air-borne birds above.

Across the highway from the fill a great international airport spreads one runway parallel to the road. One herring gull, beating upward across the nose of a climbing airliner, can be sucked into one of the plane's mammoth jet pods where, dying, it may snuff out a hundred lives in a thunderous catastrophe. The public authority that owns the airport has shown its uneasiness over the proximity of gulls to jet planes, but no government has clear, final power to determine how great the danger is or what should be done about it. The question hovers over the landfill rather like the gulls themselves.

The strange possibility that buried refuse can reach up from the ground, as it were, to snatch an airliner from the sky, symbolically suggests the complex scope of industrial man's unprecedented need to shed the substances he has used but no longer wants. When men were farmers the problem was simpler; they threw away what they could not eat, and patched, mended, spliced, and sewed their other possessions forever. Industrial society discards a flood of objects so torrential that it may well drown us. Each year, in the United States, the trash contains a smaller and smaller portion of organic residues, which gradually change into humus, and a bigger and bigger portion of change-resistant, man-made artifacts and potions: old machines and their parts, bits of cities knocked down or dug up to be discarded, plastic containers in which men deliver their goods to one another, useless when emptied, tubs of chemicals that have served their purpose and represent the now-worthless distillate of vast quantities of raw materials extracted from the earth.

For an added irony, consider that the attempt to salvage useful flotsam from the flood founders on the very productivity that originally created it. A system capable of producing eight million automobiles a year must run smoothly; it cannot be slowed down to adjust to the slight irregularity in its operation that re-used components might cause. A labor force that is paid enough to buy back its produce cannot be put to work digging for valuable sherds in the wrack of last year's mechanical marvels, or yesterday's.

A calm marble statue with head and arms missing may well be the supreme symbol of the Greek desire to achieve order and moderation in a turbulent world. The descriptive modern artifact may well be the automobile hulk with shattered windows and missing wheels, the object of supreme romantic love reduced to a cause for mere embarrassment in only ten years.

Everyone remembers the glowing pride that suffused the family lined up along its driveway as Dad arrived from the dealer's in his new car; we reeled at the fresh scent of the synthetic leather, a perfume that vanished almost as quickly as the glow of a martini. The new car's glory is so brief that the first fender dent affects us like the clap of doom. How evanescent our life is! In the movie *Goldfinger* violent death for hundreds of male and female agents evoked not a quiver from the audiences, but the premature pressing of a mint-new Lincoln Continental into a block of scrap metal brought gasps of horror. By the time Dad turns into his driveway for the first time, his car has lost perhaps one-third of its value. Within a year it is no longer even thought of as new; within ten years it has become completely valueless. Some of its components—the wheels and tires, for example —may bring a few pennies from a scrap dealer, but not enough to pay anyone to remove them. The body is virtually worthless at the moment of its obsequies, even though it still holds several electric motors, intricately machined pistons and gears, laminated safety glass, to mention only a few bits of junk that could not have been purchased for an emperor's treasure only a hundred years ago. They will be buried now under twelve feet of other trash, there to remain until some day when, the relative values of labor and natural resources having changed, they will be dug up to provide raw materials for no-one-knows-what new artifacts to please no-one-knows-how-many hundreds of millions of men and women, who will then be discarding no-one-knows-what miraculous products not yet invented, until the globe—unless already terminated for some other reason—will consist only of a mass of discarded material in which all the elements needed to sustain organic life will be locked in a permanent but sterile chemical embrace. But automobiles—Americans throw away more than four million of them a year—are only a small part of America's garbage heaps. No figures are readily available to indicate the number of refrigerators and other major mechanical appliances discarded each year, but these, too, constitute a tremendous total of technical complexity, weight and bulk.

A visit to a landfill operation, or a drive through the streets of an American city during "Clean-up Week"—an annual period in some cities when residents are permitted to discard without penalty *any* object, however large, for disposal by the sanitation department or sanitary contractors—will quickly indicate that Americans also throw away sofas, mattresses, lamps, bent gutters and leaders from their houses, jarfuls of flammable paint thinners and cleaning fluids, and broken clocks, radios, television sets. During clean-up week these objects are piled on the

(PHOTO BY CHARLES GATEWOOD)

curbs, a melancholy fringe along the trimmed edges of suburbia.

And then there is the simple daily disgorging of soda-pop bottles, soup cans, cardboard and plastic containers, orange peels. Statisticians estimate that the average American home produces four and a half pounds of solid waste per person per day, more by far than any other nation.

This rough tally of identifiable municipal wastes has skipped the anonymous commercial and industrial waste products that constitute the largest single segment of the disposable tonnage: vast quantities of fly ash, the residue of pulverized coal that has been burned under electric generating-station boilers; debris from construction and demolition sites; by-product chemicals perhaps too degraded for any commercial re-use, but flammable nonetheless and hence a nuisance in a sanitary landfill; restaurant garbage; rock and dirt dug up from excavation sites within the city.

Modern man can no longer avoid the con-

sequences of his own productivity: all these things must be put *somewhere*. Almost every city in the nation is embroiled in some sort of controversy over the final disposition of its own waste, but the vigor of the arguments cannot stretch the possibilities for disposal. There remain only four possibilities on this planet, if one dismisses the likelihood of shooting the earthly waste out into space. Of the four the most sanguine hope is that waste can be reclaimed for future use. Hardly a month passes without a happy announcement that someone has developed a method for turning garbage into topsoil, or mining it for small quantities of rich metals like gold and silver. So far no reclaiming system has proved economically attractive to American mayors, under the local ground rules that govern this subject. This comes as bad news to those who remember that when they pulled K.P. in the army they were expected to divide wastes carefully into separate cans, presumably to facilitate the re-use of fats for explosives, paper products for new paper manufacture, and bones for chemicals and soap. The army system depended upon the availability of low-paid and underemployed laborers with a plethora of sergeants aching to keep their charges busy.

When reclamation is not feasible, some solid wastes can be disposed of in the air. They need only to be combined with oxygen; that is to say, burned. Large-scale municipal incinerators can, in theory, be designed to operate with great efficiency at very high temperatures. Such incinerators would not at all resemble the messy steel wigwams, now in use in many dumps, that merely create a slightly improved draft in a smelly bonfire. Since paper and paper products constitute almost half of present solid waste, a large, efficient furnace could be designed to burn this material at a temperature of 3,000 degrees Fahrenheit. Such a furnace would require no other fuel than the combustibles contained in the waste. It could actually generate enough heat to serve some useful purpose, perhaps making steam to warm nearby apartments. An efficient incinerator produces neither smoke nor odor, but is costly to build and requires expert supervision and maintenance.

Even the most efficient and smoke-free incinerator, however, creates an invisible residue in the form of carbon-dioxide gas, the result of combustion. If all the solid wastes in the world were burned daily, a considerable quantity of carbon dioxide would be added to the volumes already produced today by the combustion of fossil fuels like coal and oil. Does this matter to anyone? The question is less easily answered than framed. But as the rate of combustion increases and, coincidentally, as the stands of forest and other plant life throughout the world decrease, the measurable carbon dioxide content of the atmosphere is increasing. Clearly the maintenance of the oxygen–carbon-dioxide balance is vital to all forms of life on this planet. Would large-scale, efficient incineration of waste affect this balance? Nobody quite knows.

If depositing wastes in the air, even under the best possible circumstances, raises questions that no one can answer, what about stowing wastes on the land? This possibility raises a different question: Which land shall be used? Traditionally, municipal sanitation commissioners and private landfill operators have chosen swamps or marshes for their landfill operations.

No one particularly wanted the wetlands. The very word *swamp* suggests uselessness. It is easy enough to convince the governing body of a city that the fill will simply be making a beautiful golf course out of a mosquito incubator. Landfill operations designed only to hide waste have not been the only consumers of wetlands, which have also disappeared to create land for housing developments, highways, and harbors. But garbage disposal is a relentless need that cannot be long deferred. Only recently has anyone begun to notice how much coastline has been changed to make room for garbage. Connecticut, for example, watched more than half its wetlands disappear before the state passed a law that lends them a measure of protection against bulkheading and fill.

Marine and ornithological biologists have been able to establish that wetlands breed far more than mosquitoes; in fact the tidal marshlands produce more usable protein per acre than the richest farm land in the world. The protein, however, is not consumed directly by men and women, an unfortunate accident, for the small aquatic animals that do consume it are not represented in the state legislatures or Congress. These small creatures are in turn eaten by shellfish or the fry of important fish, including menhaden, winter flounder, and striped bass. Decline in the productivity of offshore fisheries can be traced to the obliteration of coastal marshes, not only because the nutrients for young fish disappear, but also due to the disappearance of the small coastal watercourses in which pelagic fish spawn and are hatched. Unfortunately, fishermen who depend on the fish population for their livelihood have only recently gained the sophistication to add their voice to those of the conservationists.

Fresh-water wetlands, also popular for landfill, are not the nuisances they have generally been taken for. They are natural sumps, gathering rainfall that penetrates the substrata of the land and keeps the water table constant. It is ironic that in some areas, Long Island for one, where natural fresh-water wetlands have been filled in for housing sites, artificial sumps have had to be dug to replace the hydrologic function. There are in many parts of the country far more suitable barren areas, productive of little wildlife, that could be used effectively for depositing solid waste if the filling operation were intelligently handled and carefully controlled. There are many big holes in America—the holes of vast mining operations—that could be filled successfully with solid wastes to everyone's benefit, but few municipalities are ready to spend the money to transport their wastes to the places where they would be welcome. Solid wastes, moving to these mines, may someday be the most dependable bulk cargo of the railroads. Used properly, these wastes can even create attractive surroundings. In the vicinity of Chicago a combination of waste and excavated material has been used to build up a hill that is now used as a ski slope. Its stability indicates that compacted fill, placed intelligently, can modify flat land and turn it into interesting landscape with unexpected recreational uses.

If the uses of land are limited, the only remaining depository is the water. But here the courts have raised a cautious hand. The Supreme Court has held that wastes cannot be simply dumped into the ocean, for no government in the United States has the right to inflict a nuisance on the beaches of its neighbors. Too much of the solid-waste load floats. The key to the constructive use of water as a final disposal site for solid waste lies in the compaction of the waste to increase its specific gravity. The Japanese have developed a press capable of compacting solid waste so tightly that it will not disintegrate. The compaction raises the specific gravity so high that the material sinks like a rock. These bundles, dumped at sea, would simply settle on the bottom, where they would not harm anything and might form artificial reefs that would be of help to the fish population. Land for unwelcome uses—monster jetports, for example—might be constructed from bundles of supercompacted waste, which would save precious wetlands and the ears and nerves of those living nearby.

Ultimately it becomes clear that our planet is limited, like any house, and that the time will come when its attic will overflow with the accumulated debris of years of habitation. There is the difference, however, that when the attic of a house fills up, one may clean it out and pay someone to take the debris away. But things cannot be carted away from the earth; our planet, as the economist Kenneth Boulding has told us, is a spaceship to which nothing can be added and from which nothing can be taken away. The ultimate problem of solid waste is not that the waste itself takes up valuable room on the spaceship but that the stock of elements is limited, and if the elements are locked into waste irretrievably, they are lost to human life. As the character of man's waste has changed—from organic compounds capable of decomposition and regeneration through the metabolic processes of life, to compounds such as plastics, which resist decomposion—so the ability of the earth to sustain life may have been impaired. It is quite possible that at some time or other so much of the needed life matter will be locked into waste that the earth will not be able to sustain the population living on it. One assumes that the earth will reach this tipping point slowly, after a long period during which raw materials will become scarcer and more expensive, the standard of living will decline, and the quality of the natural environment deteriorate. And one assumes that, given warning, mankind will do something to stave off disaster.

But even with ample warning there is little to suggest that men will be able to change direction. At stake here is man's ability, nay willingness, to control his own productivity, to measure the seriousness of the waste that will result from each extension of his productivity, each new artifact, each new human life. The control over inventiveness, love, and hunger that would be required in order to utilize natural resources wisely and avoid crossing the balance point might well destroy so many of the human values that man would be incapable of asserting this control. Will men prefer to drown in the waste of their pleasures? Or will they prefer to control them in the hope of prolonging life? This, nothing less, is the question that lies burning at the bottom of the dump.

section two PLANS

Introduction

ENOUGH has been said: we are without doubt in serious trouble. Then what are we doing about it? This section takes a look at some specific attempts to deal with the urgent problems of the cities.

We start off with Christopher Alexander, who at first glance doesn't seem to deal with these problems at all. He has almost nothing say about race or poverty, or subcultures of violence, or the decay of the inner core. In a curious way he always seems, in speaking of planning, to have an individual in mind. But notice what his essay is really talking about most of the time: the problem of alienation that lies beneath the surface of so many urban desperations. He is talking about people who don't have a sufficient sense of what they are or what they're worth, and certainly very little sense of meaning or power in their community. He gives long lists of hypothetical but specific examples showing what design and planning can actually do both to enlarge people's lives and to improve their cities. He is talking about *how* to plan.

Alexander's essay is followed by a series of essays on three very different, highly specialized communities recently built or being built in urban areas: Resurrection City, the temporary housing settlement put up in 1968 for the Poor People's March in Washington; the student center at Berkeley, California, designed to facilitate use by the students, and some say excessively successful in achieving this goal; and Thamesmead, near London, an example of urban construction on a scale so huge as to revolutionize the building process by industrializing it.

The final two essays have to do with planning and the business community, and in particular with certain new zoning techniques designed to keep the urban economy rolling along, but side by side with, rather than at the expense of, its cultural life. In the case of New York's theater district, these techniques are having a very promising kind of success. Although the negotiations have been admittedly strenuous on both governmental and private sides, most of those involved have reached the point of mutual congratulations. Meanwhile, the legal grounds for the concept of special districting are slowly but surely evolving in our courts of law.

—W. McQ.

6

Major Changes in Environmental Form Required by Social and Psychological Demands

Christopher Alexander

I

THERE is a strange dichotomy between the present architecture and planning professions. On the one hand, the architects are in the habit of creating completely mad idealistic utopias. These utopias often have little meaning, they are unlikely to be implemented; often no one in his right mind would want to implement them. They are personal dreams, not anchored in reality. Archigram's city on legs is an extreme example.

One the other hand, the current generation of city and regional planners—and the regional scientists are included—have established a tradition of boring attention to detailed facts, and extrapolation from these facts. The future, as seen by planners, is merely a tidier version of the present. While architects dream of utterly unimaginable futures, the planners talk about piecemeal incremental planning. The visionary architecture is imaginative, daring, but completely mad. The planners' plans are utterly and boringly sane; though based on facts, they offer no comprehensive vision of a better future.

We may strengthen these statements. It is no exaggeration to say that many of the most imaginative utopian architects actually dislike

Apart from his duties in the Department of Architecture, University of California at Berkeley, Professor Alexander is Director of the Center for Environmental Structure.

This address was delivered at the Second International Symposium on Regional Development held in Tokyo in September 1968, under the auspices of the Japan Center for Area Development Research.

facts, and have a kind of supercilious disregard for them. And it is no exaggeration either to say that the kind of data gathering which planners most often do, since it is based on data about the status quo, tends to reinforce the status quo; and that planners—perhaps because of their concern with this kind of data—tend to have a rather conservative attitude.

This split is more serious than it seems. It is more than a mere difference of philosophy between the two professions. What it amounts to is this. We have not found a way of making a coherent, criticizable and empirically founded statement about the kind of future we want for the living of life in cities. So long as the split between utopians and data gatherers persists, it will not be possible to make such a statement. The reason is obvious. A statement of this kind will require vital imagination about man's future, based on empirical insights about the really deep forces in a man's life.

The possibility of constructing serious utopias in this sense is being set back, at present, by two beliefs—widely held by planners in the United States.

1. The first of these beliefs says that the physical form of the environment has very little effect on behavior—hence, that the physical form of the environment is not very important socially. According to this view we can tolerate architecture as a kind of amusement which has to do with beauty—the sugar on the cake—but we are supposed to recognize that it really has very little to do with the problem of making cities better to live in. Since most of the "com-

prehensive" urban utopias have been physical ones, designed by architects, this belief functions as a kind of backhand attack on utopian thinking.

2. The second belief—not so explicitly stated as the first—says that psychological insights, while no doubt interesting, are as yet too vaguely formulated to have any serious bearing on urban form. According to this view concern with the nature of life cannot have any serious bearing on the day-to-day work of the urban and regional planner.

As we shall see, both of these beliefs, though clothed in scientific reasonableness, are in fact merely offshoots of the more general refusal of city planners today to make a concrete statement of what life is all about. Let me say a few more words about each of these beliefs.

What about the first belief, that the physical environment has little effect on behavior? This belief has come into play only during the last few years when planners and architects have been claiming that they can influence people's well-being by manipulating the physical environment. A typical statement was Neutra's: "Let me design a house for a happily married couple, and I can have them divorced within six months." This sort of arrogance naturally invited suspicion. People have begun to quote the famous Hawthorne experiment—where it was shown that the crucial variable, responsible for increased production and worker well-being in an electric plant, was the attitude of management, not the pleasantness of the physical environment. Another famous study of workers in northern California examined their life-style while they were living in a high-density slum in Richmond, and then three years later, their life-style when they were living in a low-density suburban area of single-family houses; their life-styles had not changed in any significant respect.

The recent statements by Webber and others, which show that social groupings are not based on spatial proximity but, rather, on communality of interest, have been widely received. The planners who take this idea to its most extreme form, say: Let the urban sprawl go on any way it wants to—what really matters are the economic and social organizations, not the spatial. This general attitude has gone so far now in the United States that many intelligent students and young professionals have become convinced that the spatial organization of cities does not really matter much and have gone into other, more obviously social, fields.

What about the second belief, that psychological problems are too subtle to be taken seriously? I have never actually seen this belief expressed in print. But it is reasonable to infer it from the subjects which planners most often deal with. In urban planning and regional science, two closely associated disciplines predominate: economics of location, and transportation theory. It is not unfair to say that 90 percent of the literature on regional science deals with one of these two topics. Even in the architectural literature, where there are occasional references to psychological questions, they are almost never seriously studied.

It is perhaps helpful to ask *why* the regional science literature is so heavily weighted toward the problems of economics and transportation. The answer is very simple. Since these are the two disciplines where reasonable models can be made with the help of arithmetic and elementary mathematics, and since the people who started out to develop regional science were enthusiastic "model builders," wanted to be scientific and precise, and loved playing with numbers, the field of urban planning was slanted in this direction. If you press a regional scientist, and ask him why he does not take social and psychological problems more seriously, he will say that he would like to, but that unfortunately these subjects are not yet sufficiently precise, and nothing sensible can be done with them.

II

I shall now give a series of examples to show that these two beliefs are mistaken and to show that, in a modest way, careful consideration of psychological problems will lead to major revisions of environmental form.

To begin with, we must face squarely just what the task of city planning is: it is, in short, the design of culture. A culture is a system of standard situations. Each of these situations specifies certain roles, certain allowed limits of behavior for the persons in these roles, and the requisite spatial setting for this behavior. Each situation thus specifies a certain physical pattern—and each pattern recurs many thousands of times in a given city. The form of the city is generated by the combination of these patterns. In this sense, the city, viewed as a purely physical system, is a direct concrete manifestation of the culture. Any attempt to change the physical organization is an indirect attempt to change the culture. That is why I say that city planning is the design of culture.

Each person in a culture lives his life by moving from situation to situation; he builds his life up as a kind of necklace by stringing together those situations which are available to him in his culture. In a successful culture, the set of situations which is available to him is sufficient to allow all the inner forces which develop in him free play. In order to criticize a culture, we must find in the lives of its members recurrent situations which expose the members to conflicts which they cannot resolve within the framework of the cultural institutions and situations that the culture normally makes available to them. We may then try to invent new institutions, or institutionalized situations, compatible with the rest of the culture, but capable of letting people resolve these conflicts for themselves.

In order to make such a criticism, we need to know something rather concrete about the inner forces which a person is typically exposed to during the course of his life: otherwise, we cannot say what kinds of conflict he will experience. Recent work in psychology and social psychology has done much to help us here. It will perhaps help to make this clear, if I first mention a very early view of human needs presented by Bronislaw Malinowski. Malinowski said that a culture is a system of institutions designed to satisfy seven basic needs: metabolism, reproduction, bodily comfort, safety, movement, growth and health.

This view does not help us to criticize the culture of a metropolitan United States at all. At this level of analysis, we have every right to be satisfied with our culture. We do have food supply, housing, transportation, schools, parks and hospitals. All we need is more of them, perhaps. But these seven basic needs give an extremely mechanistic view of man's nature. More recent study of needs has shown us a rather more complex picture. Consider, for example, the work of Alexander Leighton, Abraham Maslow, and Erik Erikson.

Leighton identifies ten basic strivings in man: physical security; sexual satisfaction; the expression of love; the expression of hostility; the securing of love; the securing of recognition; the expression of spontaneity; orientation in terms of one's place in society; the securing and maintenance of membership in a definite human group; and the sense of belonging to a moral order and being right in what one does.

If we assume that these ten strivings are at work in adults, then it already becomes rather clearer that our present culture does not always provide an adequate system of institutions for the expression of these strivings. And, as Leighton says, frustration of these strivings leads not to physical death, but to psychiatric disorder and to spiritual death.

Maslow has described a hierarchical system of evolutionary needs. According to his view, once the basic system of food and drink needs has been met, the system of security and safety needs comes into play. Once these safety needs are being met, a system of need for affection comes into play; and once this system of affection needs is being met, the individual experiences a need for self-actualization—development of the self. In advanced economies the earlier systems are usually met, and the later systems are the most important. The last of all, the effort toward self-actualization, is a system which is very inadequately met by people in modern Western culture, and the culture does little to support it.

Erikson takes a developmental view, according to which each person goes through eight major stages during the course of his life. At each stage the person is fighting a particular spiritual battle: Erikson calls them crises. A healthy person must win each of these battles in order to be able to go on to the next; if any one of the crises is met unsuccessfully, development cannot go on to the next stage: the person gets stuck. The eight stages are:

Basic trust—mistrust	Infant
Autonomy—shame/doubt	Infant
Initiative—guilt	Child
Industry—inferiority	Child
Identity—role confusion	Teenager
Intimacy—isolation	Young adult
Generativity—stagnation	Adult
Ego integrity—despair	Old age

Again, there is abundant clinical evidence to show that the system of institutions which our culture provides does not give each person a reasonable chance of meeting each of these crises successfully.

With the help of these notions, I shall now state a number of typical recurrent problems which cannot be solved within the framework of our existing culture. In each case I shall propose a pattern which may help to solve the problem. (Many of these patterns were developed at the Center for Environmental Structure, Berkeley.) I define a pattern as a new cultural institution, together with the physical and spatial changes needed to provide a setting for this new institution. These patterns are intended for the present culture of metropolitan United States. (I do not know whether they would be appropriate for metropolitan Japan. I do not even know whether the problems they are based on occur in Japan. Such changes must, of course, always be specific to one particular culture.)

In each case, I have tried to put each of these proposals on an empirical basis. I do not claim that any one of these patterns is correct as stated. I am merely trying to show the order

of magnitude of the changes which careful consideration of psychological issues will lead to. However, to make this point, it is important to show that these patterns are not merely products of idle dreaming, and are not merely "utopian" in the bad old architectural sense. I shall therefore propose one or more experiments which could be carried out in connection with each of these patterns, to test its validity.

Each pattern is stated in three parts: (a) a brief summary of the pattern itself; (b) a brief summary of the problem which the pattern solves (with notes showing the relevant concepts in Leighton, Erikson and Maslow; (c) a collection of short refutable hypotheses which, when made more precise, could be used to test the validity of the pattern.

The statements are very sketchy—no more than shorthand. After the statements of the individual patterns, I describe a city where all twenty patterns are present together.

III

1. CELLS. Many small residential areas (diameter 200-2,000 feet), each one a different

subculture—the total variety of subcultures far greater than today, and also the variety of subcultures per square mile greater than today (Hendricks, Alexander).

People seek their own kind. Character formation. Self-actualization. Require support of "same kind of people." This requires great variety of people. Also requires exposure to many other types of people. Requires safety affection all OK (Maslow, self-actualization; Leighton, orientation).

Hypotheses:

a) Physical barrier helps formation of more distinct subculture.
   Homogeneous continuous development prevents formation of subcultures.
b) Support of differentiated subculture helps character formation.
c) Exposure of variety of different subcultures allows fuller choice, and therefore leads to self-actualization.
d) Subcultures latent in modern city are very numerous.
e) Provision of appropriate facilities will induce formation of subculture.

2. ROADS. Cellular network of one-way high-speed arteries (parallel, cellular, hexagonal—doesn't matter); (Walkey, Hershdorfer, Alexander). People seek greater average speeds, and will stick to private vehicles as far as possible. Contact. Spontaneity (Leighton, expression of love, securing of love, spontaneity).

Hypotheses:

a) For a given arrangement of origin destinations a network of largely one-way arteries optimizes flow (i.e., average speed); (Hershdorfer).
b) Capacity of such arterial loops is very large—can clear as many as 8,000 cars per hour (Walkey).
c) Friendship satisfaction varies with the number of acquaintances who can be reached in five minutes.
d) Average number of planned versus unplanned encounters correlates with disorders of spostaneity (clinical).

3. SMALL GROUP WORK. Scattered semi-autonomous employment—each large organization consisting of many smaller units—loosely connected by phone, etc. Each one largely autonomous.

Efficiency of work. Understanding of the purpose of work. Autonomy, self-determination. Self-respect. Split work/play (Erikson, generativity; Maslow, self-actualization; Leighton, membership in definite human group).

Hypotheses:

a) Work efficiency improves under small work conditions.
b) Small work groups report better satisfaction on the part of workers.
c) Work quality, quantity, and worker satisfaction decrease as number of levels of administrative hierarchy increases.
d) Number of cases of mental illness in individual or his family correlated with number of levels of hierarchy above him.
e) Spatial centralization of work effort not correlated with overall efficiency of output.
f) Split in work/play has an effect on mental picture of the world. Test by Osgood's method.
g) Test resentment of wives, children, on not knowing the purpose or details of husbands' work.
h) Under present circumstances few real friends at work. Depth of friendships at work correlated with size of autonomous group.
i) Work efficiency and involvement go up when work/play cycle is freed to each individual's own rhythm (Schnelle).

4. WINDOWS. Every workplace has windows overlooking areas of life. This has huge implications either for building shape (exterior windows) or for mixed land use (interior windows); (Alexander, Ishikawa, Silverstein).

People need refreshment—the opportunity to break out of the immediate social world. Can't keep getting up and going somewhere.

Hypotheses:

a) In windowless rooms, projective tests show bad state of mind.
b) Rooms with windows, if only of sky or other buildings, would show similar results, less acute.
c) Window significant to worker as a source of "change" not daylight (Markus).

5. OLD-AGE ISLANDS. Each one holds about 75 people (50-100). Scattered as widely as possible, so that they occur in every type of

neighborhood—i.e., every type of cell (Falor).

On the one hand, economies of scale—shared facilities, etc. On the other hand, need for interaction with rest of society—both for old and for young. At present old people forced into large relatively isolated aggregations by cost and by old-age cities (Erikson, ego integrity—despair; Leighton, human group).

Hypotheses:

a) Disease incidence higher among adults who are separated from the young (Liverpool).

b) Fear of death higher among young people with little contact with old people.

c) Old-age trauma (retirement) worse for people who have not had contact with the old.

d) Old people want to live where other old people are: how large must colony be before this want dies out?

e) Retirement trauma improved if people can go on living in the same general type of neighborhood (Falor).

6. CRUISING STRIP (context: rich, low density). Every metropolitan area has cruising strips —a strip, many lanes, no through traffic, hotdogs, etc., sidewalks, between lanes, lights, special parking, many stops possible. Strips spaced at about 20-mile intervals (Goldberg).

Teenagers need a place to meet. Houses not suitable. Schools closed. Large crowds come together by car. Police a problem today. Boys' clubs etc., won't work (Erikson, identity—role confusion).

Hypotheses:

a) Increase in the number of persons taking part in this activity.

b) Where such strips exist, thousands of persons take part.

c) Teenagers will mention express need to meet in public, unhindered by adults in interview, etc.

d) Negative correlation between teenage crime and attendance at such gatherings.

7. PUBLIC DISCUSSION PLACES. Frequently spaced: on the sidewalk circular rooms about 10 feet in diameter—discussion only. Sidewalk adapted to hold it (McCoy).

Loneliness: No avenues for meeting. Open talk (Leighton, moral order—right in what one does; Maslow, self-actualization).

Hypotheses:

a) If a place clearly designated as talking place, people will go there.

b) People have a need to talk to people—but don't know how to enter into serious talk with them.

c) High attendance at T-group type meetings (Synanon, etc).

8. SCHOOLS OPEN TO THE CITY, connected with other functions, not closed. Integrated with work-study in commercial institutions (Hoare and Silverstein).

Adolescent feels disconnected from society. Compare with village culture. Hence no possibility of identity formation; and disenchantment (Leighton, recognition; Erikson, identity).

Hypotheses:

a) Feeling of teenage alienation inversely correlated with degree of work-study.

b) Gradual mastery of real tasks correlated with strong identity formation (cf. East African example); (clinical).

c) Correlation of learning speed with relevance of material (Bruner).

d) Negative correlation between teenage alienation and effective participation in social institutions during childhood.

9. UNIVERSITY. Loose aggregation of small centers. Mainly small-group work. Use of all members of society in this process. Especially women, old people. No closed campus.

All people involved in the process of education. Adult education. Learning—teaching. Handing on insights to next generation (anthropology). Women's university in Los Angeles. Chinese commune. Life a process, going in and out of university continuously. Budget will not permit seminar type s/f ratio under present circumstances. Giving courses as common as taking them (Leighton, orientation; Erikson, generativity).

Hypotheses:

a) Research shifting more and more to small centers and institutes.

b) Increase in adult education.

c) More learned by teacher than by student.

d) Greatest influence on education had in small group study (midwest).

e) Satisfaction of adults (note especially

women and old) related to the extent to which they see themselves as handing on information, culture, etc., to next generation.

10. GROUP HOUSES. Dwellings where group of people, married and/or single, live in commune.

Family too small. Tensions. Huxley Island. Need for more mixed, less intense, contact—balancing out tensions; close contact with more people (Erikson, intimacy; Leighton, hostility).
Hypotheses:
a) Increasing tendency for people to seek such arrangements today (music groups, spread of kibbutzim, *Telluride,* summer houses).
b) Correlation of mental health with average size of household (indirect evidence of this in high mental health of Italian and Hong Kong areas).

11. SEE-THROUGH LIVING ROOM; porch; direct contact between every dwelling and public thorough fare. More private pavilions (Alexander).

Need to be in touch with the community. Contact. Possibility of dropping in. Privacy a matter of choice (Erikson, intimacy—isolation; Leighton, spontaneity).
Hypotheses:
a) Distance from street correlates with incidence of nervous disorders and upper respiratory disorders (Medical Journal).
b) Reports of loneliness correlated with distance from street (confirmed by British studies).
c) Correlation of isolation and indices of mental trouble (Faris, etc.).

12. THICK WALLS. Every lived-in room has walls of materials which are easy to mold and adapt and form permanently to individual and habits. Hence owned dwellings: condominium (Alexander).

People seek feeling of relation to environment; they need the possibility of local adaptation. Present building types make it hard.
Hypotheses:
a) People modify their dwellings as much as they are able to.
b) The personal character of a room, as perceived by inhabitants, resides mainly in the walls.

c) Depressed results of impersonal room character. Rate of turnover in personnel. Projective tests (Maslow-Mintz).
d) Self-esteem greater in a place which one has influenced (correlation of self-esteem with other indices of well-being). Ego-strength.

13. THE TEENAGE ROOM/COTTAGE/STUDIO. Teenage a period of exploration and identity-seeking—new in industrial society, since choice of adult life not automatic. Requires possibility of exploration while at home (Silverstein).
Hypotheses:
a) Relation between parents and teenage children better if children have place of their own, private access (clinical/subjective reports).
b) Where room close to parents children report constrained feeling.
c) Incidence of runaways higher in homes where this relation does not exist; lower in homes where it does.

14. CHILD CARE. In areas where families with small children live, each house opens off a common area which is entirely enclosed—connected to nursery supervision.
Small children need each other in play.
Danger to them on streets.
Parents want to go out.
Hypotheses:
a) Greater incidence of mental illness among children who have no playmates in first five years.
b) Correlation between mental trouble for child and nonactivity of mother (when mother is educated); (Mead).
c) Even where there are efficient nurseries, away from home, amount of use is considerably reduced (Denmark).
d) Incidence of child trouble caused by conflict by keeping child in, against wishes (cf. reports of how wonderfully manageable children are when they can play together in unlimited amounts).

15. DENSITY OF RESIDENCES at different distances from local community facilities and centers: as nearly as possible: 50 percent within two blocks, 25 percent within six blocks, 25 percent more than six blocks (Loetterle).
Expressed preferences. Close ones still want

gardens, etc. Deeper significance not clear. Guess introvert-extrovert dimension.

Hypotheses:

a) Distribution statistics of vacancies and houses for sale conforms to pattern.

b) More disorders among people whose introvert-extrovert rating is mismatched with their dwelling location.

16. CITY HALL SMALL (max. population, 40,000), and highly accessible place for discussion, complaint, political action. Cf. multi-service centers (Alexander, Ishikawa, Silverstein).

Political effectiveness. Small units. Culture of poverty (Erikson, generativity; Leighton, moral order, spontaneity, orientation).

Hypotheses:

a) Need for political action exists; compare well-being of those with involvement with those without it (check across cultures).

b) Hopelessness is correlated with noneffectiveness.

c) Effectiveness of citizens a function of the size of community.

d) Involvement correlated with ease of access to city hall, and possibility of starting programs there.

e) Maximum size of institution still capable of retaining informal atmosphere, freedom from red-tape, is about twenty persons.

17. RELIGIOUS CENTER extended displays where picture of desired urban life can evolve, and be discussed and criticized freely.

All cultures have religion. One function is to provide a communal world view, with community participation, which connects each man's picture of his own life to that of the community.

Hypotheses:

a) Correlation between mental health and ability of person to state a connection between his own life and the structure of the larger world.

18. TREES. Special fixed inviolable locations very frequently spaced throughout the city.

The need for a relationship with trees. Contemplation. Especially old trees. Length of time for trees to grow versus rate of demolition and construction in urban areas. Contemplating existence and permanence as opposed to action.

Hypotheses:

a) House price correlated with presence of trees in neighborhood.

b) Reverence for trees correlated with age of the trees.

c) Ill effects of long-term isolation from nature.

d) Part played by trees in convalescent process (medical evidence).

e) Person able to lose himself more completely in the presence of a tree, than without tree (may also apply to rivers, ocean, etc.—but these are rare and far apart).

19. PECKHAM HEALTH CENTER. Place which makes much of birth process. Pre-, post-natal clinic, swimming, etc.

Birth. Surround it with importance. Effect on the mother, hence on the child, if this is not done (Erikson, basic trust-mistrust).

Hypotheses:

a) Correlation between attitude of mother to birth, before birth, and mental well-being of child afterward.

b) Correlation between importance given to birth as an event, pre and post, and the well-being of the child.

20. DEATH. Funerals, cemeteries, etc. More respect for dead.

Longer and more complicated process of burial.

Need to absorb the death of those you love. Death rites. Virtual absence of death rites in our own culture.

Hypotheses:

a) If death not "lived through" psychologically, trouble likely (clinical evidence); (Lindemann).

b) Negative correlation between clinical problems traceable to death of loved ones; and relative importance of death rites in different cultures.

IV

These patterns are only a few of hundreds of similar large-scale patterns which must be combined to create the full form of an urban environment. Nor have I mentioned the literally thousands of patterns at smaller scales, which will combine to give the detailed form of buildings. And I have not described the combinatory rules which allow us to put these few patterns together. However, few as they are, they already begin to define a radically different city from the cities we live in today.

There is no Central Business District (CBD). The city consists of hundreds of small residential islands, each with a different subculture. Density is high at the edge of these islands, and falls off toward the center of each one. The islands are widely separated, and surrounded, by a sea of employment and communal facilities. Also winding around the islands there are nets of high-speed one-way arteries. All employment is radically decentralized—even when a corporation is large, it consists of many small autonomous group-run workshops. The university and schools are woven in and out of the entire fabric of the city. They do not exist as distinct entities. The process of education is going on all the time, and involves all members of the culture. Houses and households have a much greater variety of size and type than they do today. Some are group houses, in which many individuals live together. At the other extreme there are individual cottages for teenagers and old people. Some houses, for families with small children, surround inaccessible, shared gardens which touch all the houses but cannot be reached directly from outside. In some cases, as for teenagers, the one-room cottages are attached to larger houses. Thus we shall find many dwelling units grouped hierarchically around slightly larger ones, and these larger ones in turn again grouped hierarchically in larger groups. None of these dwellings will be high-rise in the modern sense—all houses will have at least some part where they come into open, visible contact with the outside. All dwellings are owned. The city is dotted with many tiny knots of trees, undisturbed by demolition or construction. Many of the cells contain colonies of old people—these colonies smaller than the basic cells themselves—where life runs a little more slowly. There are many kinds of highly specialized places devoted to public meeting—the teenage cruising strip, the covered discussion seats, and the new kind of highly accessible city hall which I described are merely examples. The detailed structure of all these buildings, especially the dwellings, is such that the final details are personal. The walls and materials are capable of remembering the touch of the inhabitants who live there—they are rich with detailed individual adaptations. The sterile thin panels of today will be unknown.

Even without making drawings, or models, or filling in the details, I think it is clear that this is a kind of city utterly different from the one in which we live today.

I do not expect you to agree with the particular patterns which I have presented—on the basis of the scant evidence I have given. That was not my purpose in this paper. What is clear is that physical conceptions as radical as the one which I have sketched out can be reached on the basis of common-sense discussion of the issues concerning human nature, as they are known to anthropologists and psychologists today. Every one of the patterns which I have described can be discussed, tested, and improved, on the basis of simple, feasible experiments. Yet the overall picture thus presented is as radical, as utopian, as the visions of classical artist-architects.

Let us review the two detailed questions with which I began: Are psychological matters too subtle to handle? Does the physical form of the environment have any effect on behavior?

First of all, these examples will hardly allow us to accept the view of regional scientists and planners who claim that economic location and transportation—because they can be quantified—are the only problems which can be competently handled. Even the material which I have presented is enough, I think, to discredit the idea that social psychology is too vague to play a useful part in city planning, or too subtle to take seriously. The issues which I have mentioned are, indeed, so unsubtle, so massive, that we tend to pass them by in our everyday lives, as being hopelessly unamenable to change. They are not subtle. We are all aware of them. In order to take these issues seriously, we need only have the courage to take them seriously. Although the scientific evidence which shows that these demands are critical is admittedly weak, this is only, I believe, because we have not so far tried to find evidence of this kind. The idea that we should consciously try to design our own culture, seems crazy at first sight—and so much so that people simply haven't been trying to gather the right kind of evidence.

Second, we come to the question: Does the

environment influence behavior? This is a curiously mechanistic and behavioristic question. Of course the physical environment, *alone,* has little effect on human behavior or welfare. Can we seriously expect that the position of a wall is going to make us happy rather than unhappy. We are not rats in a conditioning experiment. But the conclusion which planners have been drawing from this obvious point—namely, that therefore the organization of the physical environment does not matter much—is false. I have given a number of examples of psychological demands, which occur in metropolitan United States. The examples show that if we take these demands seriously, and try to invent cultural institutions which deal with these demands, we shall then have to make major physical changes in the environment. In every case, the argument which connects the psychological demands with the change in spatial pattern is simple and common sense. What does this prove? It does not prove that the environment has an effect upon behavior. I have not claimed, in any one of the examples, that the form of buildings *alone* will have an influence on people's lives, on their behavior, or on their needs. In every case, the pattern of walls or doors or buildings that I have specified, is specified along with some kind of social change. The environmental change, without the social, would accomplish nothing. But the reverse is also true. These social changes cannot be made unless the physical changes are made with them. There is no more point in trying to make the social change without the physical than vice versa.

Let me finally stress, once again, the extremely tentative nature of the patterns which I have proposed, and the empirical results which I have based them on. Experiments in social psychology are notoriously difficult, and always subject to interpretation. However, even the scant evidence which I have presented has clear implications. And, I believe, once it is made clear that new patterns may be derived from these empirical insights, this will greatly sharpen our ability to find evidence. The evidence which I have cited so far has accumulated more or less randomly. If patterns of the type I have described are defined first, and empirical studies made second, with the process of empirical observation specifically designed to refute, or support, hypotheses connected with individual patterns, the whole process will be greatly sharpened.

But I do not apologize for the tentative nature of the patterns. Indeed, in a way it expresses rather clearly their most important feature: the fact that they are set up to be criticized. They are deliberately open to criticism. They invite it.

Each one is stated in such a way that it can be criticized by experiment and observation. This gives each person the chance to disagree with the patterns on the basis of public, empirical findings—there is therefore every prospect that we shall one day be able to define patterns which we agree on. These patterns therefore have an enormous advantage over the private visions of an architect. However vulnerable they may seem today, they raise the prospect of finding form for the environment that is so firmly based on the demands of human nature, that planners and architects will all be able to agree on it. This is a prospect which current methods of architecture and planning cannot look forward to.

7

Planning and Using Resurrection City

John Wiebenson

RESURRECTION City was the dwelling place, on the Mall, of about 2,800 demonstrators brought to Washington, D.C., as part of Martin Luther King, Jr.'s, "Poor People's Campaign of 1968." Rains and organizational difficulties within the city and the campaign eventually caused severe problems; yet at the peak of its development it was a demonstration of people building for themselves with enthusiasm and pride. Though temporary, Resurrection City is a useful model of the community development process in action.

Resurrection City was built and occupied, then emptied and dismantled, within forty-three days during May and June of 1968. These were rainy days in the nation's capital, days made more grim by the assassinations of Martin Luther King, Jr., and Robert F. Kennedy.

Rev. Dr. King called Resurrection City into being as part of his "Poor People's Campaign of 1968." He claimed the country was blind to the existence of the poor and to their food, housing, and medical problems. Resurrection City and the campaign were intended to make the poor "visible" by bringing representatives to

John Wiebenson graduated from Harvard College and then served in the Engineer Corps. After receiving a graduate degree in architecture, he worked for several San Francisco architects and then with four colleagues started an architecture and planning firm there. Since 1967, he has been an Associate Professor at the University of Maryland's new School of Architecture and a guest critic at Yale.

Reprinted by permission of the *Journal of the American Institute of Planners,* Vol. 35, No. 6 (November 1969).

Washington where, during the life of the city, they would be seen by Congressmen and, via the press and TV, by the rest of the country.

This study will discuss the planning, construction, and use of Resurrection City from the vantage point of one of the members of the advisory committee on buildings and community plans. Main topics of consideration will include organization for planning, construction systems, community systems, and conclusions about this example of the community development process.

ORGANIZATION FOR PLANNING

About a month before the original starting date for building Resurrection City, a committee was formed to give advice on buildings and community plans.[1] Originally, our committee was to advise on occupancy and layout of donated tents. But, like so many donations, the tents never appeared. We were soon asked for more and more advice, and eventually some of us helped to build or helped campaign leaders to negotiate with the government for the site. As the Structures Committee, we worked with other committees for food, medicine, procurement and storage, services, transportation, legal aid, and nonpoor involvement. Most committee members came from the Washington area, and most were white professionals, but there were many black professionals and local poor as well.

Committees operated under the direction of Anthony Henry, a community organizer on leave of absence from a program in Chicago. Henry, as Local Coordinator, headed the weekly meetings of committee chairmen, and was also the liaison with the leaders of the Southern Christian Leadership Conference (who controlled finances and major decisions, but who remained out of town until immediately before the city was built). Basically, then, we were part of a large body of part-time planners working fairly closely with the local representative of a distant and rather scattered client.

Residents were recruited from all over the country, but mostly from the rural south and the large cities of the northeast and midwest. Most of the whites came from the Appalachian highlands. They were all ages, but mostly they were young. There were Indians, whites, Puerto Ricans, and Mexican-Americans among them, but most were blacks. Nobody knew how many would come, and estimates varied between 3,000 and 5,000, once getting as high as 15,000. Actually, the city was to hold about 2,800, primarily because the Mexican-Americans never lived there.

Our first move as the Structures Committee was to collect as much information as we could about residents, building materials, and site conditions. Since limited data were available, we filled in the gaps with assumptions. Our basic assumption about the residents grew out of the fact that they were coming from diverse backgrounds to dwell, briefly, in a community imbedded in what would be for them an alien environment. Therefore, we felt they would need the city's formal and programmatic framework to be both complete and explicit. This framework would have to respond to a wide variety of needs as the residents would require not only arrangements for security and health, but also conditions that facilitated neighborly relationships. Since we assumed that a resident's "day" would be devoted not only to eating, sleeping, and demonstrating, structures to house informal activities would also be needed. Finally, we assumed that three-quarters of the residents would be single, and the others would be in families that might include children.

The site for the city was to be within the Washington area, but its specific location was not pinned down until about three days before it was to begin. However, since the Structures Committee had been asked to report on the various open, publicly owned spaces in Washington in terms of their size, symbolism, distance to government buildings, and environmental qualities, we were able to assume that it would be one of five locations.

It was intended that Resurrection City would be built from donated materials and labor. It was not until quite late that it became apparent that people were going to donate more money than goods. In fact, except for 300 gallons of paint, virtually no building materials were donated. Donated labor, on the other hand, turned out in quantities exceeding everyone's expectations. Although there was less help from organized labor than was hoped, many church and neighborhood groups and individuals wanted to help build. Because of their numbers and enthusiasm, the problem with workers was how to use them all.

We organized our information in terms of problem areas and problem responses with attention to security, health, and social needs (see Fig. 1). This analysis was used for work within the Structures Committee as well as for work with other committees. Next we started developing plans for construction and community systems, which were only tentative but which would help us to advise on site selection, utilities, and schedules for materials and labor.

CONSTRUCTION SYSTEMS

The primary goals of the construction systems were: (1) shelter and services for the residents soon after their arrival; (2) severe economy of materials; (3) full use of all labor resources; (4) durability; and (5) protection from the weather. This suggested that shelter structures should be made of components prefabricated by volunteers and assembled by residents. Because of our population assumptions, we developed two types—one for families and one for dormitories, housing five or six people. Some larger, more complex structures, which could not be easily prefabricated, were also needed, so these were rented—chemical toilets, tents for dining halls, and refrigerated trucks for food storage. All other construction took place at the site.

Testing of designs was carried out on two fronts. First, we checked them against other designs, but since there were few precedents

This low aerial shot shows activity in Resurrection City. Prefabricated structures
are in various stages of construction with completed units in upper right.
Large tent in lower right was used as a dining area and general meeting
hall. (WIDE WORLD PHOTOS)

FIG. 1.   *Problem Areas and Responses*

PROBLEM AREAS | PROBLEM RESPONSES

SECURITY

- EXTERNAL HAZARDS
- INTERNAL HAZARDS

- SYSTEM OF LEADERS
- COMMUNITY FORM
- RAPID INFORMATION
  (LOUD SPEAKERS)
- LIGHTING SYSTEMS
- FIRE FIGHTING
  EQUIPMENT
- SPACE BETWEEN UNITS

HEALTH

- SANITATION
- MEDICATION
- DINING
- EXERCISE
- PEST CONTROL
- SHELTER

- PROGRAMS & SERVICES
- COMMUNITY FORM
- SITE DEVELOPMENT
- UTILITIES LAYOUT
- SANITARY FACILITIES
- INFORMATION
  (POSTERS & LEADERS)
- CONSTRUCTION SYSTEMS

SOCIETY

- COMMUNITY IDENTITY
- COMMUNITY GOALS
- CONTACT
- INDIVIDUAL IDENTITY

- PROGRAMS & SERVICES
- COMMUNITY FORM
- INFORMATION
  (POSTERS & LEADERS)
- UNIT ADAPTATION

(army camps, migratory worker camps, and the like), we used a sketch problem at Howard University's Department of Architecture to provide alternative models for building and planning. In addition, interested Washington architects were asked to submit their proposals. Next, shelter prototypes were built to test materials, use, methods of construction, and durability. A number of changes were suggested by these tests and checks.

The final shelter units were triangular in section, with floor and roof panels of plywood on 2 × 4's. A plastic membrane was used at the ridges to admit light without loss of privacy and to make a simple waterproof joint. The larger structures to be built at the city for service functions were also designed of lumber and plywood and had floors to prevent weather problems. Originally, we had hoped to find a construction system that would permit a kind of covered arcade for the main service spine. Such possibilities as telephone poles, with canvas for roof and partitions, were considered. However, our assumptions of available construction skills and money led us to more conventional solutions. Basically, construction systems were to use the highest possible technology for planning and the lowest possible for building.

Shelter unit components were trucked to the site near the Lincoln Memorial on May 13, The day before, volunteers, using plans we had made, had started painting marks on the grass to locate construction. (The marks had to be repainted two days later when park lawnmowers came through.) Then, immediately after Rev. Ralph Abernathy drove a ceremonial spike, "foremen" trained by the yard supervisor helped the poor people and local volunteers erect shelters from the laid-out components. Many units were put up during these first few days. Most builders increased their efficiency by forming teams to accomplish a specific task: there were floor-and-frame teams, skylight teams, and door teams. Later, shelters were made by those who would inhabit them. Foremen were no longer needed, for new arrivals simply used existing shelters as guides, paying attention to even minor points of construction.

During this period of major construction (lasting for the first week or two of the city's life), the committee tried to have at least one member at the site during the entire day. Most

Building a dormitory shelter unit. (DUTCH PHOTOS–CLARA WATKINS)

Camp life in Washington (WIDE WORLD PHOTOS)

Communications: one of the services located in main street. (DUTCH PHOTOS—CLARA WATKINS)

construction problems were simple and easily handled, such as changing details in large buildings to help the carpenters. Other problems, arising from organizational difficulties within the city and the campaign, were more complicated, and some were never solved. It was never possible, for example, to put in proper drainage systems for showers and sinks, and people had to be bussed to baths.

Helping with construction made it possible for members of the committee to see how people could build their own shelters with enthusiasm and pride. Some, usually those from the rural south, built slowly and individually; those from large cities seemed to have more experience in working together, and they built rapidly in teams. The New York crowd, for example, was able to put up shelters at a rate of about one unit per fifteen minutes per three-man team. The shelters belonged to their users, and after assembling them, many personal adaptations were made, ranging from painting names or designs (squares, stars, dot patterns, and faces were most popular) to making special doors or windows. Some even adapted the components, using the implicit system of geometry, to make second stories, or, before the rains came, sundecks. The materials were available, and people used them.

COMMUNITY SYSTEMS

In developing the community plan for Resurrection City, the Structures Committee tried to provide for spaces, services, and identity at several scales. The smallest scale was the single shelter unit that housed one family or, as a dormitory, five or six people. The next scale was nine shelter units (about 50 people) formed into a compound that backed onto a shower and toilet "core." Then, groups of four compounds (about 200 people) were formed with a leader's shack (also used for group storage and supplies) at its entranceway. Finally, a group of about 900 people would share a dining tent at their location on the Main Street. "Main Street," the central community spine, was to hold all other services and to tie the diverse elements together, both functionally and symbolically (see Fig. 2).

This plan was only a guide, to be adapted when the site was finally made known. Actually, the site selected required only a few changes in the plan: most of the compounds south of Main Street did have to be adjusted to fit between trees, for this area was heavily wooded. Other factors caused greater change. Because of equipment shortages, only the dining tent already up at the western end of the city could be operated. Then, the public agency that supplied the medical and dental trailers required that they be placed outside the city (contrary to our plans and to those of the volunteer doctors, too). Several other service buildings scheduled for Main Street also failed to appear, further reducing its possible level of activities.

But, Main Street was still the public place. Because community services were located here, and because it went the length of the city, this was the place of greatest traffic—basically pedestrian. New services would naturally locate here. When a couple of Diggers (a San Francisco group organized to provide free goods) arrived, they put up their bakery here. In good weather, this became a meeting place; when looking for someone, or when looking for company, people would go to this public way. On the morning of Robert Kennedy's assassination, this is where many stood, quietly, waiting for news.

Main Street was not only the public place but also the communication spine. Telephones for offices, pay phones for residents, mail, and notices were here. Loudspeakers for rapid communitywide spread of information were also here (but, through continuous use, were soon no longer "heard"). Newspapers, both from inside and outside, were available at City Hall, near the center of Main Street. Visiting Congressmen and celebrities walked its length, sometimes joining in a town meeting held there. At one end, it opened, through a guarded gate, into a parking area where reporters and curious onlookers might wait.

Another kind of communication, a sort of "bridge" between the city and the outside world, occurred away from Main Street, beside the northern perimeter fence. Passers-by would stop here to read the walls of several shelters that had been covered with enough slogans to turn them into billboards. Then, quite naturally, they would fall into conversation with residents standing within the fence. On sunny days, there were always groups on each side of the fence talking to one another.

The problems that limited public construction

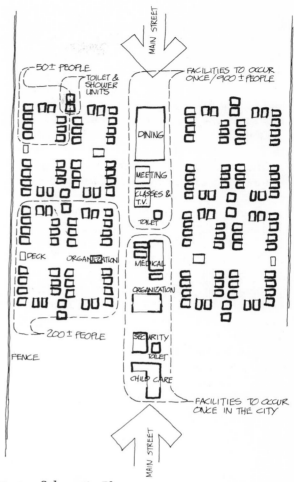

FIG. 2.   *Schematic Plan*

also prevented organizing the building of leaders' and group storage shacks. However, cohesive groups, usually those from the big cities, simply built their own. Our city plans called for these places for local organization because we had sought to provide facilities for a strong organizational fabric at local *and* city scales. However, only those groups that came organized were able to operate that way. These groups were sometimes criticized for being too independent. Indeed, some had their own marshals and did their own cooking. But, during the first week or two, these groups were solving their own problems and were helping other people as well. For example, on the first Sunday after Resurrection City's occupation (a chaotic day when nearly 1,000 people arrived in the first of the rain), some of the New York crowd carried plywood on their cars, delivering it where people needed it to build. These groups did retreat from the city as time passed; some even retreated behind guarded fences. But, this is how they had survived at home, and as problems in the city grew, it was one way to survive here.

There was a similar range between success and failure in the organizations for city services. Food and child care, for example, met their immediate goals, but many others did not. Among these was the security service, initially handled by the marshals, a group of city residents. Soon, failures and excesses of duty occurred (mainly affecting the less cohesive groups), and attempts were made to improve the organization from within. However, lack of support from above doomed these attempts, prompting a young resident from Detroit to form the "Tent City Rangers." The Rangers solved some security problems, and they provided other services, such as rush transportation, as well. But, there was more a sense of competition than of cooperation between the marshals and the Rangers, and, amid occasional announcements from City Hall that the Rangers would soon be disbanded, security continued to be a problem.

Organizational difficulties at the city scale were, with the amorphous political structure,

probably unavoidable. Town meetings were held from time to time, and efforts were made to form a City Council. Neither held power; they operated as forums. Major decisions could be made only by campaign leaders, and they were seldom in the city. The City Manager, for example, was not only the official charged with coordinating services and activities within the city, but he also served as Demonstration Leader. This effectively prevented his being able to follow through on problems. (One of the series of City Managers, after ordering gravel for the muddy Main Street, then had to go lead a demonstration. Almost immediately, one of his staff canceled the order. This was the sequence of many attempts to solve problems.)

Thus, the city became a loose assembly of groups and services, some organized and some not. Communication paths would shift from time to time, but "average" paths are charted in Fig. 3, with broken lines to show frequently broken communication paths, dotted lines for little-used paths, and crossed lines for conflicts and short-circuits in paths. Such a chart shows a shifting, complex lattice. Organizational communication became a tool few residents could use.

If the structure of Resurrection City did not

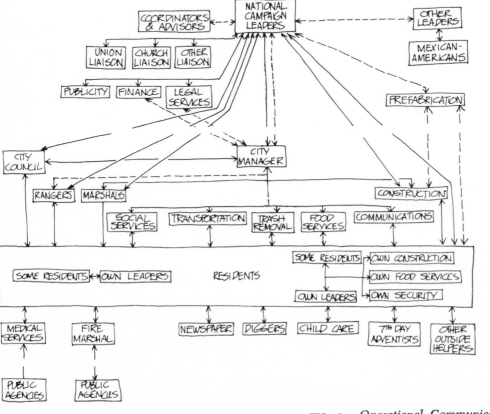

FIG. 3.   *Operational Communications Paths*

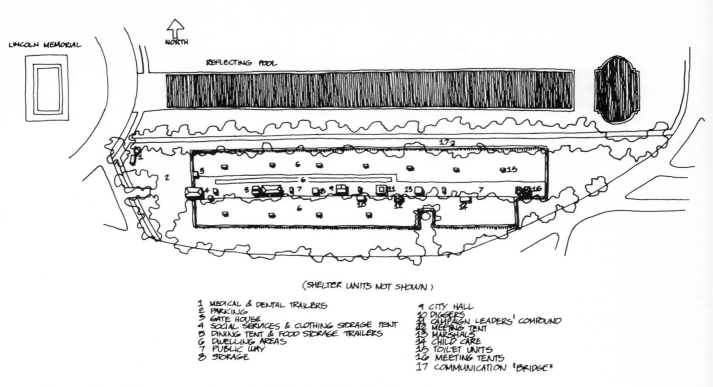

LINCOLN MEMORIAL

NORTH

REFLECTING POOL

(SHELTER UNITS NOT SHOWN)

1 MEDICAL & DENTAL TRAILERS
2 PARKING
3 GATE HOUSE
4 SOCIAL SERVICES & CLOTHING STORAGE TENT
5 DINING TENT & FOOD STORAGE TRAILERS
6 DWELLING AREAS
7 PUBLIC WAY
8 STORAGE

9 CITY HALL
10 DIGGERS
11 CAMPAIGN LEADERS' COMPOUND
12 MEETING TENT
13 MARSHALS
14 CHILD CARE
15 TOILET UNITS
16 MEETING TENTS
17 COMMUNICATION "BRIDGE"

Fig. 4. *Plan of Resurrection City as Built (Shelter Units Not Shown)*

make it possible to organize improvements, it did not hinder individuals and small groups from making improvements on their own. Many marshals (some only teenagers) took this, their first real responsibility, seriously. They worked twenty hours a day, keeping at their jobs day after day. A handful of local electricians took leaves of absence from their jobs and worked for weeks at wiring the city, stopped only by rain or, for a while, by limited power service. An outside church group donated their own labor and materials for building the Child Care Center, which was then staffed by resident and outside volunteers. A skilled carpenter came in regularly to help at building until material and organizational problems stopped construction. Then, in order to continue helping, he became a Tent City Ranger. And, during the time when prefabrication and building were taking place, many people helped others to build.

Systems of territories and barriers developed in terms of use and events. The city, as built (Fig. 4), could be compared with socially developed territorial and border systems (Figs. 5 and 6), since people operated in fairly nonoverlapping spaces. Group areas could be classified in terms of territorial possession ranging from "very private" (cohesive groups) to "private"

(noncohesive groups in the woods) to "private/ public" (noncohesive groups in the open) to "public" (Main Street). Originally, the only "impenetrable" border was to have been the fence around the city, but as conditions deteriorated, many edges between territories were also made into borders meant to challenge crossing.

Some of the levels of penetration operated because of function. For example, the dining tent with its many doors and services was an inviting place to enter. Similarly, much of the southern edge of Main Street was inviting because thick groves of trees and soft patches of grass suggested passing through would be pleasant. Still, the dense growth permitted even noncohesive groups to live privately there. The perimeter fence was both a real and a symbolic barrier. To the north, west, and east, it was in clear view, and beyond it, curious outsiders and reporters could be seen. These sides were heavily guarded. However, to the south, the fence was obscured by dense woods. There were even some extensive gaps in the fence there, but with the woods as a strong visual barrier, guards seldom patrolled this side.

As time passed, these territories and barriers, whether real or symbolic, became more fixed, channeling and limiting activities and contacts. At the smaller scale of an individual shelter unit, there was always a strong sense of possession. Their inhabitants owned them, and uninvited entry by outsiders was strongly resented. People put in doors that could be made more secure than the canvas ones provided. Owners usually wrote their names on their shelters. Similarly, cohesive groups identified themselves. People from Detroit, for example, painted large signs reading "Motown" on their shelters. Yet, there were no signs in areas where the less well-organized lived. Nor did Resurrection City, as a community, have a large sign announcing its presence.

The fence had been put up to keep potential threats at a distance. But, it also happened that, when looking over the fence at the throngs of curious (or sometimes threatening) outsiders, a resident could identify himself as part of Resurrection City. He could see, across the fence, the people, the city, and the society to which he did not belong. This was identity gained through exclusion, a kind of group self-awareness that was easy to develop, for he knew it at home. The other kind of community identity, gained through participation, was hard to find after the period of major construction passed. Some found it anyway: the Rangers, some marshals, those in food or child-care services, and a few others. A community needs a format for participation, such as helping one's neighbor to build. Resurrection City offered only a few others, mostly based on special roles.

IMPLICATIONS FOR THE COMMUNITY DEVELOPMENT PROCESS

The members of the Structures Committee were deeply impressed by the enthusiasm with which people built for themselves and for each other. The construction systems lent themselves to prefabrication and assembly by the skilled and the unskilled, the poor and the nonpoor, alike. This resulted in great pride of accomplishment and pleasure of ownership. If people can so easily be helped to build their own shelters, then it would seem easy to develop construction systems that go beyond current "self-help" programs to permit people to build their own housing. "Kits" of materials and simple directions could solve many building problems, even in our center cities.[2]

We were also impressed with the use of compounds in the city. All the residential areas were to be formed from systems of compounds strung along the linear Main Street, and it turned out that cohesive groups who built without knowing the plan would still form compounds. In addition, these highly organized groups would have facilities, such as cooking or child care, for all their members in the common space formed by the compound. The less well-organized groups, however, sometimes lost their compounds. For example, one day some marshals rearranged enough shelter units to create a lengthy alley parallel to, and just north of, the Main Street. This effectively destroyed any private group

Key in Fig. 4 also applies to Figs. 5 and 6.

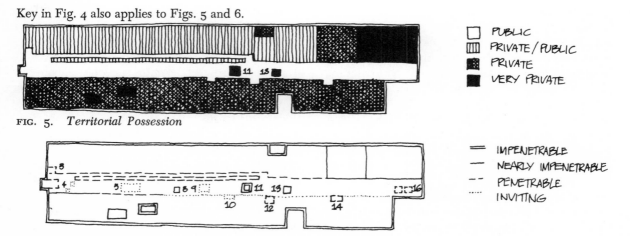

FIG. 5. *Territorial Possession*

FIG. 6. *Border Crossing*

This aerial view shows supporters of the Poor People's Campaign ringing the reflecting pool and wading into its waters as they gather at the Lincoln Memorial, foreground. In background is the Washington Monument and beyond it is the Capitol. At right is Resurrection City. (WIDE WORLD PHOTOS)

spaces these residents had. Since the units were light enough to be shifted, like large pieces of furniture, their owners could have reformed their spaces. But, being no better organized than those removed by our freeway systems, the alley remained, and traffic passed their front doors.

We were further impressed with how naturally (1) new services, like the Diggers' bakery, could come into the city and plug into a gap in the Main Street, and (2) individuals and strong groups would use paint to identify their walls. There was, in some areas, a sense of place and participation seldom seen in slums or public housing. Perhaps people in other cities could benefit from similar opportunities to develop place, group, and individual identification.

As problems increased, building came to a halt, and people withdrew from the community. Soon, qualities making this a special city disappeared. The city was gradually becoming similar to communities all over the country.

At the start, some members of the organization had wanted the city to be an actual demonstration of the problems of the poor. Others had wanted the city to be a demonstration of what could happen in poverty areas through development of real food, housing, medical, and training programs. As it happened, despite medical and dental trailers, doctors, dieticians, planners, administrators, and workers, Resurrection City became more a demonstration of conditions that exist rather than those that could be.

However, this was not a demonstration of conditions found only in poverty areas. The fence that closed the city in (and off) was based on fear. The withdrawal of the organized groups into self-sufficient enclaves was based on fear and on their despair of successfully participating in community events. Fences and fear, withdrawal and despair describe ghetto, suburb, and downtown apartment building alike. Resurrection City had, in a matter of weeks, become a demonstration model of the current American community.

The only way the city could develop these conditions so rapidly was to start early in developing many of their causes: security services of mixed effectiveness and responsibility; inability to develop participatory government; inability to encourage growth of group structures among the disorganized; inability to develop rapid response and follow-through to changing needs.

People had come to Resurrection City, as people have come to other American communities, seeking many things. These included excitement and reward, but primarily they came seeking a new and improved destiny. The momentum of their expectations made it possible for them to build places to live and to withstand early storms, despite predictions that the place would have to be abandoned. There was pride in proving the predictions wrong. More storms came, but growing organizational difficulties, adversities that were more difficult to withstand, also came. Resurrection City, like other American communities, lost its high expectations. The population dropped from around 2,800 to about 500, and those who stayed found other ways to withdraw.

Still, as in most American communities, many people kept trying to make things work. These persistent menders were like the people who had helped build the city, hoping that with this effort some problems could be fixed in America, even after the riots following King's assassination. Those who stayed in the city were, just at the end, starting to build again.

The end came in late June, little more than six weeks after the beginning. The city was emptied, and its inhabitants dispersed. Its buildings were taken down to be sold to a contractor from Tennessee. Sod was rolled out where mud had been. The area was returned to its parklike character, a place of grass and trees and flags, a place for monuments and memorials.

NOTES

1. Members of the Structures Committee were: James Goodell (then at Urban America), Kenneth Jadin (Department of Architecture, Howard University), Tunney Lee (architect and planner from Washington, D.C.), and John Wiebenson, (School of Architecture, University of Maryland).

2. A concern for tapping the little-used resources of the individual builder's energy and initiative was expressed by John C. Turner, "Barriers and Channels for Housing Development in Modernizing Countries," *Journal of the American Institute of Planners*, XXXIII (May 1967), 167–81. This excellent study of a Peruvian squatters' city describes the potential (and official blocks to the potential) found in underdeveloped countries. A similar potential exists in underdeveloped neighborhoods in more advanced countries.

8

Center of Action

Roger Montgomery

At noon, October 1, 1964, when Mario Savio climbed on top a police car and triggered the Free Speech Movement, student dissent in America crystallized in Sproul Plaza at the University of California. This was the students' Haymarket Square, a then new civic space sensitively laid out by a competition-winning design team. Vernon DeMars, his partner Don Reay, Donald Hardison, and Lawrence Halprin had designed the Berkeley Student Center intentionally to serve as the social focus for the university community. They succeeded and then some.

The student center has been growing piece by piece since 1961: Sproul Plaza, the Student Union building, the Dining Commons, Lower Sproul Plaza, Eshleman Hall student activities office building, and the recently completed Zellerbach Hall (students prefer King Hall) auditorium and theater. Most of the time, these facilities serve peaceful, happy, often culturally improving functions. They do this very well indeed.

What makes Berkeley's center different from other campus centers? Two things, mainly. The university planners made a perfect location choice which the designers matched by a splendidly responsive design concept. This made it the "natural center" for people to meet, for things to happen. Both the plan concept and its architectural detail was approached as if pro-

Roger Montgomery is professor of urban design in the Department of Architecture and the Department of City and Regional Planning at Berkeley.

viding a stage for human drama—a "behavior setting" is the currently *in* phrase.

This corresponds to Lewis Mumford's view of architectural purpose. What he wrote years ago in *The Culture of Cities* might as well have been the program for the Berkeley Student Center. If we substitute "center" for "city," Mumford writes: "It is in the center [city], the center [city] as theater, that man's purposive activities are formulated and worked out, through conflicting and cooperating personalities, events, groups, into more significant culminations."

SKEPTICAL REACTIONS

Architecture as behavior setting is not a very popular subject among professionals, who mainly stick to more tectonic values or admit user needs only in terms of narrow, "functional" considerations. Lewis Mumford has observed: "There is a tendency in our age to regard the mechanical functions as the dominant ones, even to view with suspicion any deliberate attempt to produce visual animation or excitement." DeMars and his colleagues have been viewed with suspicion ever since 1957 when the design appeared.

Initially the project generated some interest from the organized profession. In its first year, while still a set of competition drawings, it received its only national prize (a P/A Design Award). But even then the jurors mainly worried about formal problems, "unity," "clutter," and some misread it totally as a "little island" walled off from campus and town.

(PHOTO BY BILL WASSON, KAISER GRAPHIC ARTS)

Nine years ago, after the first part of the project was up and in use, Alan Temko, then a *Forum* associate editor, wrote a major critique of it (Oct. '61 issue). In that review he came close to predicting its success while simultaneously condemning it as architecture.

Temko found the site plan "excellent," "adroitly organized," "deliberately city-like," and having affinities "most notably with the Piazza of San Marco in Venice." Nevertheless he found the architecture of the first two structures "fatally at odds," "a clutter of forms," marked by "anarchic detailing," even "carelessness tinged with sentimentality." (Oh horror of horrors!)

TEN YEARS OF HARD USE

In the time since Temko wrote these words, almost a decade has passed and the Berkeley Student Center has been completed. A generation of students has come and gone. The Free Speech Movement has been followed by countless others. A new generation of students—and faculty—has been radicalized by the events of May 15, 1969, when the Alameda County sheriff's deputies fired on students—killing one, maiming others—and of May 20, 1969, when a California National Guard helicopter blanketed the Student Center with CS gas, a chemical warfare agent outlawed by the Geneva Convention. Between crises, all manner of people have inhabited its spaces. In daily life it has become one of the most used places in the Bay Region.

By now almost everyone—students and town-folk, architects and nonarchitects, radicals and conservatives, old folks and young—digs the general layout of the center. Its openings—compositionally and in terms of use; its sequential elasticity in time—people have used it for nearly ten years, yet it has only recently been formally completed; its easy accommodation of an immense multiplicity of clients, users, and designers; all make it a classic textbook work of urban design.

A SUCCESSFUL SITE DESIGN

The center occupies a former city block of business property and the streets which once bounded the block on three sides. This block lay between the stiff white stone hulk of Sproul Hall administration building on the eastern or uphill side, and the squat, homely men's gym sprawled across the west end. The site sloped down more than two full story heights east to west between these two monuments.

The designers took the direct approach. They made a big space in the middle, on the middle level. The functions of union, dining commons, offices and theater which many architects would have shoe-horned into a single box were disposed separately instead to define the space. This had the advantages of making buildings which did not seem outsize in contrast to their neighbors, which phased easily in time, and which made the *space*, not the architecture, the real center of attention.

Under this big plaza DeMars and his col-

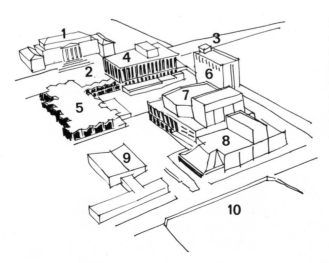

The Student Center links the campus (picture on page 70) to the town of Berkeley. Classical Sproul Hall (1) faces the center across Upper Sproul Plaza (2) which leads out to Telegraph Avenue (3). The center buildings include the Student Union (4), the Dining Commons (5), Eshleman Hall (6), Zellerbach Hall (7), and the Playhouse (8). The Alumni Building (9) and the gym (10) predate the center development.

leagues put parking and building services, entered neatly at grade to the west. And still farther west a piece of the old street right-of-way gives entrance to the gym, the existing Alumni House and the new small drama theater, the Playhouse. Eshleman Hall, an eight-story office building, forms the southern street edge along Bancroft where town and campus meet. On the north the Dining Commons forms a softer, less definite boundary along Strawberry Creek only partly masking the view of the campus behind.

The most active edge of the big plaza occurs on the east where the Union Building straddles the story-height step between this space and Upper Sproul Plaza. Inside the Union and on through the Commons parallel to the line of this step lies the interior street along which the designers have strung most of the daily services provided in the center.

Between the Union building and Sproul Hall lies the linear space, more street than square, which has come to be known as Upper Sproul Plaza. It is here that Mario Savio first spoke to the world, and it is here that the most intense everyday life of the campus is concentrated.

Upper Sproul, which runs on the old Telegraph Avenue right-of-way, connects the historic campus portal, Sather Gate, with the town and the world beyond. Telegraph, which begins (or ends) here, runs straight for nearly five miles to the heart of Oakland, but it is the four blocks immediately south of the student center which form the campus-oriented shopping area.

ORGANIZED AROUND SIX AXES

A row of bollards across Telegraph at Bancroft marks the new campus entrance at the corner of the Student Union. This was intended as a Hyde Park corner by the designers and so it has become. Pushcart peddlers, religious orators, and all manner of street life clot this gateway.

Upper Sproul Plaza is about 550 ft. long, but only 75 to 100 ft. wide, and forms a transition space between town and campus. There, both elements mix in an improbable linear room—actually a chain of softly defined spaces—which forms the chief axis of the design.

This axis is the most active and important of the six axes which organize the plan. Each of the axes has clear visual and functional purposes. The second axis in importance is the longest: it extends from Sproul Hall to the gym, tumbling down a monumental stair from the Upper Plaza, running along the north edge of the lower Plaza, then flowing down another broad stair, cranking to the north so that it hits bottom aligned with the gym's symmetrical façade.

A third axis, less clearly defined, organizes the main space around the center line of the theater façade. Its influence instantly locates speakers and organizes activities in space. The ribbon of balconies and terraces which runs around the plaza focuses on this axis. They make it function as an outdoor arena—a scene of tremendous power when 6,000 to 8,000 people assembled there in the rain to hear Herbert Marcuse.

Two diagonal axes also work in the ordering of Lower Sproul Plaza. One enters from the town at the southeast corner and moves across the square toward the big trees along the creek on the lower part of the campus. The other diagonal forms one of the scenic high points of the center. As it enters from the town at the southwest corner it goes under a covered walk and emerges dramatically targeted on the Campanile, the best-known feature of the campus, framed between the Union and the Commons.

The last of the major axes runs *indoors* as a real, live "activity spine" through the lower level of the Commons and Union buildings. It ties together shops, the main cafeteria, recreation rooms, barber shop, post office and check cashing service, all-hours snack bar (designed self-consciously as a hangout), and finally a great two-level student store. DeMars and his collaborators gave the store an enclosed small-shopping-center layout, with the various departments in open-fronted pouches off the main interior street.

SELF-CONSCIOUS TOWNSCAPE

This account of the axes only begins to explore the richness of the site design realized in the Berkeley Student Center. What does all this compositional richness mean? In an era caught up with other themes—systems building, mega-

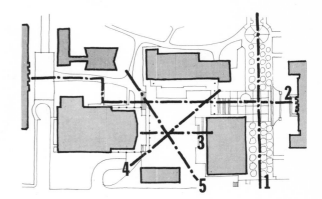

The center is laid out around several axes
(plan above). The Upper Sproul Plaza axis 1
follows the line of Telegraph Avenue, the
traditional approach to the campus. A cross axis
2 runs down from Sproul Hall to the gym, linking
the upper and lower plazas at Sproul Stair
(photo below). The center's two largest buildings
are lined up along a parallel axis 3. Two
diagonals 4, 5 cross the lower plaza, one aimed
at the symbolic campanile (photo at left). A
sixth runs indoors through the lower levels of
the Student Union and the Dining Commons
(plans on page 74).

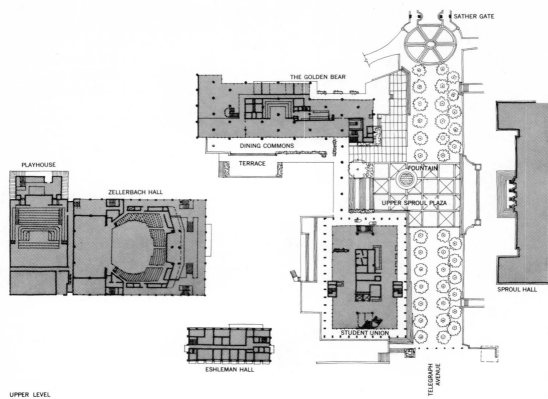

THE GOLDEN BEAR

PLAYHOUSE

ZELLERBACH HALL

DINING COMMONS

TERRACE

FOUNTAIN

UPPER SPROUL PLAZA

SPROUL HALL

SATHER GATE

STUDENT UNION

ESHLEMAN HALL

TELEGRAPH AVENUE

UPPER LEVEL

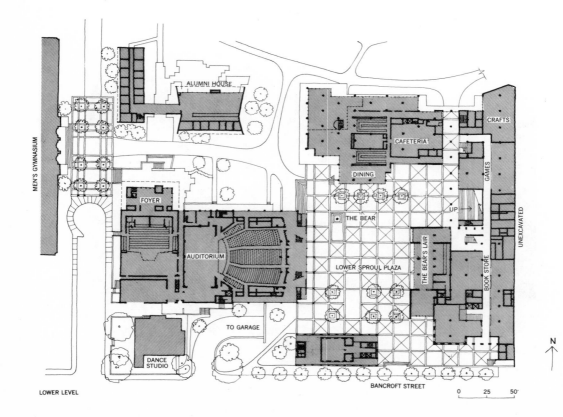

ALUMNI HOUSE

CRAFTS

CAFETERIA

DINING

MEN'S GYMNASIUM

FOYER

GAMES

THE BEAR

UP

AUDITORIUM

THE BEAR'S LAIR

LOWER SPROUL PLAZA

BOOK STORE

UNEXCAVATED

TO GARAGE

DANCE STUDIO

BANCROFT STREET

N

0   25   50'

LOWER LEVEL

structures, and a narrow behavioral-environmental determination—this sounds like turning the clock back to the townscape enthusiasm of the late 1940s. And so perhaps it is.

DeMars recalls: "Much thought and very positive goals shaped these spaces. They were meant to accommodate people—encourage them to be there and tarry. Loggias and overhangs at the people level offer friendly shelter and the steps of the Union and the auditorium are there for sitting and to raise the back rows of spectators a bit for 'events' taking place in the open, and so they are used." And he admits: "We were very interested in the whole vocabulary of considerations that Gorden Cullen discussed in his book *Townscape*, published in 1961, the year the Commons and Student Union were completed."

Donald Reay, another of the collaborating designers, reinforces DeMars' recollection of the design intentions. In 1957, Reay had recently come to the United States. Before that he had designed the center of Stevenage, one of the first round of British new towns. He was steeped in the townscape spirit that then pervaded English architecture.

Reay remembers that the design group always had Piazza San Marco before them, drawn to the same scale. The main plaza at the student center turned out to be almost exactly the size of the Piazza. Both spaces measure about 250 ft. by 150 ft.

Another aspect of the townscape movement shows up in the detail of the public spaces. When Temko wrote about it, he found it "easy to grasp the intention of the architects to transmit the mellow, variegated charm of the European cityscape into American terms . . . to install stage scenery," to scatter "cylindrical kiosks stuck with placards just like those on Paris boulevards."

Kiosks, pavements, benches, all manner of street furniture, trees, fountains, and the bottom edges of buildings, have all been treated with loving care. Some will find the results "cutesy." *The fact is the designers have produced thousands of different places to sit outdoors on a seven-acre site half covered by buildings.* They have made an environment with a visual wealth corresponding to the wealth of ways it gets used.

DeMars, who more than the other designers has lived with the project over the fourteen years of its existence, exhibits a fascination with special effects in the Hollywood sense. He made sure the Union was decorated with spiral-striped flag poles and heraldic shields, that a golden bear announces the Golden Bear Restaurant in the Commons, that the entrances to the internal activity-shopping street have appropriate graphics.

It seems perfectly clear that this self-conscious townscape has produced an unusually adaptable setting for social action. From early morning until well into the evening, 365 days a year, indoors and out, it forms the central stage on which the university community plays out its life. And other communities too: the plazalike spaces of the Student Center resemble more than anything else the summer-time street-park culture of Washington Square in New York and Dupont Circle in Washington.

THE CENTER AS ARCHITECTURE

Time has taken the edge off Temko's discontents with this design. Even he has mellowed. He eats frequently in the Golden Bear and freely admits that the center's success as social space outweighs his reservations about its architecture.

Not only have the critics relaxed, but the architecture has improved. As Don Reay puts it: "The theater is very much better due to the fact it took longer and we had some very good designers involved in it with us." He ascribes much of what disturbed people about the Union and Commons to "a function of time." These buildings went almost immediately from competition plates to working drawings. The theater took ten years to jell.

Zellerbach Hall, in both its main auditorium and its small playhouse, exhibits a more architectonic organization than the earlier buildings. In detailing, too, the wealth of materials is still there, but somehow managed in a more orderly way. The decorative detail vastly enhances the main spaces, particularly the magnificently festive banners by Betty DeMars which hang in the main lobby. The auditorium makes a noble new room for a university which sadly lacks such spaces.

Mechanically, the architects feel they have

Zellerbach Hall (above) closes the big lower plaza on the east side. Its banner-decked lobby (left) looks out toward the Student Union. Lighting and acoustical treatment of the main auditorium inside (below) are incorporated into sculptural side walls and balustrades. (PHOTOS BY DENNIS GALLOWAY)

achieved a high level of success in layout and equipment in Zellerbach. Unfortunately, this discussion of the Berkeley Student Center as urban design cannot report properly on the theater technology of the auditorium and play-house. Here it simply remains to be said, it is a joy to witness performances in these spaces.

SOME LESSONS LEARNED

One main facility in the center has been totally redesigned by Hardison. The student store was torn out during 1968-1969 and re-constructed to follow the interior street concept set forth in the competition design. Apparently the store's original management could not ima-gine the store departmentalized as open-front small stores along a busy pedestrian street. Their original discount-store layout, with checkout counters at the entrances to the lower level of the Union, did not work. It is gone now. The interior activity spine is complete. Its detailing exhibits more confident tectonics and materials use. The center improves with remodeling, a testimony both to the strength of original con-cepts, and to the skillful design of the changes. Again, as Don Reay says: "Nine years show."

Altogether the center now follows with as-tonishing precision the exact outlines set forth in the hectic few weeks of the competition charette.

The jury which unanimously selected the De-Mars-Hardison entry, praised it then in these thoughtful words: "Although competitions may

Attached to the rear of Zellerbach Hall is the Playhouse (below), its mass minimized by the downward sweep of its tentlike roof. The Zellerbach auditorium lobby (above) is in itself a kind of theater.
(PHOTOS BY DENNIS GALLOWAY)

not always be the best method of selecting an architect, it is fair to say that in no other way could such an extraordinary solution be found for such a complex problem."

The student center proves against all criticism that it *is* possible to build a great urban space in the last half of the twentieth century. Vincent Scully was recently reported to have dismissed this possibility in our cyberneticized world. DeMars, Hardison, Reay and Halprin have proved Scully wrong.

Some younger architects may take heart and reassert the validity of townscape for people on foot. It seems sad to think of a generation of architects caught up in a drawing-room abstraction which makes socially valid art of the Las Vegas Strip.

Another lesson from the Berkeley Student Center concerns the importance of constructional and style purity in the urban design context. This project strongly suggests that successful public space can be achieved independent of some of the conventional architectural verities. To reread Alan Temko's 1961 criticism of its tectonic failures is to confront their relative irrelevance in urban design. Here the dominant issue is what Sigfried Giedion called "social imagination," just as it was in Laclede Town.

A FINAL IRONY

DeMars spends a lot of time in the center he played such a leading role in creating. He uses almost any excuse to walk the half mile from his office for lunch. Obviously he is terribly pleased and proud. He has every right to be.

But Vernon is troubled too. He loved his university just the way it was before FSM, Mario Savio, Eldridge Cleaver, the People's Park people, the University Administration, campus cops, sheriffs' deputies and Governor Reagan found Berkeley the perfect stage for their confrontation politics. A troubling thought enters DeMars' mind and the minds of every thoughtful observer: perhaps if it had been just another building group—perhaps if it had been just another campus or civic center untouched by social imagination—the student movement in America would not have found Berkeley such a perfect strike base.

There lies the irony: the very success of the student center as urban design may have contributed the fatal blow to a great university.

Or it may not. The civilizing influence of the center may have prevented worse events. John Kenyon, sometime Berkeley correspondent for the *St. Louis Post Dispatch*, writes: ". . . during last May's National Guard occupation it was hard to doubt its civilizing effect. Lower Sproul Plaza provided a quiet setting for a day-long ecology teach-in, while the tree-shaded concourse with its fountain allowed for cavorting and comic happenings that would have led to quick arrest on the public street."

Truth lies in both views. The Berkeley Student Center's success as urban space must often catalyze action. More often, it simply provides a stage for everyday human association, the drama of everyday life in Berkeley. What more could we ask for? That, after all, is the highest purpose of urban design.

9

Thamesmead

THAMESMEAD is a piece of housing history under construction, under pressure. Its very site is somewhat staggering. The 1,600 acres include a former arsenal, with the sturdy name Woolwich, bombed out in two wars, girdled with marshland with the poetic name Erith. Within the second most populous city in the world, London, it includes some four miles of riverfront. Back up a rise, overlooking the site, are the ruins of a medieval abbey.

But all else within view is a townscape as tedious as tea with milk. It is, on the one hand, bluntly industrial, like the Ford Motor plant at Dagenham across the Thames, and, on the other hand, trivially conventional, with rows and rows of rowhouses stretching endlessly between here and the central city. Some is old, much is new—sometimes where the old was bombed out during World War II.

In this dull landscape, Thamesmead is an event of geographic proportions. Its high-rise apartments spear up twelve stories, but that is not the real point. The towers alone might possess the tediousness familiar to governmental housing projects around the world. Instead, the powerful lift of Thamesmead results from the deliberate contrast of towers with acres of well-knit low-rise housing of two basic types. The first type, five stories tall, is composed of two duplex apartments stacked over a raised ground floor. The other type is three-story rowhouses.

Because building regulations in this marshy locality forbid residential occupancy of the

Reproduced from the July/August 1969 issue of *The Architectural Forum*, copyright © 1969 by Whitney Publications, Inc.

ground level, even after filling, the first stage of Thamesmead has materialized the old planners' dream of separating cars from the people by strata, leaving the bottom range for the precious metal beasts and some storage, and beginning living space one level up. Much of the pedestrian circulation has been raised as well. With its first stage almost finished, Thamesmead achieves the pleasant architectural balance of Reston, Va., but at larger scale, without the toylike character.

When completed, Thamesmead will house some 60,000 people, about the same number as America's single largest state-aided project, New York City's environmentally starved Co-op City. Thamesmead is entirely government-sponsored, at present a project for subsidized tenants, but it will be broadened to include at least 20 percent of private participation. It is all being shaped by the Greater London Council's own architectural and planning staff. And finally, but not least, it is being put together by means of systems building, out of large concrete slab assemblies precast under indoor industrial conditions in a hangarlike, on-site factory owned by the governmental client. It is the largest single systems building undertaking so far in Western Europe.

APPROACHING SYSTEMS WITH CARE

The Greater London Council was out to prove things on various scales of values when it undertook Thamesmead. The GLC, successor government to the old London County Council, is one of the world's largest landlords, owning a

*Aerial view of Thamesmead construction,
Stage I. In the center are eight 13-story
towers, some of which, finished and
occupied, are shown in photo below.
Directly behind them are the three-story
rowhouses. Running parallel to the road in
the foreground are five-story linear, duplex
houses, a closeup of which is shown
in photo on page 81.* (PHOTOS COURTESY
HOLLAND & HANNEN AND CUBITTS/AERIAL
PHOTO BY HANDFORD PHOTOGRAPHY; OTHERS
BY F. R. LOGAN LTD.)

total of some 260,000 dwelling units, most of them built between the two world wars. The 3,000-man architectural construction staff of the GLC is responsible also for all municipal structures in the London area: firehouses, schools, colleges, magistrates' courts, sewage treatment plants—everything public. The responsibility is not only for managing and making contracts, but for designing. The organization is able to raise money by bond issue without too much difficulty and, indeed, is rather resented by the poorer county authorities throughout Britain because the GLC can build to higher standards.

It was with the higher standards that the GLC designers began; only secondary was the determination to execute the plans by means of systems building. The GLC planners and designers evidently decided to try to satisfy people living in a city, rather than a theoretical social stereotype. In the preceding several years, there had been widespread public and professional reaction against family housing solutions with total emphasis on high-rise. Having laid the city out, including schools, stores, health facilities, space for industry, etc., they designed the first 4,000 housing units with diversity in mind.

The shapers were the chief architect of the GLC, Sir Hubert Bennett, with, as principal associates, J. Whittle, J. G. H. C. Cairns, W. J. Appleton, and D. T. Groves. They next arrived at a firm sketch design for the housing, set high performance specifications for materials, and had surveyors estimate costs.

Then entered the industrial approach. In Britain, as throughout Europe—and possibly, before long, throughout the United States too—the main reason for the systems approach is the saving of labor. Building craftsmen are in such short supply in Britain that completing the first stage of Thamesmead might have necessitated bringing in craftsmen from all over the island if done conventionally. Cost entered too; the GLC knew that systems building should be cheaper, but not exactly by how much.

TO SHARE SAVINGS

This was the method established: the GLC proposed for Thamesmead a business arrangement in which the contractor would, in effect, operate a systems setup *for* the GLC, with the client paying for the factory and equipment, including special cranes. If GLC's cost analysts discovered that there were substantial savings in systems building by this pattern, the contractor would share the benefit by a bonus arrangement up to 25 percent of the savings. If systems cost ran higher than the estimated conventional costs in the "target cost-value" scheme, the contractor would have to accept a lower fee.

Lowest bidder of the three invited contractors

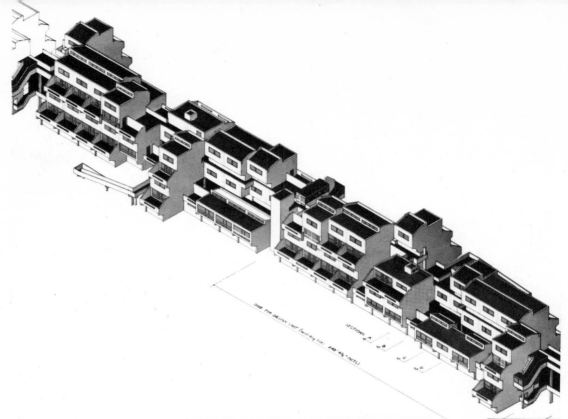

LINEAR HOUSING · AXONOMETRIC   ERITH I

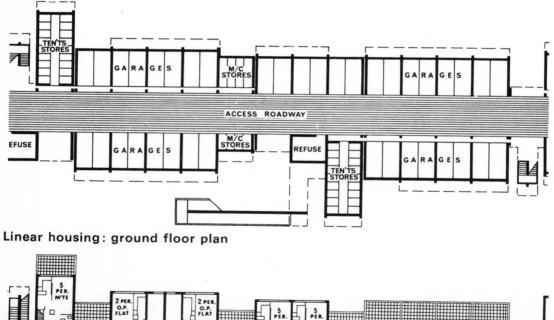

Linear housing: ground floor plan

Linear housing: first floor plan

was Holland & Hannen and Cubitts, one of the big six in Britain, who are licensees for the French system developed by Balency & Schuhl. The Balency system, like the other two widespread French systems, consists of large concrete load-bearing wall slabs, with cast-in heating, window frames, plumbing, electrical conduits, and finishes, factory-formed in heated steel molds. The GLC architectural section then collaborated with Cubitts engineers and production men and with the engineers of Balency & Schuhl, to adapt the system to the Thamesmead design.

But while these working drawings were being done, construction was already under way on the large factory to house the systems building process on the Thamesmead site, roads were being built for the special vans which would carry the concrete sections to the first stage, and construction had begun also on the first residential units, which were the five-story stacked duplexes. This meant that the earliest Thamesmead housing was not truly systems-built, but was what the British themselves refer to as Rat-trad, for rationalized-traditional. It was yard-cast, not made indoors, and was erected with the assistance of scaffolding.

What this early start achieved was the setting of architectural quality. It cost extra; rationalized-traditional construction saves man hours, but at nothing the rate that the fully industrialized method can, as has been shown at Thamesmead since completion of the factory. All the Thamesmead tower flats and the row-housing have been craned into place straight from the stacking yard by way of delivery vans. The first Rat-trad duplex units will not be duplicated, but have been redesigned to be completely factory fabricated, which has meant a certain amount of simplification in their panels. But the architectural point was made.

CRITICISM AND RUMORS

There is considerable criticism of Thamesmead in professional circles in London, with objections centering on the whole idea of building such a large, even if varied, project, and on cost

Isometric drawing (page 82, above) and floor plans of the linear houses (page 82, below) and a typical four-apartment floor plan of the towers (right).

rumors. The GLC admits that the cost of the early units was up, but no higher than might be expected in setting up a large manufacturing process. The British national government has instituted a national yardstick for subsidized housing, and Thamesmead's costs are above it, at about £5,500 construction costs and £1,500 land costs per average unit. But those yardstick figures were set after Thamesmead had been qualified for national assistance. Now, with the factory running full blast, it is expected that unit costs will be brought down considerably, rather than rising as is more usual. For one thing, the costs of the molds will be written off after the first 4,000 units have been made, although they will still be usable for thousands of more units. Another object of write-off will be the big cranes. Belt-tightening will be going on all over England, and Thamesmead will be much more capable of doing it than projects undertaken conventionally. Until the long-range economies of full production and write-off of capital investments appear, however, it may be that some of Thamesmead's notable amenities may be pinched, such as the landscaping around its lakes, the first of which has already been installed.

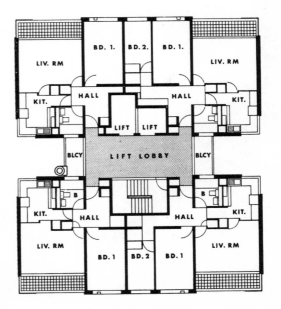

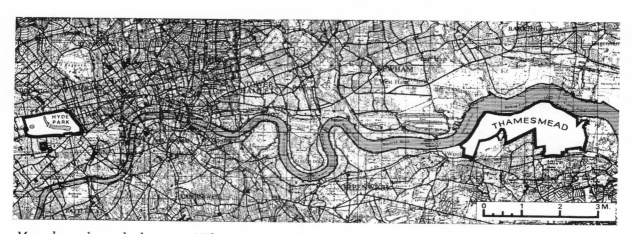

Map above shows the location of Thamesmead in the London conurbation and its size compared with Hyde Park.

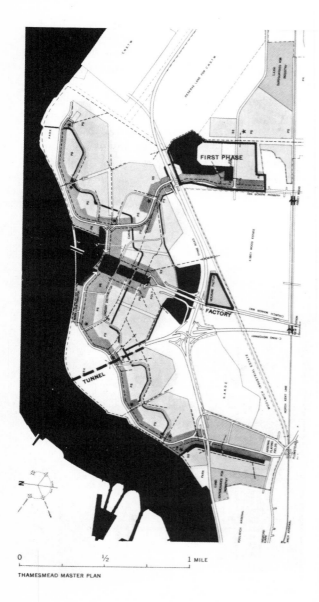

THAMESMEAD MASTER PLAN

Thamesmead was started small, if 4,000 dwelling units can be considered small. The first stage is well back from the normal path of the river, near the commuting railroad to center London.

THE SITE PLAN SURVIVES

A considerably greater tension about the future of Thamesmead was relieved not long ago when a governmental decision was made to dig a tunnel under the Thames near the middle of the project. This had been the original intent of the planners, but a suspension bridge seemed more probable for a time when it became evident that it would save millions of pounds over the tunnel. It would also have murdered Thamesmead's site plan, of course.

Another lift came not long ago when Sir Hubert Bennett's design team was awarded the 1969 award for architecture and town planning by the *Union Internationale des Architectes* for Thamesmead. Bennett, a Yorkshireman, evinced polite pleasure, but professed no illusions that Thamesmead itself was yet won. "We have got to hang on to the conception—to the piece of sculpture—and that is going to be a problem for fifteen years. We have got to ensure that over that period it will get better and better, not worse and worse." If this professional and his colleagues can keep the end product of their housing factory up to the 1968 and 1969 models, these architects and planners will be winning a good many more prizes from the world's urbanists. Thamesmead is a piece of housing history under construction, under pressure.

10

How New York's Zoning Was Changed to Induce the Construction of Legitimate Theaters

Richard Weinstein

I WAS among the first architects in the New York Department of City Planning Urban Design Group when it was established in 1967. The zoning resolution of 1961 and its procedures seemed to us obscure, technical, and infinitely detached from the problems of the city.

Someone brought to our attention an application for a zoning change on the site of the old Astor Hotel at Times Square and 44th Street. At that time, we were just settling into our jobs, and occasionally, without any predictable pattern, certain buildings would be referred to us by the department's zoning engineering section, perhaps out of the feeling that the passing of something attractive, like the Astor, should evoke a response from the Urban Design Group, whose mission was related to maintaining the attractiveness of city sites.

THE ASTOR HOTEL SITE

Someone told us that Mayor John Lindsay liked the legitimate theater, and was afraid that an office-building boom on Broadway would lead to the destruction of the theater district. Wouldn't it be nice, we thought, if somehow we could build a new theater on the Astor site?

We quickly learned that the power of advising the City Planning Commission on questions of zoning was of great interest to developers. In this case, a group of developers, builders of

flamboyant temperament, were delighted to meet with us on the subject of their application. They came armed with a senior partner of an established architectural firm. When we suggested that the construction of a new theater be incorporated into their office building they pounded the table. Their architect swore that such a project would be impossible, invoked the canons of architectural form, and ended every statement by proving that you could not combine a theater and an office building. Having been trained as architects ourselves, we recognized in our professional adversary the same taste for argument which we, not too long ago, had enjoyed as students. We therefore ended the meeting by expressing the hope that the problem would be given further study, invoking the lofty purpose of public benefit.

This call to civic virtue immediately resulted in a call by the developer to the Chairman of the City Planning Commission. Chairman Elliott, in turn, called us for reassurance that over and above the Mayor's love for the theater, it was indeed possible to build a theater and an office building on the same site. Chairman Elliott, propped up by our resolution, told the other side to proceed with their studies, and everybody went to the drawing board. In a few weeks, another meeting was scheduled.

The developers presented a fantastically inflated theater which would have been difficult to fit into the Central Park reservoir, while we, on the other hand, produced what I like to think of as a rational, sensible proposal. We had done some homework and consulted informally with people in the theater community, who gave us advice on theater design and backstage, inside dope on the Broadway scene. This gossip, together with the inevitable jokes and scandalous rumors, went a long way toward making our investigations of the zoning resolution more meaningful. This second meeting in which various drawings and statistical proofs were exchanged, ended (in our judgment) in a standoff, despite the ritual table pounding, an oath that a theater would never be erected on this property, and a statement that there wasn't enough rentable floor area in the world to compensate for the cost of such a ridiculous proposal.

By now, it was obvious to everyone that a theater could be built on the property if the city could permit enough FAR (Floor Area Ratio: the relationship between [1] the area of permitted floor space in a structure and [2] the area of the lot on which it is situated) to pay for the theater. Another meeting was scheduled, at which the city was to receive an analysis of how much additional FAR would be required.

We began to put together a team of people to help us in the coming negotiations. One of my colleagues suggested a friend of his who was a structural engineer with an interest in computers. We also chose a major real-estate firm that acted as a consultant to the city, the planning commission's legal counsel, the member of the Department of City Planning staff who had been largely responsible for drafting the language of the 1961 zoning resolutions, a member of the planning commission who had a great penchant for cutting up zoning texts with scissors and then reassembling them with Scotch tape, which gave a kind of Talmudic-scroll effect to our work sessions. To season the sessions, I arranged occasional visits from figures in the theater world, who at least gave a boost to our spirits when they did not inspire confidence.

It became necessary for me to inform myself on the economics of theater operation and on the mystique of mixed-use concentration upon which the life of Broadway depends. My principal tutor was Harold Prince, the producer of *West Side Story, Fiddler on the Roof, Cabaret,* and other shows and a close personal friend of the Mayor's. He was later to play a pivotal role in organizing support for the Theater District Zoning Amendment.

At our next meeting, we were threatened by the developers with the "lobster building," a mindless, ominous, faceless structure, legal under existing zoning, with two low, clawlike appendages (doubtless both of them would have been banks) pinching a small plaza between them. In contrast to this crustacean we were offered an earlier proposal depicted in a lyrical water-color rendering, a conventional office tower with a large plaza on Times Square. The third alternative was a gigantic office building with a theater behind it, this one of conventional size.

We told the developer that the most we could offer him was a floor-area bonus of up to 20 percent more space above the current zoning ceiling, the waiving of height and setback regulations, and the use of full provisions for a plaza without the provision of a plaza as defined in the zoning resolution.

At this meeting the developers moved from indignation to pathos. We were told by the builder in charge of the project that he loved the theater, that he would even like to build a theater, that his wife, an ex-actress, would like him to build the theater, but that the economics of the project simply would not work at a 20 percent bonus or a maximum 21.6 FAR. We held firm, and they held firm, and the whole dilemma was then escalated to the Mayor.

The next meeting took place in the Mayor's office in the basement of Gracie Mansion. I had never met the Mayor before, so when Chairman Elliott was called to another meeting at the last minute, I was understandably edgy. It was true that by this time I had added to my training a course in building economics, accounting, zoning law, and real estate, but I certainly did not feel a match for the builders until I saw them give the meeting room the same nervous once-over I had.

The Mayor reassured me by his candid confession that he did not know if we could pull this thing off, and by his general unsureness of the process we had been going through. No trace of this showed during the meeting. The Mayor displayed a sure sense of where to mix dramatic firmness with good humor, and justified the method of carrot and stick by appealing to the significance of the precedent we would be setting. He said: "Every day of my life I ask people to do something which is in the

One Astor Plaza in the course of construction. The theater can be seen at the foot of the picture. (PHOTO BY J. ALEX LANGLEY)

interest of the city. Sometimes it makes them richer, sometimes it makes them poorer. I don't know how this will affect you, but I do know that a theater on this site is in the interest of the city, and today the finger is on your shoulder."

The three buildings, in abstract model form, were presented, with a fourth, the city's proposal. While the builders were presenting their case, the Mayor slipped me a note which said: "Which is ours?" I scribbled back the answer and the meeting proceeded smoothly; Scotch and water celebrated its triumphant conclusion. This meeting served to convince the developers that the city was serious.

Encouraged by the forceful backing of the Mayor, both sides set to work in earnest to arrive at an accommodation. Endless versions of the buildings were studied by the design group and presented to the commission: the theater behind, the theater under, the theater in front, the theater above. Complications thickened when I discovered that the chief designer for the developers' architect was an old classmate. This produced a series of agonizing midnight phone calls, strained by the requirement of professional propriety, in which pompous public declarations on both sides were gradually modified by the private exchange of hunches and partial disclosures. "Last offer" followed "last offer"; minutes of earlier meetings arrived after new and critical meetings were finished. Some of these meetings took place in the developers' posh, leather-filled offices on top of their building as night fell on the view of Central Park, all dusky through tinted glass.

Meanwhile, our computer was comparing different building envelopes: the "lobster" against "the plaza" against the theater building (the theater with its bonus of office space) to establish for us that all three buildings were equally profitable.

The last, last offer was to be made by us to the developers in a 10 P.M. meeting, this time in Essex House at the apartment of the builder married to the ex-actress. It was after dinner, and the plan was to brief the Chairman of the Planning Commission on the way to the meeting. We picked up the chairman at Newark airport, somewhat tired after a working trip, and raced back to the city. I hopelessly tried to take him through my maze of charts, drawings, and computer printouts. The Chairman kept asking me where we came out, and I kept answering in subordinate clauses which systematically canceled out the meaning of every preceding thought. In this state of confusion we coldly confronted the dilemma of every public official, the necessity to act on policy with only a partial vision of the truth. Partial vision or not, we had to decide as we strode down a corridor, high in the Essex House, toward the apartment. The question was asked me for the last time; and in reply I quoted something not too relevant from Shakespeare, and rang the bell.

The comforting sight of whiskey and cut glass and the lateness of the hour combined to produce a reassuring mood. It did not seem possible that these pleasant surroundings could produce yet another noisy confrontation. In fact, the proceedings were very low-key. In fact, there was an atmosphere of restrained and discreet good fellowship. Obviously, everyone had already decided on his position in advance; the developers were no doubt content that they had secured at least some concessions from the city with the 20 percent bonus. We were relieved to find them willing to accept our top figure. We knew that we would have to face severe criticism on the size of the bonus, and felt slightly shaky on this point ourselves. Later events, however, showed that we had underestimated the cost of the theater, so any possibility of an excessive profit was neutralized.

THEATER DISTRICT ZONING AMENDMENT

We then moved into the second phase of the project, which was to end in a hearing before the Board of Estimate, New York City's governing body, on the Theater District Zoning Amendment legislation. It was necessary to amend the zoning resolution before we even considered the application for a 20 percent floor-area bonus on the Astor site.

The major theme of this second adventure was announced in the elevator on the way down from the Essex House apartment. Who was to get ownership of the new theater? Would it go to the Shubert empire, which owned theaters immediately behind the plot? The ex-actress in a moment of levity remarked that having worked in Shubert theaters herself, she would go as far as divorce before she let her husband allow the Shuberts to manage the theater. The focus of our problem thus shifted to the intrigues of the theater business itself.

The Shuberts, in a consent decree [1] following an antitrust action against them by the Justice Department, where they were held subject to an antimonopoly proceeding [2] (they owned or operated more than 50 percent of the theaters in New York, as well as key road tryout houses), were made subject to restrictions in connection with their acquisition or operation of any more theaters. In our judgment, the Shubert interests, fearing the competition of new houses, did everything they could to discredit the proposed Theater District. Their attack was led by a lawyer who played, in our eyes, what Broadway calls the "heavy."

We began to mobilize for the coming public hearings. It was essential that a broad range of people whose lives were affected by the theater should get together to make an effective statement of support for the zoning amendment.

Harold Prince played a central role in this endeavor, and became the focus of the operation. At one point, shortly before the public hearing, Prince called a meeting at Sardi's Restaurant to which he invited about sixty people broadly representing the theater industry. The purpose of this meeting was to brief those who were to testify on the nature of public hearings, where City Hall was, how you get your name on the list of speakers, how not to offend the dignity of the Board of Estimate with too much show business and schmaltz. Some instinct prompted Prince to close the meeting early. The room was hardly clear when Shubert representatives arrived. They found Prince and one or two others. I am told that, covering their disappointment, they asked Prince to read their statement to the Board of Estimate. He mumbled something about feeding his children and departed. This was a minor act of heroism, as *Fiddler on the Roof* and *Cabaret* were, at this time, both playing in the Shuberts' best theaters. About this time, rumors began circulating that David Merrick, jealous of Prince's hold on

the Shuberts' two best houses, was interceding on behalf of the Shuberts behind the scenes at the Board of Estimate.

In the meantime, plans went ahead to get everyone down to the public hearing. A risky business, since the hearing was at 10 A.M. and most theater people get up in the afternoon. Two star witnesses were Angela Lansbury and Diana Sands. The story is that two limousines were dispatched, one person in each, assigned to wake up the star, give her coffee, dress her, give her some more coffee, and put her in the limousine for the trip downtown.

By a miracle of logistics, about fifty people gathered at a prearranged spot next to City Hall at 9:30 A.M. They were so astounded to see each other at that hour (after a final briefing) they moved with a spirit of solidarity, the most glamorous lobby ever assembled for a public hearing, into the Board of Estimate chambers.

The Mayor presided, and Planning Commission Chairman Elliott was placed near the lectern with two fat law books containing the consent decree and Supreme Court reports prominently tucked under his arm. The Shuberts spoke first. The speech was an effective attack on the proposed legislation, and gave the Board of Estimate a number of ways to delay support, and in effect, ruin our chances on the Astor site by delaying the project.

While the Chairman was making his forceful reply to the Shuberts, the Mayor sent me a note saying that the theater people should make it brief. I relayed this information to Prince, who put our alternate prearranged plan into effect. When he was called upon to testify (bright red from stage fright), he introduced a few speakers: Angela Lansbury, Diana Sands, Fredrick O'Neil of Actors Equity. They each made a brief statement. Then Prince rose again, to read the names of those present, who stood up as their names were called instead of reading their statements. This resulted in a most dignified and impressive demonstration of support for the legislation. The Mayor then announced that David Merrick was in the chamber and wished to speak.

The unpredictable Mr. Merrick went to the microphone and the room became extremely quiet. After a few preliminaries, he came out in favor of the Theater District Zoning Amendment. There was applause, hat throwing, and kissing. And there was a unanimous affirmative vote by the Board of Estimate giving the green light to the first construction of new legitimate theaters in the theater district in over forty years.

In an interesting postscript, a Shubert representative called me not long thereafter with a proposal for a combined theater-office building taking advantage of the new legislation. To my surprise and joy, their theater, on the basis of early sketches, promised to be the best yet.

NOTES

1. *United States v. Shubert* 1956 CCH Trade Cas. ¶68,272.

2. *United States v. Shubert* 75 S.Ct. 277 (1955).

11

Special Districts: A Departure from the Concept of Uniform Controls

Allen Fonoroff

CONCEPTS OF THE SPECIAL DISTRICT

THEORETICALLY, if not in practice, zoning controls have attempted to solve difficult land use and development problems in furtherance of community objectives within the constitutional guarantees of a democratic society. The basic tripartite classification of land as residential, commercial, or industrial—a characteristic of most zoning ordinances—is based on an assumption that these uses of land ordinarily cannot exist side by side without detriment to the community.

More recently, under the growing emphasis on the compatibility of various land uses, and under the realization that these are unique characteristics which distinguish one community from another, that tripartite dimension has given way to "special districting." In cities throughout the nation, there now are civic center zones,[1] flood plain zones, green belt zones, educational institution zones, historical zones,[2] design control zones, and, more recently, in New York City, a Theater District and a Special Lincoln Square District (cf. Chap. 10, above).

As development becomes more complex, there is an attempt to achieve better land use patterns to accomplish the specific purposes necessary for all aspects of the general welfare. Cities now preserve scenic values; controls exist to preserve historic, cultural, and aesthetic values.

From *The New Zoning*, edited by Norman Marcus and Marilyn W. Groves, copyright © 1970 by The Center for New York City Affairs, New School for Social Research. Used by permission of Praeger Publishers, Inc.

Bulk controls have been adjusted to achieve various community objectives, such as increased open space, low-cost housing, and cultural establishments. In New York, the Lincoln Square District that surrounds the city's cultural center and the Special Theater District along Broadway are extensions of that concept. This is as it should be inasmuch as land use controls are merely an expression of planning policy.

PRIVATE PROPERTY

The common law and the constitutional rights and obligations that are a part of the ownership of land have shaped the growth of the United States. But these property rights and obligations have changed significantly over the years to reflect the economic and social needs of the people, and it has never been possible for a landowner to do freely as he pleased even though the contrary has often been emotionally announced with citations.

The continuing complex economic and social problems that confront the United States today require a flexible rather than dogmatic approach to refining the concepts of private property and the public interest. The ability of land use controls to meet judicial scrutiny depends upon the "justice" of the restriction. The questions to be decided are whether the restriction is a reasonable method of achieving reasonable objectives, whether the expected public benefit justifies the restriction, whether the property owner is able to secure a reasonable use of his land, and whether the regulation is clear and unambiguous.

ENABLING LEGISLATION

It hardly bears repeating that adequate enabling legislation is an invaluable asset to special district zoning. Ideally, enabling legislation should set forth the power of the municipality to formulate a plan for a given area, including authorization to create controls to accomplish specific purposes and objectives of the plan.[3] The controls, and perhaps the plan, should be subject to public hearings and procedural due process. As an added benefit, enabling legislation may authorize the municipality to acquire, by gift, grant, condemnation, or devise, a fee or any lessee interest, including development rights, within the district. For example, a recent amendment to New York's General City Law, the Bard Act, empowers every city to:

. . . provide for places, buildings, structures, works of art, and other objects having a special character or special historical or aesthetic interest or value, special conditions or regulations for their protection, enhancement, perpetuation or use, which may include appropriate and reasonable control of the use or appearance of neighboring private property within public view, or both. In any such instance such measures, if adopted in the exercise of the police power, shall be reasonable and appropriate to the purpose, or if constituting a taking of private property, shall provide for due compensation which may include the limitation or remission of taxes.[4]

SUBSTANTIVE DUE PROCESS

The special district and the objectives of the plan for the district not only lay the groundwork for the selection of land use controls; they also provide the framework by which the controls will be judged. To meet constitutional objections, mandatory controls must satisfy two constitutional requirements: (1) substantive due process, and (2) equal protection.

The due process clause is the yardstick against which all social and economic legislation is measured to determine "reasonableness." In the specific field of land use control, the reasonableness of any legislative enactment depends heavily on the criteria set forth in a plan. Accordingly, "planning lawyers" and planners have a special responsibility to develop physi-

cal, social, economic, and legal criteria to support community planning objectives, and, based on these, to deveolp constitutional theory to support the planning controls.

So far as the requirement of due process is concerned, and in the absence of other constitutional restriction, a state is free to adopt whatever economic policy may reasonably be deemed to promote public welfare, and to enforce that policy by legislation adapted to its purpose. . . . If the laws passed are seen to have a reasonable relation to a proper legislative purpose, and are neither arbitrary nor discriminatory, the requirements of due process are satisfied.[5]

To be sure, it will be impossible to develop controls that satisfy all landowners. Some will endure hardships for the benefit of the community. This was succinctly stated by the New York Court of Appeals in *Shepard v. Skaneateles:*

Zoning laws, enacted as they are to promote the health, safety and welfare of the community as a whole . . . necessarily entail hardships and difficulties for some individual owners. No zoning plan can possibly provide for the general good and at the same time so accommodate the private interest that everyone is satisfied. While precise delimitation is impossible, cardinal is the principal that what is best for the body politic in the long run must prevail over the interests of particular individuals. . . . There must, however, be a proper balance between the welfare of the public and the rights of the private owner. The zoning regulation . . . may neither deprive an individual owner "of all beneficial use of his property" . . . nor impose upon him a "special hardship unnecessarily and unreasonably."[6]

If a particular use or an arrangement of buildings is likely to be harmful to the development of surrounding land uses, there is likely to be no due process objection to its regulation or even to its total prohibition.[7] However, if mandatory controls are used to implement the plan for a special district—and the harm being attacked by the plan is not the typical nuisance case presented in *Hadacheck v. Sebastian,*[8] or *Miller v. Schoene,*[9]—the reasonableness of the plan is put at issue. Can the police power be interpreted to recognize that within the context of a larger comprehensive plan the general welfare requires a plan for a smaller special district and that construction or use contrary to that

MANHATTAN

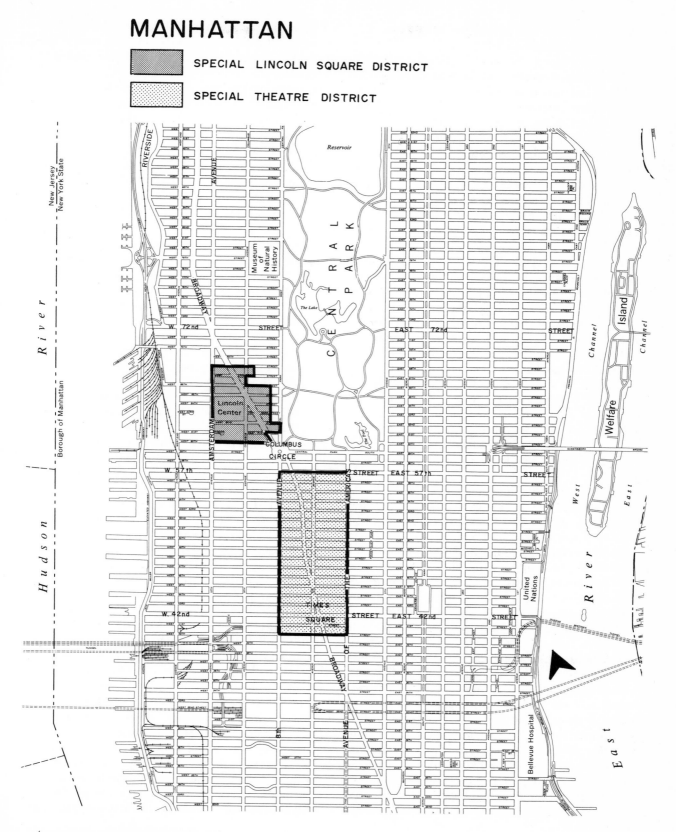

▨ SPECIAL LINCOLN SQUARE DISTRICT

▨ SPECIAL THEATRE DISTRICT

(MAP DRAWN BY JOSEPH LORUSSO)

plan is harmful and therefore subject to reasonable regulation?

Another major question to be asked is whether the mandatory controls in fact accomplish the purposes of the plan. There must be a causal relationship between the property owners' activity and the harm to be prevented. For example, the public investment in streets and open space requires protection not only from the usual traffic menaces—speed, overweight trucks, etc.—but also from congestion of people and vehicles. It would seem reasonable to expect that a design concept or set of bulk controls related to this end ought to receive judicial approval.

There is a very limited amount of case law dealing directly with this subject, and an answer to the constitutional questions must proceed by analogy with similar kinds of controls, such as various types of height regulation devices to ensure light and air. A lengthy discussion is not required to show that reasonable regulations of the height of buildings and other structures will be sustained by the courts so long as they are designed to implement the objectives of a plan and promote the general welfare and other aspects of the police power.[10] The special height regulations of the Lincoln Square special district would seem to meet any constitutional question.

Another close analogy to mandatory controls in special districts is the development of the law concerned with aesthetic regulations. The use of the police power to regulate aesthetics has been the subject of much litigation, for it raises significant constitutional questions.

Government clearly may act in the interests of aesthetics when exercising its power of eminent domain.[11] However, special district regulations that restrict the use of land do not involve a "taking," and therefore do not require compensation. Although the U.S. Supreme Court has not chosen to speak definitively on the subject of aesthetics and the police power, a strong trend has developed within state and federal court decisions that indicates that beauty will soon enter the halls of justice unassisted by the crutches of public health and public safety.[12] Aesthetic considerations have broad effects beyond health, safety, and morals, and are a very important element of the general welfare. To so narrowly dissect the meaning of general welfare as to exclude these considerations is contrary to the vast body of knowledge in economics, sociology, and other behavioral sciences.[13]

Regulating the use of land so that it remains "open space" or conforms to a particular land use pattern also raises constitutional questions of reasonableness. From time to time, some municipalities have attempted to zone private property for an "exclusive" purpose.[14] The constitutional question to be answered in this situation is whether the landowner has an expectation of receiving a reasonable return on his investment—the land.

The issues raised by these questions, when applied to special districts, can successfully meet the constitutional questions where the owner of land has some latitude and choice with respect to its use and development within carefully defined areas of regulation. Obviously, no attempt should be made to "freeze" land in its natural state either by prohibiting all use or so restrictively regulating land as to render it valueless.[15]

In deciding constitutional questions, the judiciary must evaluate conflicting social values. Every restriction on the use of real property is measured against society's desire to achieve the objective for which the restriction is imposed. The courts have exercised extreme care in evaluating land use regulations. In the early history, aesthetics was excluded as a legitimate objective of the police power. Today, the courts hold that aesthetic considerations may be taken into account along with other valid considerations.[16]

Some courts have taken a very strong position in finding a viable relationship between aesthetic values and the economic health of a community. "There are areas in which aesthetics and economics coalesce, areas in which a discordant sight is as hard an economic fact as an annoying odor or sound."[17] The rationale for this and other decisions rests firmly on the propositions that the aesthetic controls were enacted to protect property values and therefore the economic health of the community.[18]

The development of criteria for judging aesthetics presents a very difficult problem: Is it possible to apply the same aesthetic yardstick to different types of aesthetic values? Obviously, regulating the design and appearance of buildings, as some communities do through boards of architectural review,[19] is quite different from regulations designed to protect a community's scenic and historic heritage. It is not the purpose here to develop standards for the administration of aesthetic regulations, but to point to the city's duty to create a comprehensive plan and the tools necessary to implement it. To do otherwise would bring irreparable damage to the total community.[20]

The preservation of aesthetic and other values described and classified in special district regulations cannot be dependent upon the hypothetical average person used by Justice Field in *People v. Stover*.[21] The destruction of these values would in some measure affect everyone.

One of the strongest and most obvious justifications for the use of aesthetics within the police power is found in the cases dealing with signs and billboards. When community indulgence in visual blight had apparently reached its saturation point, civic reaction manifested itself in an attack on the unsightly billboards.[22] Community appearance lost the initial skirmish as the courts tenaciously held to the doctrine that aesthetic considerations were beyond the scope of the police power.[23] A different handle was required if the door to the sanctum of the police power was to be opened. Such a handle was fashioned, but it was based upon a legal fiction that is still very much in use today, adding nothing but confusion to the concept of the police power. Again, the U.S. Supreme Court showed the way. In 1899, the Massachusetts legislature limited the height of buildings in the vicinity of the State House primarily to preserve a beautiful setting for public structures in which the public had invested its funds. When the limitation was challenged, the Court's decision, in *Welch v. Swasey*,[24] was based on public safety, in that height regulations were required to protect the public against the danger of fire. Aesthetics, however, were not to be completely ignored. Regulations otherwise rooted in the public health, safety, and morals sometimes also had an aesthetic objective.

It was not long after *Welch v. Swasey* that the courts reinforced the attempt to preserve community appearance. The police power was available to regulate billboards because, if unregulated, these devices provided a danger to public health, safety, and morals. That the bill-

boards were also ugly, and that their ugliness played a part in stimulating the enactment of restrictive legislation, was not fatal to the exercise of the police power.[25]

Through the years, courts have shown an increased willingness to recognize and give effect to aesthetic considerations.[26] Perhaps the strongest statement by a state court is that of the Supreme Judicial Court of Massachusetts.[27] In answer to an argument that the sign regulations were promulgated primarily to protect scenic beauty, the Court said:

Grandeur and beauty of scenery contribute highly important factors to the public welfare of the state. To preserve such landscape from defacement promotes the public welfare and is a public purpose.

Even if the rules and regulations of billboards and other advertising devices did not rest upon the safety of public travel and the promotion of the comfort of travelers by exclusion of undesired intrusion, we think that the preservation of scenic beauty and places of historical interest would be a sufficient support for them. Considerations of taste and fitness may be a proper basis for action in granting and in denying permits for locations for advertising devices.[28]

Adding weight to this body of authority are several cases decided by Florida's Supreme Court upholding sign regulations designed to improve community appearance.[29]

Aesthetic considerations have played an important role in legislation regulating junkyards, topsoil removal,[30] sand, stone, and gravel operations,[31] and similar types of open land uses. Through zoning and other types of land use controls, these uses have been regulated and even prohibted. The Oregon Supreme Court upheld the total exclusion of automobile wrecking yards from Oregon City.[32] The Court stated the principal question: "Whether the city can wholly exclude a use of property on the sole ground that the use is offensive to aesthetic sensibilities," and gave its answer: "Aesthetic considerations alone may warrant an exercise of the police power."[33]

In upholding a statute prohibiting unscreened junkyards near highways, Kentucky's highest court rested its decision of the proposition that aesthetics is a proper basis for police power regulations.[34] In view of the most recent decisions, and the new impetus provided by the federal government, it is most probable that the courts will continue to give a more positive appraisal of the value of aesthetics.

It is fair to conclude that a statute designed to protect and promote the economic well-being of a political subdivision and thus the general welfare of its people, and which sets out a course of action, all of which is directed at a classification reasonably related to the statutory purpose, is a valid and constitutional exercise of the police power.

EQUAL PROTECTION

A complaining landowner may argue that mandatory controls within a special district are unfair to him and, because of their limited application, constitute an illegal classification. Simply stated, the issue is that others within the district, in a similar position, are not similarly regulated. The key to this argument is a showing that the controls and the distinctions are related to the legitimate objectives to be achieved, and that the distinctions are one way of promoting the legislative purpose.[35]

The "uniformity" requirement of zoning law is simply that equal treatment must be given to all similarly situated property within a district.[36] The constitutional guarantee of equal protection does not require the universal application of legislative act, and distinctions may properly be made in the application of regulations.[37] Similarly, the legislature is not required to be omniscient and to solve a problem completely in one legislative pronouncement.[38]

If the key questions noted above can be answered, it is reasonable to expect favorable action by the courts.[39] These problems, in turn, raise other issues which must be thought through carefully. Obviously, a community cannot solve all of its development problems by use of the police power. Alternatives for implementing specific community goals must also be sought through other governmental powers.

ALTERNATIVE APPROACHES

Eminent Domain

Greater opportunities must be made to utilize the possibilities of compensation.[40] To the ex-

tent that partial compensation is a possibility, it relieves many courts of the unenviable choice of either upholding a regulation which in fact is a taking of considerable rights or rejecting a regulation and thereby leaving the future use of the land to the developer. Difficult as it is, funds must be found so that acquisition, full and partial, may be employed in appropriate circumstances. For example:

Fee Simple. The acquisition of land in fee simple, and its retention in public ownership.

Fee Simple and Right of Occupancy and Use. The acquisition of land subject to a right of occupancy and use of such lands or part thereof by the grantor.

Fee Simple and Resale. The acquisition of land in fee simple and the reconveyance of such land and of rights and interests therein to the former owner or to others, subject to specified covenants, restrictions, conditions, or affirmative requirements designed to protect the public interest and to accomplish the purposes of the special district.

Fee Simple and Leaseback. The acquistion of land in fee simple, and either the transfer for a life term or the lease for a period of years of such land or of rights and interests therein back to the grantor or to other.

Less Than Fee. The acquisition and retention of any right or interest in land less than a fee.

Lease. The lease of land for a term of years, with or without an option to purchase.

Option to Purchase. The acquisition of an option to purchase land and rights and interests therein.

Special Assessment Districts

American cities have long used special assessments to finance local improveemnts. With appropriate changes in the state constitutions and enabling statutes where necessary, it would appear to be feasible to so structure a special district to accomplish its planned purposes by levying special assessments to defray the costs of the planned benefits. If the special district for which mandatory controls are required is viable, then clearly there is a public benefit to be achieved. The extraordinary costs of achieving the benefits of such a district can then be assessed against all those benefiting. Of course, it is essential that all procedural requirements are met in establishing the district and the assessment and, further, that there be clear proof of the benefits to be achieved.

The purpose of the discussion here is merely to suggest a method of financing and implementing a plan for a special use district without relying entirely upon the police power to enforce mandatory controls.[41]

All these devices can be used to implement the community's objectives as expressed in its comprehensive plan. The problems inherent in each device can be minimized by careful planning and administration.

The argument for these alternative approaches can be made on the grounds of fairness. It is basically unfair for those benefiting from the mandatory controls of special districts not to share in their costs. Moreover, if it is constitutional to compel landowners to pay for a special district that enhances value and provides material benefit, it should also be constitutional to prevent landowners from using their land in some alternative form which would be detrimental to community values as well as property values.

NOTES

1. E.g., City of Detroit Zoning Ordinance, §A-13 (1968).
2. E.g., Phila. Zoning & Planning Code, §R14-2005 (1959); Mass. Laws ch. 601 (1955).
3. See, e.g., A Model Land Development Code (Tentative Draft No. 11, *Amer. Law Instit.* (1968).
4. §20 subd. 25 (a) (McKinney 1968) (repealed 1968; subject matter now covered in N.Y. Gen. Mun. L §96-a).
5. *Nebbia v. New York,* 291 U.S. 502, 537, 54 S.Ct. 505, 516 (1934).
6. 300 N.Y. 115, 118, 89 N.E.2d 619, 620, 91 N.Y.S.2d 187 (1959).
7. *Euclid v. Ambler Realty Co.,* 272 U.S. 365, 47 S.Ct. 114 (1926).
8. 239 U.S. 394, 36 S.Ct. 143 (1915).
9. 276 U.S. 272, 48 S.Ct. 246 (1928).
10. *Welch v. Swasey,* 214 U.S. 91, 29 S.Ct. 567 (1909).
11. C.J.S. *Eminent Domain* §31,63 (1965); compare with 101 C.J.S. *Zoning* §48 (1958).
12. Price, *Billboard Regulation Along the Interstate Highway System,* 8 Kan. L. Rev. 81 (1959); Comment, *The Role of Aesthetics in the Exercise of Police Power and its Application to South Dakota's Highway Beautification Statute,* 11 S. D. L. Rev. 157 (1966); cf. Comment, *Control of Outdoor Advertising; State Implementation of Federal Law and Standards,* 38 Neb. L. Rev. 541

(1959); 13 *Syracuse L. Rev.* 325 (1961); 110 *U. Pa. L. Rev.* 899 (1962).
13. See generally, Dukeminier, *Zoning for Aesthetic Objectives: A Reappraisal,* 20 *Law & Contemp. Prob.* 218 (1955).
14. *McCarthy v. City of Manhattan Beach,* 41 Cal.2d 879, 264 P.2d 932 (1953), cert. denied, 348 U.S. 817, 75 S.Ct. 29 (1954); *Vernon Park Realty Co. v. City of Mt. Vernon,* 307 N.Y. 493, 121 N.E.2d 517, 125 N.Y.S.2d 112 (1954); cf. *Greenhills Home Owners Corp. v. Village of Greenhills,* 5 Ohio St.2d 207, 215 N.E.2d 403 (1963).
15. See, e.g., *Morris County Land Improvement Co. v. Parsippany-Troy Hills Tp.,* 40 N.J. 539, 193 A.2d 232 (1963); *Kozesnik v. Montgomery Township,* 24 N.J. 154, 182, 131 A.2d I, 16 (1957); *City of Plainfield v. Borough of Middlesex,* 69 N.J. Super. 136, 173 A.2d 785 (L. Div. 1961); *Arverne Bay Constr. Co. v. Thatcher,* 278 N.Y. 222, 15 N.E.2d 587, 294 N.Y.S. 926 (1938).
16. See *Cromwell v. Ferrier,* 19 N.Y.2d 263, 225 N.E.2d 749, 279 N.Y.S.2d 22 (1967); *People v. Stover,* 12 N.Y.2d 462, 191 N.E.2d 272, 240 N.Y.S.2d 734, appeal dismissed, 375 U.S. 43, 84 S.Ct. 147 (1963).
17. *United Advertising Corp. v. Borough of Metuchen* 42 N.J. 1, 5, 198 A.2d 447, 449 (1964).
18. *State ex rel. Saveland Park Holding Corp. v. Wieland,* 269 Wis. 262, 69 N.W.2d 217 (1955); see *Hanking v. Borough of Rockleigh,* 55 N.J. Super. 132, 150 A.2d 63 (App. Div. 1959); *Borough of Point Pleasant Beach v. Point Pleasant Pavilion Inc.,* 3 N.J. Super. 222, 66 A.2d 40 (App. Div. 1949).
19. E.g., *Reid v. Architectural Bd. of Review of City of Cleveland Heights, Ohio,* 192 N.E.2d 74 (Ct. App., Ohio 1963).
20. See *Udell v. Haas,* 21 N.Y.2d 463, 235 N.E.2d 897, 288 N.Y.S.2d 888 (1968).
21. See *People v. Stover, supra* at 12 N.Y.2d 468, 191 N.E.2d at 276. See also *Cromwell v. Ferrier, supra.*
22. Profitt, *Public Aesthetics and the Billboard,* 16 Cornell L.Q. 151 (1931).
23. *City of Passaic v. Paterson Bill Posting, Adv. & Sign Painting Co.,* 72 N.J.L. 28 62 A. 267 (Ct. Err. & App. 1905).
24. 214 U.S. 91, 29 S.Ct. 567 (1909).
25. *St. Louis Gunning Advertisement Co. v. City of St. Louis,* 235 Mo. 99, 137 S.W. 929 (1911), appeal dismissed per stipulation, 231 U.S. 761, 34 S.Ct. 325 (1913). See also *Thomas Cusack Co. v. City of Chicago,* 242 U.S. 526, 37 S.Ct. 190 (1917); *Murphy, Inc. v. Town of Westport,* 131 Conn. 292, 40 A.2d 177 (1944); *People v. Wolf,* 127 Misc. 382, 216 N.Y.S. 741 (Nassau Co. Ct.), rev'd, 220 App. Div. 71, 220 N.Y.S. 656 (1926), appeal dismissed, 247 N.Y. 189, 159 N.E. 907, 220 N.Y.S. 656 (1928).
26. *General Outdoor Advertising Co. v. City of Indianapolis,* 202 Ind. 85, 172 N.E. 309 (1930) (prohibiting billboards within 500 feet of park, parkway, or blvd.); *Preferred Tires, Inc. v. Village of Hempstead,* 173 Misc. 1017, 19 N.Y.S.2d 374 (Sup. Ct. 1940) (prohibiting all vertical signs over any sidewalk or street). See also *Merritt v. Peters,* 65 So.2d 861 (Fla. 1953); *Commonwealth v. Trimmer,* 53 Dauphin Co. Rep. 91 (Pa. 1942);

Churchill & Tait v. Rafferty, 32 Philip. I. Rep. 580
(1915), appeal dismissed, 248 U.S. 591, 39 S.Ct. 19
(1918).

27. *General Outdoor Advertising Co. v. Dept. of Pub.
Works,* 289 Mass. 149, 193 N.E. 799 (1935), appeal
dismissed, 297 U.S. 725, 56 S.Ct. 495 (1935).

28. *Id.* at 185, 187, 193 N.E. at 816-17.

29. E.g., *Sunad, Inc. v. City of Sarasota,* 122 So.2d
611 (Fla. 1960); *Dade Co. v. Gould,* 99 So.2d 236 (Fla.
1957); *International Co. v. City of Miami Beach,* 90
So.2d 906 (Fla. 1956); *City of Miami Beach v. Ocean
& Inland Co.,* 147 Fla. 480, 3, So.2d 364 (1941).

30. *Krantz v. Town of Amherst,* 192 Misc. 912, 80
N.Y.S.2d 812 (Sup. Ct. 1948); *Lizza & Sons, Inc. v.
Town of Hempstead,* 19 Misc.2d 403, 69 N.Y.S.2d 296
(Sup. Ct. 1946), aff'd., 272 App. Div. 921, 71 N.Y.S.2d
14 (1947).

31. *Town of Burlington v. Dunn,* 318 Mass. 216, 61
N.E.2d 243, cert. denied, 326 U.S. 729, 66 S.Ct. 51
(1945). See also *Town of Billerica v. Quinn,* 320 Mass.
687, 71 N.E.2d 235 (1947).

32. *Oregon City v. Hartke,* 240 Ore. 35, 400 P.2d 255
(1965).

33. *Id.* at 46, 49, 400 P.2d at 261, 262.

34. *Jasper v. Commonwealth,* 375 S.W.2d 709 (Ky.
1964). See also *Delmar v. Planning & Zoning Bd.,* 19

Conn. Supp. 21, 109 A.2d 604 (Ct. C.P. New Haven Co.
1954).

35. Compare *Morey v. Doud,* 354 U.S. 457, 77 S.Ct.
1344 (1957) with *Tigner v. Texas,* 310 U.S. 141, 60
S.Ct. 879 (1940).

36. See *State v. North W. Prep. School. Inc.,* 228
Minn. 363, 37 N.W.2d 370 (1949); *St. Cassian's Cath.
Church v. Allen,* 40 N.J. 46, 190 A.2d 667 (1963); *State
ex rel Wisconsin Luth. High School Conf. v. Sinar,* 267
Wis. 91, 65 N.W.2d 43 (1954).

37. *Railway Express Agency, Inc. v. New York,* 336
U.S. 106, 69 S.Ct. 463, 466 (1949).

38. *Carroll v. Greenwich Ins. Co.,* 199 U.S. 401, 26
S.Ct. 66 (1905).

39. See Williams, *Planning Law and the Supreme
Court:* II, 13 *Zoning Digest* 97 (Apr., 1961) for an excellent discussion of the Equal Protection Clause and
planning.

40. See *Vermont Scenery Preservation,* Central Planning Office, Vt. These possibilities were suggested in
proposed legislation prepared by the author and Norman
Williams, Jr., Professor of Planning, Rutgers University.

41. For a detailed discussion of special assessment
districts, see G. Lefcoe, *Land Development Law* (1966);
D. Mandelker, *Managing Our Urban Environment* (1966).

section three ISSUES

Introduction

ADVOCACY planning, a term unheard of a decade ago, has in the past few years been discussed more thoroughly—certainly more heatedly—than any other single concept in planning. A substantial part of the disagreement concerns the meaning of the term. What is an advocate planner? What is he supposed to do?

He is supposed to plan, presumably, bringing to bear his extensive technical training and expertise. But also he is supposed to advocate—in short, to be a politician, a task he is not trained for but tends to get more and more enthusiastic about as he goes along. In actual practice, in fact, advocacy planning has in most cases proved to be more advocacy than planning, with few projects designed and even fewer built, but with numerous, often successful, protests to its credit.

Here lies its weakness, say its critics. To which its proponents reply that, on the contrary, here is its strength. To these proponents, the first job of advocacy planning is to change not the environment but the power structure, to wrest the right of decision away from government and business and hand it over to the neighborhoods.

All in all it is a difficult role, certainly an insecure one. Among other tasks, the advocate planner is supposed to rouse the community to take action on its problems, but increasingly it seems to be turning against him in the process. More and more, and with growing bitterness, the ghettos are saying No to the white, university-trained planner who comes in to represent their needs before the establishment. They're ready to do their own representing, thanks—also their own catalyzing, their own energizing, and while they're at it, their own planning.

In fact, advocacy planning may turn out to be only a transitional stage—and a largely intellectual one at that—as the cities move away from the traditional planning practices—from on high, by decree—that have done so little, while trying so hard, for the Roxburys and Wattses and Bedford Stuyvesants of America. Whether these communities can do any better on their own remains to be seen; meanwhile, participatory planning by the neighborhood itself appears to be very much the wave of the future.

The first two essays in Section Three deal with the general idea of advocacy and the ways in which it hopes to remedy the failings of our more traditional planning machinery.

We next read a report of an American Institute of Architects/Association of Collegiate Schools of Architecture (AIA/ACSA) conference that met to consider the role of universities in advocacy planning. The hostility of the arguments that took place, by turns hilarious and chilling, demonstrates once more how advocacy, whatever its successes, has so far failed in the simple but significant matter of defining itself.

To build, or to ventilate the hostilities? One wonders again, when reading the angry ultimatum from the community to the new department store that Gimbels executives are building in the center of Yorkville on Manhattan Island, and for which they were some time ago granted a zoning variance. Toilets cleaned hourly in the adjacent subway station, public phones guaranteed to work for a block in all directions, plus the maintenance of two free nursery schools inside the store—these are only some of the challenges Gimbels is presumed eager to take on in order to be at peace with its fiery new neighbors. To anyone unfamiliar with advocacy, but all too familiar with the customary department-store service nowadays, it can only sound like madness.

We end more quietly, with a story of advocacy and community participation on a Boston playground. This is a case in which something actually got built, possibly because the builders, a group of neighborhood children, had a bigger stake in doing than in militating. In fact the participation part of it was a great success; it was the advocacy that failed, as the advocate-author sorrowfully admits.
—W. McQ.

12

Advocacy and the Urban Poor

Marshall Kaplan

To DATE, the city planning profession has played a peripheral role in American urban life. Planners have, for the most part, attempted to apply the value system of others to a set of facts which they can aggregate, analyze, and (under guidance) forge into a set of alternative programs and strategies. This separation of fact and value parallels the planning profession's historical fear of mixing in politics, an inheritance from the "good government" era.

The primary tool of the planner, the general plan, exemplified this fear. Rather than conflicts and competing interests of urban life, the general plan reflected consensus and acceptance of a corporate or utilitarian view of the city. Rather than class and/or caste, the general plan usually perceived only infrastructure and land use. Rather than priorities among functions, projects, and claims of competing real-world groups, the general plan dealt with abstraction: complete rationality, comprehensivity, and equality.

. . . although such an approach can be described, it cannot be practiced except for relatively simple problems and even then only in a somewhat modified

Marshall Kaplan, AIP, a principal in the planning firm of Marshall Kaplan, Gans, and Kahn, has provided technical assistance to the cities of Oakland and Honolulu in completing their successful Model Cities applications; has consulted to the Bedford-Stuyvesant project; and has worked with the National Advisory Commission on Civil Disorders. Previously he was Assistant Director of the Community Development Project at the University of California and coauthored *The Community Builders*.

Reprinted by permission of the *Journal of the American Institute of Planners*, Vol. 35, No. 2 (March 1969).

form. It assumes intellectual capacities and sources of information that men simply do not possess and it is even more absurd as an approach to policy when the time and money that can be allocated to a policy problem is limited, as is always the case.[1]

CHANGING DEFINITIONS OF LOCAL GOVERNMENT AND PLANNING

The advent of the War on Poverty, followed by the Model Cities program, offered welcome opportunities to *redefine* urban planning. The original Office of Economic Opportunity (OEO) mandate not only pointed out "hidden" poverty in our central cities, but also, at least implicitly, recognized that community interests may not equate with group interests.[2] The phrase, "maximum feasible participation" of the poor was purposely utilized—to the surprise of most congressmen and mayors, as well as most early progenitors of the war—to build in communities countervailing structures within which the poor (or their supposed representatives) could compete for limited public and private goods and services. In many cases, such as Oakland,[3] this "advocacy" took place internal to city hall, while in others, such as San Francisco, it took place outside city hall.

Both the War on Poverty and the Model Cities program view resource distribution as a prime function of city government. Both opt for a local political system where dialogue concerning resource allocation is a way of life and incremental decision-making a process and product. Rather than utilitarian objectives, the War on Poverty and the Model Cities program suggest specific class and/or caste objectives along with local government recognition of these objectives.

Decision-making concerning resource allocation—public or private—is premised in both programs as a resultant of constantly competing and shifting objectives. Both attempt to present a frame of reference where competing objectives and interests can be debated and resolved through adaptation, compromise, negotiation, and even contention. Both recognize the historical weaknesses of the poor in playing the resource allocation game, and both consciously attempt to redress this balance and to assure the poor an improved delivery system and some involvement in deciding content of and maintaining control over that system. In these terms, planning must be concerned with the microenvironment of specific neighborhoods, blocks, and people. The programs require a planning process directed toward functional priorities, a modest planning period, and precisely defined, achievable products.[4] It is a process oriented to achievement of immediate and predictable results, rather than presentation of long-term and somewhat speculative proposals. Finally, the planner is asked to plan *with*, not *for*, the recipients of his technical beneficence—joining fact and value.

ADVOCACY PLANNING MODELS

Implementation of the War on Poverty and the Model Cities program has lent renewed vigor to debate in the planning profession concerning advocacy planning.[5] The term has recently been used to describe professional planners whose clients are the "have-nots" in our society. Unfortunately, neither the term nor the role it implies is ever precisely described. Its vagueness and threatening connotations have sent undue fear into the hearts of federal as well as local officials (particularly redevelopment directors), who view advocates as obstacles to progress. Indeed, self-chosen (or anointed) advocates often mistakenly see themselves as generals in a singular war against an undefined establishment. Clearly both are wrong. Neither the perspective of the official who must compute success in terms of units produced rather than people benefited and who

must meet project deadlines, nor the ideas of the ideologically oriented, antiestablishment technician should prevail in chartering this new avenue of professional endeavor. Since the term *advocacy* is borrowed from the legal profession, we may look to that profession for at least an initial, if partial, definition of role and process. The legal advocate is responsible for defending, prosecuting, and, in many instances, "brokering" the system for clients. In the latter role, he advises of the relationship between the law and individual or group objectives and programs and, at times, pleads these objectives. Arbiters exist in the form of judges, juries, or quasi-judicial commissions. Advocates for contending parties join issues when "facts" or laws are differently interpreted.

The planning advocate functions in much the same context. His role is to defend or prosecute the interests of his clients. The planning advocate links resource and strategy alternatives to objectives and joins issues at the request of his client when others' interpretation of facts overlooks, minimizes, or negatively affects his clients' interests. Like an attorney, the planning advocate has several strategies to choose from to achieve his clients' goals—independence, coalition, negotiation, contention, and so forth. Communities' political systems are final arbiters. Resolution of issues is not absolute or final but usually incremental. As in the legal profession, clients' defined objectives, priorities, and ultimate strategies take precedence over those of the professional as long as the professional-client relationship exists, but the professional can always opt out if selected value systems and defined courses of action cause moral or professional anguish.

While the planner can learn much from the contextual framework within which the legal advocate functions, the analogy provides only limited insight. Most planners, like many lawyers, work for public agencies. If one accepts the notion that the community interest is, in effect, often the interest of the dominant political voice in the community or the aggregation of many individual and group interests, then the planner/public employer relationship is not completely analogous to the planner/client relationship. Within the strictures of institutional responsibility, the planner attempts to articulate values, priorities, and programs. These are not usually given to him by his employer; if they are, they will often be so general that they elude precise definition. This suggests a role for an *inside* advocate—a planner who is linked by choice to a *constituency* rather than a *client*.[6] He defines his role in much the same way as the *outside* advocate. Because he lacks a direct relationship to a client, the planner accepting the role of inside advocate often is—and should be—subject to criticism from: (1) constituents who want to participate directly in decision-making going on inside the organization and who feel the planner should not, or is not able to, represent them; (2) those within the organization who question the planner's ability to mix a commitment to a constituency with a loyalty to an employer; and (3) the planner, who often doubts the merit, efficacy, and ethics of his role. Given the increased role of the technician in decision-making and the resulting difficulty in developing a workable model of participating democracy, the difficult road of the inside advocate should be traveled by at least a few.

The role of the advocate, whether on the inside or outside, rests on several seemingly readily provable assumptions:

1. The present distribution of public or private resources in American cities favors the haves, not the have-nots.

2. Even when resources are *directed* at the poor or the ghettos, they fail to reflect articulated resident needs and priorities.

3. In most cities, resource distribution results not from a rational, but from an adaptive and incremental, decision-making process in which ghetto residents and groups play only a minimal role.

4. The public interest in most urban areas reflects not a unitary concept but the outcome of a political dialogue between group and individual values and interests, favoring the dominant.

5. Aggregation and analysis of facts involve, more often than not, the application of value systems. One set of facts can suggest different conclusions to different planners. Decisions to amend or exclude facts often stem from individual value perspectives and lead to less than a complete exploration of alternatives.

6. The key to effective citizen involvement in ghetto rebuilding efforts appears to relate quite closely to the ability of citizens to convert local aspirations into highly visible, creditable projects that affect the public and private resource stream.

If the above assumptions are accepted and linked to a value system which defines poverty and discrimination (class and caste) as the number one priority of urban America, then advocacy, whether of the inside or outside variety, is a claim on the professional. The planner, public or private, has a responsibility to articulate alternatives to reflect clearly the impact of resource allocation decisions on the poor. Further, he has at least minimal responsibility for presenting program alternatives within his particular frame of reference which indicate a benefit/cost relationship in favor of the poor. In essence, traditional concern for general amenities, aesthetics, access, health, and so on, should be complemented, if not subsumed, by concern for physical, social, and economic priorities of the poor and the translation of these priorities into effective programs.

This might be asked of many professionals, particularly those committed to using their technical expertise to convert the probability of an American tragedy into the possibility of an American dream. Objectives would clearly be:

1. Direction of existing and new public and private resources to meet priorities and needs of the client/constituent group.

2. Matching available resources to realizable client/constituent objectives.

3. Insertion of the many and varied value systems of the client/constituent into the local decision-making process.

4. Entering ghetto groups and individuals into the local decision-making process.

5. Exposition and discussion of alternatives pertaining to resource allocation decisions and their impact on client/constituent objectives, priorities, and needs.

While many "case study" articles have been written describing personal experiences in advocacy, generally they have not been rigorous efforts at evaluation.[7] Certainly, the profession needs a better understanding of these new roles. Some recent experiences of my consulting firm offer interesting alternative advocacy models. We have been involved in professional-client relationships with ghetto groups in which it was clear that our position was to lend technical assistance to their objectives. We have also been involved in client relationships with cities in which it was made clear by us that our position would be one of advocating what we thought to be the interests of the poor as best we could determine them. The former might be called *directed advocacy* (advocacy with a client); the latter, *nondirected advocacy* (advocacy with a constituency). In between directed and nondirected roles we have served in many hybrid capacities. For example, we were asked *by* one city to work *with* a local group of low-income residents to assist them in translating objectives and priorities into viable programs. Each of these models posed many problems—not all technical.

HUNTERS POINT—DIRECTED ADVOCACY

Hunters Point, an area on the southeastern edge of San Francisco, contains barrack-style "temporary" housing units that were built in the early 1940s to house shipyard workers. These units, now converted into public housing, are in a dilapidated condition and are occupied by an essentially black population. The Redevelopment Agency is collaborating with a local citizens' group, the Joint Housing Committee, to plan a Title I urban renewal project. Ultimately all existing wartime units will be replaced by a variety of low- and moderate-income housing.

Just after the Redevolpment Agency initiated the Part I Survey and Planning Contract, we were asked to consult with the OEO-funded Bayview-Hunters Point Nonprofit Community Development Corporation. The Corporation, fearful of displacement and relocation, defined its function as watching over planning done by the Agency and developing low-income housing opportunities for local residents. Many of its members thought the Joint Housing Committee had been co-opted by the Agency and was not really an "equal partner" in the planning process. This was never an easy issue to resolve. Some members of the Corporation also served on the Joint Housing Committee, and linkage between the groups varied in intensity over time.

Initially the Corporation asked us to prepare a report defining possible housing objectives and programs. One program we suggested was immediate initiation of a community-owned housing development on ten acres of vacant land in the one-hundred-acre urban renewal project area. This required a redefinition of Title I boundaries to exclude the land in question, and forfeiture by the community of some Title I write-down benefits. Completion of the project would have provided the community with locally owned new units earlier—we thought—than the Title I program could have. Since the city owned the land and Section 23 leased-housing benefits could be utilized, the Title I subsidy would be of only marginal import. The proposal was certainly debatable, but we and the Corporation thought the benefit-cost relationship was clearly on the side of the residents.

With the client's seeming acquiescence, we released the report.[8] While the document contained numerous proposals, the Redevelopment Agency, through its Director, responded only to the one described above. Indeed, the Director vociferously reacted to the press prior to reading the report. Regardless of the merits of his later position, the intensity of his premature attack served to set the stage for an open public dialogue and helped strengthen community support for the client group. At this point then, the Development Corporation had achieved two of its initial objectives—entrance into the resource allocation game with respect to their environment and creation of more visible community support.

Some of the arguments raised following release of the report illustrate issues of rationality and comprehensiveness discussed previously. In criticizing the proposal, the Agency's consultant, an outstanding local architect, raised the "problem of building housing units at the entrance of the Hunters Point site." We countered by suggesting that this was a proper use, given the Agency's commitment to making this a residential community with options to present residents. It is illustrative to note that the now published Agency plan also shows similar residential use. The Agency stressed that to carve ten acres out from under the redevolpment plan would hurt the "overall" planning program and would, in effect, destroy the "rationality" of the anticipated project plan. This argument revolves around the sanctity of the general plan, its inviolability to change and amendment, as

Right: Hunters Point Housing, to be replaced. (PHOTO COURTESY SAN FRANCISCO REDEVELOPMENT AGENCY)

Below: Hunters Point low-to-moderate-income housing to come. Foundations already under way. (DRAWING COURTESY SAN FRANCISCO REDEVELOPMENT AGENCY)

well as the priority granted physical as opposed to social and economic objectives. Yet since renewal boundaries are changed every day during the planning process and since the Hunters Point planning process had not even begun, the situation seemed to afford considerable flexibilty for the public planners. Although other issues were raised by the Agency in contending with our client's plan, none made the plan irrelevant.

The Corporation, by asking us to release the report prior to submission to city hall, chose *contention* as a means of energizing their own organization and assuring that their value system and interpretation of facts entered the public dialogue. This was done successfully. Yet, while contending with one public body, the Redevelopment Agency, they were trying to cement alliances with other public bodies and private groups as well as attempting to strengthen their own base in the community. Victory was not absolute for either party: a compromise, reflecting selective trade-offs amenable to both, was forced because the parties involved were uncertain of their strength. Essentially, the Agency secured an agreement from the Corporation not to seek through the San Francisco Board of Supervisors a redefinition of project boundaries, while the Corporation secured the "right" to participate as sponsor and a commitment from the Agency assuring early land disposition.

Contention was easier to engender than reconciliation. The compromise resulted from many bargaining sessions involving city officials, Redevelopment Agency staff, federal officials, our firm, and representatives of the client group. When the compromise was "advocated" before the client's executive board as the best possible political and technical resolution, it was not unanimously received. Some wanted to continue the fight thinking more could be won; others wanted to continue the fight thinking that even if all were lost, the organization would be strengthened. Our role in the community was threatened because of our strongly articulated position in favor of accepting the compromise. We indicated that this was the best the client could get under the circumstances (political and technical) and that we believed success in achieving the compromise and in later developing the units would do more to strengthen the organization than continuing the conflict.

Life was not easy during those few days. Our ability to work with the client was jeopardized for a time. Given the alienation, suspicion, and hostility between the client and the Agency, the feeling of some Corporation members was understandable. Given what we felt to be our knowledge of the redevelopment process, we had no other position to take. Final judgment as to the correctness of our position, as opposed to the position of some in the client group, must remain open. Similarly, what we would have done had the client chosen to disregard our advice can only be the subject of speculation. The internal issue was resolved and the compromise finally ratified by a majority.

OAKLAND—NONDIRECTED ADVOCACY

Nondirected advocacy best describes our work on the Oakland Model Cities application. It is fair to say that in Oakland, as in most other large cities, the poor, particularly blacks, feel alienated from, if not completely outside of, the decision-making process on allocation of resources. Indeed, the physical ecology of Oakland—hills occupied by affluent whites, separated by limited-access freeways from flatlands occupied by blacks—mirrors residents' views of the social and political ecology.

Our role in assisting a city-county task force in preparing a succesful Model City application was preceded by and directly related to our work with the Redevelopment Agency to restructure the physical environment with minimal displacement and maximum resident equity options. Basically this involved aggregating the backyards of blocks in which lots were long and narrow and building housing in this aggregated space. Once new housing was built, phased displacement of nonrehabilitatble frontyard housing would begin.

Our *values* on minimizing relocation were based on interviews with residents and several factual analyses of the impact of prior urban renewal plans in Oakland and other cities. They were supported by the (then) new Redevelopment Agency Director. The report was cast in a style which was thought to coincide with the as yet unofficial Model Cities program. Publication of this document, as well as increased concern of the City Manager with the problems of coordinating federal programs, created an initial base upon which to build the Model Cities application. To prepare the application, the city manager created a joint city-county task force and asked us to serve as staff consultants. The strains, crosscurrents, tensions, and resolution of tensions engendered in the process of preparing the application reflected the historic institutional and political milieu in Oakland, a milieu which has led to an alienation of the black community from city hall.

The Model City guidelines stressed meaningful citizen participation during the pre-application period. Yet Housing for Urban Development (HUD) allowed cities only four months from publication of criteria to submission of proposal. While there was no doubt that Oakland might have chosen other alternatives to gain citizen involvement, given the juxtaposition of time pressures and difficulties in defining successful participation models, the city made, we felt, a reasonable and honest attempt to involve citizens. They chose to rely on interviews for initial priority definitions and the Community Action Agency for dialogue and ultimate resident *ratification.*

Model Cities legislation and criteria provided the normative frame of reference for the pre-application work program. This was quite different from earlier federally financed planning efforts. We saw our role as assisting the city to develop objectives, priorities, and programs consistent with program guidelines and with (what we thought to be) resident priorities, but our position as consultant to the Task Force was blurred, and we were thought of, and thought of ourselves, as staff to the Task Force. We provided an evaluative reference point for Task Force proposals, particularly those which appeared on cursory examination to depart from Model City and resident guidelines.

Even had Oakland not been a successful applicant, the Model Cities pre-application process would still have been worth the effort. While no basic changes were made in either institutions or delivery systems during this short period, tentative public commitments were made to rearrange some local priorities and programs. For the first time all department heads consistently participated in a process which focused their attention on the needs of a particular area and a participating group. While some proposals articulated in the document may reflect a marginal commitment by one or more

local departments, these proposals at least provide residents fresh opportunities for dialogue along with a frame of reference for citizen planning and, if needed, a bargaining position. The application committed the city to providing financial help to the Model Neighborhood Group so that the group can select their own technical assistance. It also accepted countervailing power as a functioning premise of the neighborhood/city relationship in the planning process.

Oakland's present difficulties in successfully initiating the planning process suggest some problems of nondirected advocacy. Although the Civil Aeronautic Authority (CAA) and its local advisory groups approved the application prior to submittal to HUD, many local neighborhood residents complained to HUD that resident involvement in the application preparation stage was minimal. What we thought was a reasonable effort at planning with citizens— given HUD's deadlines and budget controls and the lack of any identifiable community group—was harshly criticized by some in the community. This criticism is probably warranted —since it is probable that resident involvement in deriving these priorities was minimal and confined primarily to ratification procedures.[9] How this involvement could have been increased is open to speculation. The application's success in securing Oakland's designation as a Model City has put residents in a better posi-

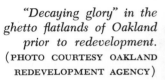

"Decaying glory" in the ghetto flatlands of Oakland prior to redevelopment. (PHOTO COURTESY OAKLAND REDEVELOPMENT AGENCY)

tion to contend with the city over planning structure. In the politics of incrementalism this is perhaps all that could be achieved.

CONCLUSIONS

Technical Assistance versus Ideology. Advocacy, when it involves the application of profesional expertise, is a synonym for technical assistance and implies evolutionary rather than revolutionary changes in institutional or delivery systems. It suggests neither contention nor coalition as a permanent reflection of relationships between public and private groups; indeed, these terms should be viewed as strategy only, not ends in themselves. Alternatives with respect to relationships will vary by issue, community, stage in the planning process, available resources, recorded priorities, and various group and individual involvements and alignments. The reintegration of fact with values is a necessary precondition for advocate planners. The value system assumed by the planner need be only basic humanism primarily concerned with expanding the choices of the poor but should not be confused with ideology because too often those with ideologies, whether of the right or of the left, use the poor. Plans premised on ideologies are, at best, irrelevant and, at worst, harmful to specific interests of the poor, for they represent unreal, often misplaced, abstractions and provide a weak base for resource allocation.

Determining Local Priorities. We feel we might have erred in assuming that we could determine local priorities for West Oakland, but we think the issue is not so much correctness or incorrectness of the estimate but, rather, the need, given Oakland's history, for direct community involvement. Even if we "hit the nail on the head" and articulated a perfect coincidence of citizen needs and proposed plans, the lack of sustained participation would have caused conflict. The perplexing problem is that the conclusions drawn from rethinking Oakland's experiences do not fit all cities. In some instances, our reading of objectives and priorities apparently conformed to that of most residents and engendered a coalition with city hall. The only conclusion we can draw, and it may be premature, is that the historical response of city government to ghetto needs and

the style of the present city government affects resident response to nondirected advocacy.

It is not easy to determine local objectives, priorities, and needs. Marginal dollar concepts fail, since all dollars are marginal; ordinal or cardinal rating systems are difficult to achieve, given prescriptive scarcity; and psychic strains resulting from decades of discrimination inhibit ready communication. Rationality is difficult to maintain, yet new techniques must be devised to complement intuition and the ultimate veto power of the client's or the professional conscience.

The White Professional in the Black Ghetto. Can white professionals work with black clients, given existing racial tensions? We have been able to do so with some limited success which we think stems from a willingness to let the client group define the initial frame of reference thus providing (1) the normative definition of our role and (2) guidelines for process and product. We have usually required written contracts containing a clause that we could be released on twenty-four hours' notice. This is done primarily to create the image and substance of a legal, not a paternal, relationship and to establish trust.

Citizen Participation. If participation is defined by numbers, nationwide efforts to engender participation have achieved only peripheral involvement of ghetto residents in local decision-making. These efforts have created a number of black leaders, including some militants, and this is perhaps no mean accomplishment. Ghetto organizations reflect most of the nuances characterizing nonghetto organizations: fluctuating and crisis-oriented membership roles; shifting and varied constituencies; and lack of member responsiveness. To these similarities are added differences of varying intensity that emanate from prescriptive social, physical, and economic environments. For example, members of many ghetto organizations are experienced in or favor only limited strategies when playing the resource allocation game. Alienation, suspicion, and hostility, compounded by lack of experience, reduce the options and limit the use of bargaining, negotiation, and compromise. Class rather than caste issues produce serious internal conflict in some groups (renters/owners) while the continuing conflict of the matriarch versus the patriarch for control and dominance creates instability. Like more affluent communities, the black community is in reality many communities, and the quest for personal leadership and recognition is apparent.

No easy answers exist for the professional as he works with his client.[10] He must continuously resolve questions of integrity. Because of the open-endedness of many assignments, he is subject to charges of being out in front or too slow to respond. He must constantly be aware of his own and his client's fallibility.

Modest claims are made for advocacy in this paper. It is basically defined as technical assistance to public and private groups premised on articulated commitment to the urban poor. Yet, the planner should not view this commitment as heroic, since it is a commitment that has become an integral part of the nationally accepted conventional wisdom.

Author's Note: This article is an amended and edited version of a paper delivered by the author before the National Conference on Social Welfare. The complete paper was printed in the *Social Welfare Forum* which was published by Columbia University Press, Winter 1969.

NOTES

1. Charles E. Lindblom, "The Science of Muddling Through," *Public Administration Review*, XIX (Spring 1959), 80.

2. For an excellent series of essays on the history of OEO and the War on Poverty, refer to Hans B. C. Spiegel (ed.), *Selected Readings Series Seven, Citizen Participation on Urban Development* (Washington, D.C.: NTL Institute for Applied Behavioral Science, May 1968).

3. Marshall Kaplan, Gans, and Kahn, *Analysis of Select Western Region Community Action Agencies, Exoneration of War on Poverty*, VII, A Report to the Subcommittee on Employment, Manpower and Poverty, U.S. Senate, Washington, D.C.

4. There are some inconsistencies in the Model Cities program criteria that suggests HUD's planners are still debating whether a long-range, rational, systemic-planning framework and process is preferable to a short term, adaptive, functional process. For example, the five-year planning forecast—certainly an incremental time period—is to be measured against long-range goals. While HUD permits cities to define functional plans and projects, they are asked to achieve an understanding of cause-and-effect relationships linking or crossing functionally defined problem areas.

5. This debate was stimulated by Paul Davidoff, "Advocacy and Pluralism in Planning," *Journal of the American Institute of Planners*, XXI (November 1965), 331–8. While I agree with Davidoff's basic premise concerning the need for advocate planners, I find his article some-

what inconsistent: he correctly posits a pluralistic decision-making process and a pluralistic definition of public will as rationalizations for advocacy but continues to support, somewhat inconsistently I think, the "comprehensive" plan as a product and the central planning function as a process. Both are derived from a unitary or utilitarian decision-making model. I find that there is at best only tenuous justification for comprehensive planning, given the present state of the arts and pluralism in urban society.

6. Linkages between inside and outside advocates for the urban poor are numerous. One astute urban commentator, Dr. Leonard Duhl, at a recent conference at Berkeley called this "the floating crap game"; while another at the same conference somewhat more pejoratively referred to the inside advocate as an institutional guerrilla. Both comments correctly suggest that relationships between outsiders and insiders are aften as important in determining the outcome of institutional decision-making as processes at work within the institution itself.

7. Peter Marris and Martin Rein, *Dilemma of Social Reform* (London: Atherton, 1967), and Sar. A. Levitan, *The Design of Federal Antipoverty Strategy* (Ann Arbor: University of Michigan, March 1967), are two publications descriptive of the inside advocate. Lisa R. Peattie, "Reflections on Advocacy Planning," *Journal of the American Institute of Planners*, XXXIV, No. 2 (March 1968), 80–7, and "Notes and Comments" on "Participation of the Poor: Section 202(a)3," *Yale Law Journal*, LXXV (March 1966), 599–629, provide two initial readings on outside advocacy.

8. No formal vote was ever taken. The organization at that time was having significant internal problems. It was difficult to achieve a quorum at meetings and the Board membership was subject to constant change. A majority of Board members asked us informally to release the report prior to submittal to city hall. We concurred. Their rationale for release was: (1) to assure and open up public dialogue; and (2) to use the dialogue to strengthen the community organization.

9. The first draft of the application reflected a pure advocacy model with separation between the city/county planning group and the citizen planning group. In essence each side had a veto. A HUD staff member questioned this separation and several members of the city/county team interpreted this as a suggestion for change and immediately proposed adding two citizens to an eleven-man planning team, without considering ramifications of this and its damage to the previously accepted advocacy model, the city/county team approved the proposal. This later became an item of contention between residents and the city. Priorities reflected in the application were never really questioned by the residents.

10. Lisa R. Peattie, "Reflections on Advocacy Planning," raises many thoughful questions about the relationships between the professional and his ghetto client. These questions focus on the degree to which the client groups reflect wider community wishes and priorities. Answers are not easy to come by, but this should not excuse the professional from service to such groups where value systems are parallel. In reality, planners face these questions with most clients, white or black.

13

Absentee Planning and the Integrated Society

James V. Cunningham

You have asked an organizer to comment on what the planners are doing, and that I will do, but I really feel I am talking with fellow urban professionals, that we are climbing the same icy mountain grasping the same slippery rope, and that my comments are on our work not your work. Because our society insists on placing each occupation in a neat pigeonhole, I am labeled an organizer while most of you in this audience are labeled planners. I have found during the past twenty years that it is often difficult to know where organizing begins and planning leaves off, and vice versa. And as I have sat in sessions on "advocacy planning" and "the riot torn city" at this conference the sense of overlap has become more intense.

The theme is physical standards and social goals. It appears that the mounting urban revolt and violence of these past three years, which is spreading to more and more cities, and the painstaking work of the National Advisory Commission on Civil Disorders, point us toward one great overriding social goal: the making of a single peaceful prosperous integrated society from two separate, bitter parts. One part is white and marked by material abundance and much unconcern. The other part is black and marked by deprivation and hostile determination.

The young black militants whose fire bombs

James V. Cunningham is lecturer in urban organizing, Graduate School of Social Work, University of Pittsburgh. This paper was read at the American Society of Planning Officials (ASPO) National Planning Conference which was held in San Francisco in May 1968.

today symbolize urban revolt are reading and responding to the writing of Frantz Fanon, Negro psychiatrist and Algerian revolutionary, who declares: "The destruction of the colonial world is no more or less than the abolition of one zone, its burial in the depths of the earth. . . ."

What Fanon spoke of was the violent expulsion of the white from the black nation. We see this happening today in America as the black militants with rocks and torch drive out the white landlord and the white businessman and "purify" their black communities, just as whites long ago "purified" their own areas with restrictive covenants, covert real estate practices, and with the rocks thrown at Martin Luther King as he marched through the white neighborhoods of Chicago in 1966.

We have two hardening zones of hostility and an uneasy nation.

Do planning and physical standards have any relevance in the face of such human chaos? In this time of urban agony they seem almost insignificant. And by themselves they probably are. What's the difference if densities are 6 or 60 white racist families to the acre? Or if neighborhood delineation isolates a black community that doesn't want to see a white man anyway? For significance it seems necessary to start not with standards but with the planner, who is in a position to have effect on how people think and act toward the city. It is he who brings standards to bear on society. It is he who can put them forward to heal or to hinder.

Under the leadership of a sensitive planner, it seems possible that physical standards can have social implications of consequence even in fusing our split cities. The planner can help ease the frustrations within a community and in so doing put himself in a position to help raise the community's sights.

When Jack Meltzer, ASPO's treasurer, was the chief planner in the renewal of Hyde Park-Kenwood in Chicago during the 1950s many of us struggled with him to locate shopping centers, select buildings for demolition, and realign streets with the aim of achieving an interracial comunity of high standards. His sensitive leadership was a major factor in Hyde Park-Kenwood becoming the only neighborhod in Chicago that has ever achieved long-term bi-racial stability. Jack Meltzer worked patiently for years in close collaboration with residents, black and white, with merchants, and institutional officials to achieve a workable plan. Physical standards were applied to make Hyde Park-Kenwood so livable that it could attract and hold middle-income families, both black and white.

Today's bitter climate makes such planning much more difficult. Blacks have become more suspicious, many whites more intransigent. The drastic urban renewal carried out in Hyde Park-Kenwood is no longer feasible or desirable for city neighborhoods. The poor must be made full partners: something we did not do in Hyde Park-Kenwood. But if the same widespread participation, the patience, the goal of an interracial community were applied to, say, Model Cities planning, this might have considerable social significance for a number of cities.

Much more important for our brutal time, probably, is the work of the consumers' planner. In Pittsburgh we have Troy West. He had his architect-design-planning shop in a high visibility storefront on Centre Avenue deep in Pittsburgh's all-black Hill District. After Dr. King's assassination, smashing, burning, looting swept up and down Centre Avenue but left Troy West's storefront untouched.

Troy West teaches architecture at Carnegie Mellon University and is a sculptor of distinction. But his greatest concern is for the development of old city neighborhoods. For a long time before he opened shop in the Hill he soaked up the neighborhood, roamed the crumbling streets, sat in the meetings of organizations, joined informal conversations in the shine parlors and restaurants. He never hid what he was or who he was. When he opened shop he was not a stranger. It is a first principle with him.

People must know the planner. Only then can he have creditability when the conversation gets around to planning standards.

West imposes nothing. This is his second principle. He waits for the people to show him the healthy things, the genuine things, the often hidden things of the neighborhood, and upon these he and the people make their plans. Many traditional standards are thrown out and particularly the suburban open-space–greensward standard. West finds his people want and need the privateness of the inner city with its mystery and small hidden places.

Troy West is working with the owners and tenants of a whole block to make courtyards and walkways of their messy, neglected little open spaces, with benches in some courts for quiet conversation. There will be space for a boxing ring and space for poetry readings and theater. A young black participant has given the main court the name, "the Court of Ideas."

Sketches for this block are emerging from numerous conversations between the planner and the people of the block. Troy West is confident this process will wipe out the present chaos of spaces in the block—a block which

Street sculpture. (PHOTO BY CHRISTINA ROTELLI, COMMUNITY DESIGN ASSOCIATES)

Gilmore Street, Lower Hill District, before redevelopment. (PHOTO BY RICHARD SAUNDERS, COURTESY CARNEGIE LIBRARY OF PITTSBURGH)

most of the city thinks of as just another piece of slum. He believes the process of planning and the changes in lives that can occur from carrying out the plan will open communication of this block with others, and of other people with him, and will move toward wider planning for the neighborhood.

Troy West's colleagues include architectural students from the university, another registered architect, a structural engineer, a sociologist, and imaginative black youths from the Hill District. As they assist the people of the neighborhood to remove some of the physical disorder from their lives, it may be possible that frustrations will be reduced. This could mean that the employment, antipoverty, and social welfare pro-

grams already in the neighborhood will get wider use and have more effect.

The Hill District where Troy West works is part of Pittsburgh's Model Cities area. Whether or not Troy West's storefront firm is retained to do some of the planning, his work with the people will have profound effect upon Pittsburghs Model Cities planning. For the people of the Hill will have something to say about Model Cities planning. And they are learning from Troy West how standards can be applied to serve their needs as they feel them. The rapport and skill of Troy West and his colleagues could be of much more value to Pittsburgh. If his storefront firm were contracted with to do the Model Cities planning for the

Hill District it would represent a planning revolution for Pittsburgh. But it could mean planning would become a home-grown process helping to heal the Hill District neighborhood rather than another outside force further aggravating it.

All of this involves the question: Who is the planner's client? The people who reside in cities have been demanding more power over the decisions that affect their lives. They have been enforcing their demands with escalating weapons of force: marches, sit-ins, picketing, political action, and violence. Legislative requirements for "maximum feasible participation" and "widespread citizen involvement" have been backing them up. The planner's client is no longer merely the businessman and the elected official. The resident, the consumer, the poor man is there, also, to be served as participating client.

And when their rights are not respected, planning and development simply will not proceed. This is the new reality which frustrates so many of us who are urban professionals. It is this frustration, I believe, which has caused so many attacks on advocacy planning at this conference. The bitter pill of shared power is a difficult one for us to swallow. As we swallow it, let us remember that the adult population with which we share power now has a median educational level of twelve years, where as recently as 1940 the adult population had only a grade school median. It now rises every year. Today's citizenry is not only better able to demand a share in power, but it is better able to exercise that share responsibly.

Standards do not always have the same meaning and reality to this wider group of clients. For instance, the high school may be judged by the poor for its ability to prepare its graduates for jobs and to place them in employment, with concerns about size of site and air conditioning shoved aside. The street may be valued more as a playground than as a channel for moving vehicles. Up to now the planner, like the architect, has been accustomed often to the powerful and affluent as his client. By accepting a wider clientele and taking the time, making the patient effort to understand the different needs and goals of this wider group, the planner becomes a professional of increased influence, able to do much more about achieving social goals.

The wider clientele can bring to the planner new knowledge. It can offer him new opportunities for opening up to this wider clientele alternatives not previously understood. He is in a position to help resolve conflicts among his clients—over the location of a playground, scattered public housing, or suburban densities which may have racial consequences.

Cleveland offers a case where physical planning is being used directly against racism. There a social scientist nun, Sister Helen Volkomener, from the city's Project Bridge, is the planner-organizer working on the racially explosive near-west side. Sister Helen has brought together Negroes, nationality whites, Puerto Ricans, and Appalachian whites—parents, clergy, and teachers—to plan for combining three declining somewhat segregated Catholic schools into one interracial, nonsectarian, nonprofit private school. This project aims to submerge racism in the achievement of quality education for the children who need it desperately. Her work has as its major emphasis using standards to ease white racism.

Unfortunately, the more familiar situation is where physical planning standards have worked against social goals. Recently, there was a flagrant case of this in the Shadyside neighborhood of Pittsburgh.

Shadyside is probably Pittsburgh's most interesting neighborhood. It is a delightful mixture of dense blocks of small, old houses and apartments, a few surviving handsome mansions, modern townhouses, and new and remodeled apartments. It has a crowded, hidden little shopping section full of distinctive shops and lively bars. Parts of it are interracial, and there is a marionette theater, a Salvation Army branch, and a Gaslight Club.

Inevitably, the discerning middle class from far and wide discovered the delightful cluster of shops and bars, and parking became difficult. The anxious merchants created a $125,000 parking fund and sought out the city planning department. The planners did a quiet study, applied traditional physical standards in the traditional manner, without consulting with residents, and came up with a plan to destroy some blocks of aged modest housing occupied by white and black families. They proposed a concrete parking lot wholly out of scale with Shadyside.

You can guess the explosion that ensued.

Neighborhood people obtained volunteer planning assistance and came up with a counterplan for a string of small lots that would have preserved scale and dislocated few families. These small lots with a network of landscaped walkways could have enhanced immensely the unique charm of Shadyside and, incidentally, probably done much more to strengthen the investment of the merchants than the city's great concrete mass.

The city planners, however, clung stubbornly to their imposed plan. They finally revised it into stages and rammed the first stage through city council. So was lost an enormous opportunity for the official planners of Pittsburgh to work with the people in strengthening one of the city's rare, stable interracial neighborhoods. The residue is unnecessary bitterness. The wrong standards were applied in the wrong way. The split in Pittsburgh was aggravated. If it weren't that the citizens of Shadyside are so polite and middle class, the project would have been stopped. I predict that in a few years even the Shadysides of America will not allow such imposed planning.

An even more dramatic and catastrophic example of this way of planning is the Columbia University gymnasium plan which would take scarce park land from the poor, a plan that seems to have been conceived without deep citizen involvement. It seems incredible in these times that a great university would go so far with a serious public interest project without knowing a part of the public would revolt against it.

Such absentee master planning is completely unacceptable in our time. (It is doubtful if it was ever relevant to urban neighborhoods at any time.) It has done violence and met fierce resistance so often it is a wonder it still gets tried in a Shadyside or a Morningside Heights. Jane Jacobs wrote its obituary ten years ago. And surely the racial rebellions of these past three years have put the seal on its grave. Yet there are signs some cities will attempt its use again in Model Cities. If this happens, the class, caste, and racial splits in our cities will be widened and new brutal events will be detonated. Traditional master planning for old residential neighborhoods is in a class with blood-letting to cure disease.

We know the alternative to master planning

but hang back from using it. It would be to supply neighborhoods with their own local planner in residence, housed in a convenient storefront, working intimately with the people of the area, answerable to an elected neighborhood board—each such board in a city then sending a voting member to the city planning commission. Financial stability should be given to such an arrangement, with irrevocable public funds supplied by local and federal sources and with the planner subject only to his local board for tenure. Model Cities opens the way for a number of cities to begin doing this right now. Such planning in non-Model City low-income areas, it would appear, would be an appropriate activity to be underwritten by poverty funds.

It may be that the Jack Meltzers, Troy Wests, and Sister Helens have to come out of non-profit organizations, church projects, and private practice—but I hope not. The great bulk of physical planning in this nation is going to be done for a long time by the planners of local government. It is here that a profound new commitment to social goals is most crucial. It is ironic that the question even has to be raised of public planners learning to have an intimate client relationship with the people of a neighborhood.

No matter how appropriate the structure is, however, each significant contemporary attempt to deal with the turmoil of the city through planning finds the critical factor to be the philosophy of the planner. Is he the supremely self-confident expert who feels he knows what's best for all and wants to be left alone to shape up a master plan which he can hand down? Or is he a man willing to listen, soak himself in a neighborhood, help people identify needs, and build on the strengths of the environment?

Secure in such roots the planner can handle physical standards for what they are: fallible man-made guides which sometimes are useful, and sometimes best ignored, and always in need of modernization.

I believe all of us involved in planning can contribute to the making of a single peaceful integrated society—but it will come from what we are and how we establish our relations with people in cities much more than from the physical standards we apply.

14

Community Involvement, Pros and Cons

Jerry Finrow

To what extent are the universities becoming involved in community action (advocacy) projects? The AIA/ACSA (American Institute of Architects/Association of Collegiate Schools of Architecture) Teachers' Seminar focused on this topic or, as the program stated, "the role of problem-centered activities in educational programs of environmental design—the need for engagement with societal issues as supplemental experience and knowledge to qualify activities in instruction, research and public service." Chairman of the seminar was Donald D. Hanson, AIA, head of the Department of Architecture of the University of Illinois, Chicago Circle.

The seminar drew about eighty persons, many of whom were active in advocacy work in their universities. While some provisions were made for small-group meetings, the seminar really was a conference with an extensive program of speakers worked out in advance. Apparently little effort was made to put together a widely representative list, and there was a definite bias toward the problems of New York, Chicago and San Francisco. The program could have been more inclusive.

The links between advocacy and teaching were seldom clearly drawn; the main thrust of the conference was toward an exploration of the state of the art of advocacy planning rather than toward the relationship between education of

Jerry Finrow is assistant professor of architecture and head of the Center for Environmental Research at the University of Oregon.

Reprinted from the April 1970 issue of the *AIA Journal*, copyright © 1970 by The American Institute of Architects.

environmental designers and community involvement.

The Reverend Jesse Jackson, head of Operation Breadbasket in Chicago, was scheduled as keynote speaker but had just been arrested for leading a demonstration. In his place, the Reverend Arthur Brazier, director of the Woodlawn Organization of Chicago, spoke to the conference topic. After establishing the basic position that the black community is fed up with the "guinea pig" attitude that universities seem to hold concerning community involvement, he went on to spell out a short history of the establishment's efforts to destroy the black community under the guise of urban renewal. He pointed out how the Chicago Southside renewal projects had made living conditions worse than before.

Community organization was seen by Reverend Mr. Brazier as the primary way of beginning to coordinate the general need objectives of the people and directing action toward attaining those objectives, the implication being that advocacy begins with understanding the goals and hopes of the people.

Brazier concluded with the statement that the profession has a staggering challenge and that somehow we must look at each project to assess its social rather than just its physical appropriateness and be willing to reject morally reprehensible projects. Further, the profession should work directly with community organizations on project development and encourage and invite discussion on projects affecting black communities.

Herbert Channick of Metropolitan Structures Inc., Chicago, spoke on urban strategy, holding that it is physically impossible for further growth to occur in urban areas. He suggested that we need to look to new town development as the only realistic solution to urban problems, given estimated growth projections, and that the federal government should initiate a land bank program for future new town development. He mentioned the present agricultural land banking system as a model.

In the area of housing, Channick pointed out, little real faith can be put in low cost methods of construction as a means to getting more housing because the methods of financing constitute such a large portion of housing costs. He saw innovations in financing as being of utmost importance and the only real way at the present time of reducing housing costs to an acceptable level for low-income people through direct-cost subsidy.

Frances Piven, assistant professor of social work at Columbia University, opened her speech with a number of theoretical questions concerning the relationship of "advocates" to the poor. Her point was basically that the poor have no legitimate power by virtue of their position in society; therefore, their only real weapon is threat of disruption of the established order.

The roots of disruption are born of disorganization and frustration with respect to their own conditions as compared with the conditions of others. If the advocate sees his role as being an organizer of the poor, working for constructive change within the society, then he is attempting to direct the disorganization and frustration into "appropriate societal channels," thus short-cutting the only power the poor have: disruption.

To this extent, she felt that advocates often feed false expectations and in some ways limit what the community might obtain by disruptive means.

The role of planner and architect advocates is substantially different from that of other professions, Miss Piven said. While doctors and lawyers bring the poor actual services that they need, architects and planners only bring promises of ways of getting housing, schools, etc. She suggested that perhaps the advocate role should be to try to assist the poor to get as much as possible out of turmoil.

Kenneth Simmons, a teacher in the Department of Architecture, University of California at Berkeley, talked about his experience with one of the earliest advocacy projects, the Architects Renewal Committee of Harlem (ARCH), of which he was a co-founder.

ARCH was established in 1964 to counter the planned urban renewal program in Harlem. With the exception of a small project in the "triangle" area of Harlem, ARCH has not actually managed to see any structures built.

The kind of work ARCH is primarily involved in relates less to architects' traditional skills and more to those of a community organizer and information-processing center. Simmons said that one service he felt ARCH has been able to give is in providing the community with information about plans of the city with respect to developments that would affect it. This typifies the role of advocacy planning: spending great amounts of time and energy trying to figure out where and how someone is going to "get you" rather than trying to create something positive.

Dr. Robert O'Block, who is with the program on technology and society at Harvard University, discussed analysis as a potential tool of the advocate. The specific project he presented was a study of the impact of rent control on housing deterioration in New York, carried out by himself and others. The results indicated that with the existing housing policy and rent control program in New York, the present housing stock will continue to deteriorate and thus increase rather than decrease the housing problem.

While the analysis itself was a very well-executed example of urban housing research, it appeared to the conference group that such thinking assists the establishment rather than the poor. Dr. O'Block pointed out that while this may sometimes be true, it nevertheless should not undermine the fact that decision-makers rely on analytical studies for information concerning the impact of their decisions.

Ernest Preacely, director of the Institute of Training and Progressive Development based in Watts, placed his hope for development of the black community in organization for positive change through black pride and nationalism. The training institute, he said, acts as a consultant in development of black organizations that are counter or parallel to existing social institutions. He felt that these were effective means of getting at the established order and, in a very special sense, disrupting it. The nonblack professional would be welcome only if he were brought in by the blacks and had a specific, useful function. Black control was seen as essential.

Hugh M. Zimmers, AIA, consultant to the AIA Task Force on Professional Responsibility to Society, presented a quick summary of the initial thinking of that group. Basically it suggested movement on four fronts: education, social aspects, politics, and creative economics. Each area offers a number of proposals for what the AIA might do to assist the poor.

Under education are programs of assistance to the unaccredited black schools of architecture in the south; a minority scholarship program; on-the-job training programs; continuing education of the profession; and high school programs to develop environmental awareness in the young. Under social aspects the proposal suggests that larger firms associate with black firms to assist them in getting projects they might not otherwise get; the establishment of an urban design team that can be called in to assist with special problems in communities; and community design centers to focus on local problems. The political programs suggest increased lobbying on the part of the AIA in order to make known the opinions of the profession. Creative economics will focus on work for the coming together of economists and architects to search for new ideas in investment and new ways of evaluating environmental solutions; and for re-evaluation of tax structures.

The seminar participants were quite upset with the proposals, which seemed to them to represent a policy of appeasement. The key comments were made by Andrew Heard, head of the Black Architects Collaborative in Chicago, who said that the entire program seemed to him to express neopaternalism and that he would personally work against this kind of thinking. He suggested that if the AIA was really serious about improving the conditions of the poor, the institute would study ways in which the money could be used more effectively rather than try to cover every special interest whether it assisted the poor or not.

By the beginning of the third day, the group had become quite familiar with the basic questions asked in connection with community involvement. However, there had been little attempt among participants to share knowledge about various projects around the country. The third day offered this opportunity.

A number of projects fell more or less into the conventional lines of advocacy work. Both the Philadelphia Experiment (Richard Plunz) and the Community Projects Laboratory of MIT (Hans Harms) reported on community involvement that was primarily student-organized. There were similar reports of little actual building success, although some small-scale projects were carried out. Questions were raised concerning the way in which community action projects should be organized to accommodate the student best. No real conclusions were reached.

Bernard Spring, AIA, of the City University of New York, took the position that the poor want to be in full control of their own planning decisions. This idea led to the development of community planning aids by some graduate students at Princeton University. The aids, when used after a short training course, give fundamental planning skills to selected members of the advocacy group.

Spring's basic thinking was that professionals should get out of poor communities because these are entirely capable of helping themselves once they have the planning skills. He suggested that the future role of the professional should be contractual in character, ensuring responsible action on both sides.

John Bailey, director of the San Francisco Design Center, brought along his staff, which also participated in the discussion. The center, Bailey related, was begun in 1967. Its initial effort was sustained by volunteers; continuing support was obtained through a grant from OEO. As with other such centers, the staff spends perhaps 30 percent of the time at drawing boards and the rest in organizing and collecting information. Services through the center are available to those who would not otherwise be able to afford them. The center's staff also works for a number of community organizations and as consultants with a great variety of expertise. No physical building has been carried out. Bailey felt that the experience had not been very encouraging and that the future does not look good.

Roger Katan of Pratt Institute took up the general question of student dissent and community action. Citing his personal experiences he suggested that universities were very conservative in this area and that it is difficult to be innovative with students in community-involved projects because of administrative restrictions.

Emilio Ambasz, associate curator of design of the Museum of Modern Art, New York, brought up the idea of an environmental university. He saw the potential for making the learning experience itself an integral part of environmental concern through universities based in poor communities.

Trying to bring the conference back to its concern with community involvement, Herman F. P. Goeters, assistant professor of architectural design at Yale University, told how students had thrown him out of his role as teacher, though allowing him to be present. The incident suggested to him that students can learn as much about power politics in class organization as in "real" context.

Andrew Heard talked about how the Black Architects Collaborative in Chicago responds to the needs for advocacy planning. BAC is unique because it represents one of the few all-black architects advocate groups in a large city. BAC, like many other advocate groups, was born of frustration and disappointment, in this case from urban renewal in Chicago's Southside. As might be expected there was a closer working relationship between BAC and the community than in many other efforts but again, little actual design work has been carried out. Its main efforts have been to stop city plans for new development.

The university's part was seen by Heard as a training ground for the blacks and the poor rather than as an agent for change by direct community involvement. He stressed the need for more black and poor teachers and paraprofessionals to assist the minority student in developing cultural awareness as well as skills to deal with the problems of his own community. If the university does use the poor community as a teaching tool, Heard said, then it should pay for its uses. He also held that a community-based advocacy effort must be controlled by people in the community; that not only black but also white areas need more community involvement; and that advocacy begins where you live.

Gerald M. McCue, FAIA (Fellow of the American Institute of Architects), head of the Department of Architecture at the University of California at Berkeley and chairman of the AIA Committee on the Future of the Profession, gave a preliminary discussion of the report of that committee, a few points from which were that current practice ethics may need revision to admit links between architectural and development services; the specialization of parts or functions already occurring need further recognition and reinforcement through the schools and through licensing laws; more public services and lobbying for environmental causes need to be carried out at the national level. Only a portion of the whole study was presented to the conference group.

Dr. Ernest Lynton, dean of Livingston College of Rutgers University, discussed work going on at Livingston to develop a new concept of an urban university. He sees the university basically as a potential agent of social change and feels that only by becoming involved in response to community problems and needs will it be redirected toward society rather than withdrawn from it. The need is for the university to go to the people where they live rather than for the people to come to the university. The implications of citizen participation is clear: the university must not use the community as a training ground but, rather, be a dispenser of skills and a center for problem-focused multidisciplinary action.

Livingston College, Dean Lynton declared, is a model of how the university can relate to poor communities without "using" them. By establishing the university in this way, he went on, one begins to reform the nature of learning, making it less elitist and less suspect to the poor. He suggested that university teachers concerned with advocate questions should deliver education rather than planning promises, and work for reformation of the nature of the institution as an advocate project of their own.

At the conclusion of the seminar a minority statement was presented and accepted (after some debate) by the attendees. It was hoped that the statement (see The Black Minority Statement below) would be a guideline for universities.

The seminar concluded with most attendants feeling that the whole experience had somehow been worth it even though it was difficult to know quite why. It had been encouraging to know that there were a number of people involved in the same difficult problems. Several of us thought it unfortunate that the Miyako Hotel had been the conference address because it had been built as a result of some of the same processes (urban renewal) that many had fought against. Others felt that there had not been enough free time left for people to get together to talk about their experiences in a less formal way.

Generally, it was felt that the seminar had not been representative of the whole spectrum of work going on in the country. Interesting work from Denver, Cincinnati, St. Louis, El Paso, Pittsburgh, etc., was never fully discussed, only alluded to. Preseminar planning organized around the interests of the attendants might have worked better rather than a program set up in advance.

Finally, there was a great deal of discussion concerning setting up some kind of permanent means of keeping in touch and sharing experiences in this field. Hanson indicated that he would put the conference material into a book and that there would be further documentation and contacts in this area.

THE BLACK MINORITY STATEMENT

The following statement is issued by the black people present at this seminar. We feel that since advocacy planning is the topic of this conference, a hard definition of advocacy emanating from the black community is required to set a correct conclusion from this seminar. "Advocacy planning is the black professionals aiding the black community in defining, giving priority to and together solving the community's problems." This statement excludes the idea of exterior forces, first, coming into the black communities and second, trying to give directions to these various communities.

Combining the irrelevance and in most cases misdirection of present architectural/planning design and teaching methods, we strongly question the input that untrained and for the most part nonminority students can give the minority community—a community in dire need of hard technical expertise. The black community does not need further study but does demand realistic

(PHOTO BY BESS BALCHEN)

committee action—the minority community in this country has been studied to death. We, the black minority here, feel it incumbent upon our unfortunate small number to speak out in this interest. In effect, you must stop using black communities as guinea pigs in the training of your white professionals. We resent any minority community being used as a training ground and a vehicle for gaining university research funding, which aids the university and not the community.

If the universities and people representing them at this seminar are really concerned and realistically committed to the idea and principles of real advocacy, it is strongly recommended that the following directions be considered and implemented:
1. Total, not token, university commitment in aiding the black/minority community by giving continuous funding and support to minority community planning groups.
2. Immediate university recruitment of black/minority faculty.
3. Immediate university recruitment of black/minority students in realistic numbers of at least one-half of incoming classes.
4. Representatives at this conference shall put their universities and proponents of advocacy in the vanguard in demanding the immediate

accreditation of all existing black schools of architecture by aiding with full university resources in helping these black schools in their development at the direction of these schools.

5. Representatives at this conference shall demand that ACSA direct the necessary resources for a black/minority seminar to involve both professionals and community in setting realistic planning standards in relation to community and educational needs.

6. In the future, if ACSA proposes to hold a conference directing itself toward problems of the poor/black/minority community, it shall (a) invite and finance full poor/black/minority participation from both professional and community sectors or (b) not hold such a neo-paternalistic gathering to develop artificial formulas to supposedly aid the poor/black/minority community.

This conference should go on record in agreement with these six points and individual schools should direct their power and prestige toward achieving these points.

The Black Minority Committee at the AIA/ ACSA conference: WILLIAM McNEIL, ERNEST PREACELY, DAVID SHARPE, MYLES STEVENS, JERRY LINDSAY, ANDREW HEARD, KENNETH SIMMONS.

15

The Yorkville Community and Gimbels

The issues of community involvement are generally fought out on a grim level—but not always. Sometimes the community involved is so articulate, so intelligent, so well equipped in ways both material and mental that the game becomes anything but grim. This was true in 1970 in one of the areas of Manhattan's favored upper East Side, when an organization of residents, formed into a group called For Yorkville, attempted to force certain concessions out of Gimbels Department Store, which was building a branch store in that area, at 86th Street and Lexington Avenue.

The building was actually under construction when the battle was joined. Gimbels had long since obtained the necessary zoning variance from the city authorities, after public hearings before both the Planning Commission and the Board of Estimate, with but little community opposition.

Yet when this new Gimbels store began rising in their midst, the community thought again, and realized the character of their neighborhood, much beloved, might indeed be changed. They determined it should not be, and launched a set of demands, widely circulated, which is printed below. The community's recommendations for physical improvements center about the subway station, onto which the new Gimbels branch would open, with requests for escalators to be paid for by the department store or the Metropolitan Transportation Authority (the subway is a very deep one at 86th and Lexington). You will see, however, that once a community makes its mind up on such deep, desperate matters as subways, it goes on to consider what kinds of films will be shown at

the movie theaters to be included in the building, and even to ponder the condition of pay-phone booths on the sidewalks around. The issues noted here have not yet been resolved between Gimbels and For Yorkville as this book goes to press, but another subsidiary group, called A Citizens Committee to Boycott Gimbels in Yorkville, has been organized, and nobody—including, probably, Gimbels—is underestimating the zing and zeal of the residents of Yorkville. —W. McQ.

STATEMENT BY FOR YORKVILLE, A COMMUNITY ORGANIZATION

THE YORKVILLE COMMUNITY AND GIMBELS

A Comprehensive List of Items of Contention Between the Yorkville Community and Gimbels East

("Gimbels East" as used hereunder refers to the structure or store that Gimbels Brothers Inc. is erecting at 86 Street and Lexington Avenue.)

1. As an indication of Gimbels' desire to avoid inflicting further psychological damage to the Yorkville Community Gimbels will remove their two signs facing Lexington Avenue which advertise the coming of Gimbels to Yorkville.
2. Gimbels will remit in full the fees paid by Planning Board #8 to Beyer-Blinder Associates for having to undertake what Gimbels should have done in the first place.

Gimbels East in the course of construction. (PHOTO BY SY SEIDMAN)

3. Subway, traffic, pedestrian and related facilities:

    a) Consideration will be given for reconceptualization of the entire store plan: for example, ground floor would be converted to entrance lobby with seats, phone booths, public toilets, dispensary, cigar-cigarette stand, post office, maps of subway system and city; fast-speed elevators would take customers up to all floors; escalators would do the same; stress would be on the easy access to Gimbels and all its floors from this comfortable and inviting lobby; many of these facilities could be incorporated on the local subway level.

    b) If first- and second-floor space are at such premium, it makes sense to eliminate the theaters or move them to higher floors where they could be reached by elevators and escalators. Their elimination, however, is more likely to be in the community's interest.

    c) In any plan adopted, an additional toll booth and turnstiles must be installed at the new Lexington entrance (under Beyer-Blinder Plan C) with appropriate enlargement of space.

    d) Gimbels will install moving stair-cases from the express-platform and local platform in the section of the subway station directly affected by Gimbels East.

    e) Internal truck-loading system must be installed at *this* time of construction.

    f) Store's ventilating and heating and air-conditioning systems are to be fed into the subway station to provide some heat and cooling to that area.

    g) Gimbels will investigate the provision of a second-floor pedestrian concourse over the sidewalk level, with walkways bridging across 86 Street and Lexington Avenue, with appropriate amenities, and will maintain same.

    h) Gimbels will work closely with the local businesses, Local Planning Board #8 and city agencies to improve the streetscape of 86 Street and Lexington Avenue, to eliminate curbside parking, alleviate traffic congestion, provide bus and taxi pull-offs, add planting and sitting areas.

i) Simultaneous cross-walk in all directions for 86 and Lexington will be studied.

j) Installation of bus stops at the corners of both Lexington and 86 Street will be studied, viz.: buses should stop at both north and south, east and west corners; bus shelters *with seats* will be provided.

k) Gimbels will consult with the Yorkville Community and have its assent always before asking any city agency for a change in the traffic patterns or traffic and parking signs.

l) Adequate toilet and hand-washing facilities for the large crowds expected are to be installed on the two subway levels and on each floor of Gimbels East.

m) The roof of Gimbels East will be converted to a city garden with related community facilities and plants which will be tended and kept in growing condition or replaced. The roof will not be left bare of such greenery.

4. Public and Customer Services: Quality of service and merchandise, treatment of employees and customers are all of concern to the Yorkville Community. Gimbels East must meet the standards required by the Community:

a) The store's dispensary will be available to the public in case of emergency; it will be accessible to entrance from the local platform of the 86 Street station as well as close to the store's elevators; it will have a direct line for use to summon ambulances in emergency.

b) A customers' nursery for children will be provided. This will be separate from the working mothers' day nursery.

c) Customers are to receive unfailing concern, service and courtesy from all employees. Employees are to be knowledgeable about their merchandise.

d) There will be a set procedure for complaints regarding overpriced merchandise.

e) There will be an adequate complaint bureau in Gimbels East for defective and inferior merchandise. This bureau will be separate and apart from the desk dealing with mere returns. Each defective item that is returned will be catalogued and marked; defective and inferior merchandise will be listed in a booklet that will be available at cost to the public quarterly; merchandise that is found defective or inferior will be withdrawn from sale or clearly marked accordingly.

f) Any restaurant within the store will serve clean, wholesome food. Its kitchen will be open to inspection to inspectors from the Department of Health and to any person in the Community who has

(PHOTO BY SY SEIDMAN)

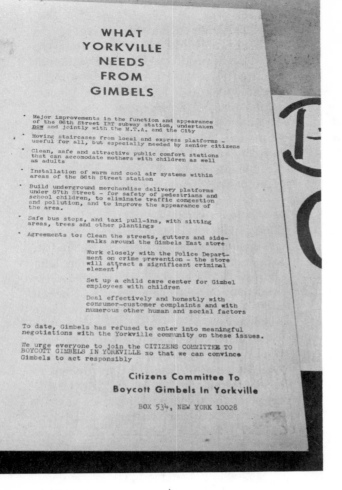

WHAT YORKVILLE NEEDS FROM GIMBELS

- Major improvements in the function and appearance of the 86th Street IRT subway station, undertaken **now** and jointly with the M.T.A. and the City

- Moving staircases from local and express platforms - useful for all, but especially needed by senior citizens

- Clean, safe and attractive public comfort stations that can accomodate mothers with children as well as adults

- Installation of warm and cool air systems within areas of the 86th Street station

- Build underground merchandise delivery platforms under 87th Street - for safety of pedestrians and school children, to eliminate traffic congestion and pollution, and to improve the appearance of the area.

- Safe bus stops, and taxi pull-ins, with sitting areas, trees and other plantings

- Agreements to: Clean the streets, gutters and sidewalks around the Gimbels East store

    Work closely with the Police Department on crime prevention - the store will attract a significant criminal element

    Set up a child care center for Gimbel employees with children

    Deal effectively and honestly with consumer-customer complaints and with numerous other human and social factors

To date, Gimbels has refused to enter into meaningful negotiations with the Yorkville community on these issues.

We urge everyone to join the CITIZENS COMMITTEE TO BOYCOTT GIMBELS IN YORKVILLE so that we can convince Gimbels to act responsibly

**Citizens Committee To
Boycott Gimbels In Yorkville**

BOX 534, NEW YORK 10028

(PHOTO BY SY SEIDMAN)

authorization to act on behalf of the Planning Board.

g) Guards are to be provided to make sure that pedestrians have adequate warning of trucks that emerge from Gimbels off-the-street underground trucking entrance.

h) Guards are to be provided to guide subway riders and customers and to be watchful of public toilets. Guards are to be knowledgeable of the general geography of the area; they are to be unfailingly courteous, and Gimbels is to agree to take action where a guard is sloppy in either dress, attitude or behavior.

i) In the movie theaters no films of violence or sadism are to be shown; pandering eroticism, lewdness, sadism or masoch-

ism or the adulation of the abnormal will not be exhibited by Gimbel or his agents outside the theaters in Gimbels East; instead such outside advertising will be strictly limited and decorous at all times.

j) Gimbels will work out an arrangement with the New York Telephone Company to see that all public phones within Gimbels East, within the subway station at 86 Street, and within a one block radius in all directions of Gimbels East are in working order. Such surveillance by the phone company will be made every 24 hours.

5. Treatment and Conditions of Employees:

a) A children's day nursery will be provided for preschool children whose mothers are working in Gimbels East; it will be staffed according to regulations and be open for public inspection.

b) Courtesy and service by employees in Gimbels East is to be paramount. A course to teach employees the importance of this approach will be instituted. Employees will be instructed in the rights of the customer to be served adequately; employees will also be taught their rights to avoid being abused by a customer and what steps to take in case of such abuse.

c) Instructors of employees will be chosen for their qualification to teach the subjects mentioned above. A college degree or a series of courses in personnel practices are not necessarily the qualifications an instructor needs to understand interpersonal relationships.

d) Employees will be treated with respect; all will receive their entitled rest times and lunch periods as outlined in union contracts.

e) Gimbels will concern itself with the physical problems of sales personnel who have to stand long hours on their feet while on duty.

f) Floor supervisors will be properly informed of their duties and will know thoroughly the administrative procedures and the merchandise within their jurisdiction. They will treat their staffs with decorum at all times.

g) The attitude of the Gimbels East office

of personnel to prospective employees will be unfailingly decent and concerned. Prospective employees, or those who are not accepted for employment, will not be kept waiting while personnel staff flaunts its power, or talks to other staff members in idle chatter, or assumes any kind of superior "you-wait-for-me" attitude. Personnel staff will never dismiss any prospective employee with the words "You don't have the experience." A written set of procedures will be available for public examination.

h) Any purely employee restaurant will serve simple, reasonable, wholesome food. Cafeteria employees of Gimbels East will be expected to act with courtesy in serving food to Gimbels retail employees. The kitchen of any employee cafeteria will be open for public examination.

i) In the event that no employee cafeteria is planned for Gimbels East adequate time for lunch or dinner in crowded neighborhood eating establishments must be permitted for employees.

6. Public Cleaning & Maintenance:

a) While open for business, Gimbels East will undertake hourly cleaning of all stairs and subway platforms throughout the 86 Street station; similarly it will undertake hourly cleaning of all gutters and sidewalks in the following areas:

    1) On both sides of Lexington Avenue between 86 and 87 Streets;

    2) On both sides of 87 and 86 Streets from Lexington Avenue to Park Avenue.

b) Sidewalk mechanical cleaner or snow-removal equipment will be of a type that does not pollute the air with carbon-monoxide or any other poison fumes.

c) Gimbels East will undertake hourly cleaning of all public toilets within the 86 Street station—both on the uptown and downtown sides, and within the store itself. All mentioned toilets will be maintained in a clean and well-lit and cheerful condition, and will receive appropriate painting and repairs as immediately as needed.

d) Garbage disposal by Gimbels East is to be arranged to avoid creation of a public nuisance; this is to include such problems as incineration, removal and accumulation.

7. Gimbels East construction problems as they relate to the Yorkville Community:

a) The construction fence around Gimbels East will be kept closed and in good repair; it will be available for suitable notices by various Yorkville Community groups while it remains in position. The signs posted on the fence will be removed or painted over after the date of their message has passed; or after a reasonable time has elapsed for public examination.

b) Gimbels will order its general contractor and his subcontractors to:

    1) obey all traffic and parking regulations around the Gimbels East site;

    2) obey all written requirements of the 1968 Building Code without exception;

    3) maintain the gutters and sidewalks around the construction site in clean & orderly condition.

c) Gimbels will ensure the hiring of minority workmen in all trade categories with the ratio being maintained of one minority construction worker out of every four men employed in each trade.

d) Neither Gimbels nor its contractual agents nor their agents will in any way use or employ poison, cancer-giving, air-polluting asbestos to cover the steel framework of Gimbels East.

8. Miscellaneous:

Gimbels will draw up a program to deal with theft of merchandise from Gimbels East, primarily by addicts who need to finance their affliction with drugs; Gimbels will outline its plans for the prevention of the increase of crime in the Yorkville area because of the arrival of Gimbels in the neighborhood. (Such crime has plagued the mid-town stores.) Gimbels will clarify how it plans to treat shop-lifters and what procedures will be used to deal with the problem. What will the police-Gimbels East relationship be in Yorkville for handling this matter?

16

The Political Collapse
of a Playground

Mayer Spivack

A FEW years ago while working as a city planner I became involved in the design and construction of a neighborhood playground located in a very dense, old, urban area near Boston. I had for some time been interested in the problem of designing physical settings for children which could provide a spectrum of play satisfactions.

My new play facility was to be constructed on the site of an older one whose originally uninteresting and meager equipment had been further incapacitated by vandalism. The city under whose auspices I was working agreed to supply tools and earth-moving equipment and specialized labor where it was required, as in the installation of water supplies and drainage pipes, and drivers for the heavy equipment.

The city also made available a small amount of money (under $2,000) from a special fund. It was our intention to build an inexpensive, appropriately designed play world with the aid of children as designers and constructors. My services were available as a kind of technical consultant to both the city and the children.

For two or three weeks prior to the beginning of construction, and while involved in measuring the site and drawing up tentative proposals for its use, I was able to observe the play and intensity of use on the old playground and to become friendly with the children.

School had let out for the summer and yet in none of my visits to the site were there ever more than three or four children on the playground. Characteristically, they would sit disconsolately in a corner against the chain link

Reprinted from the July 1969 *Landscape Architecture Quarterly*.

fence in the shade—for it was already quite hot on that black desert—or they would ride bicycles in lazy figure 8's, obviously bored. The space was huge in relation to the scale of a child, and totally flat. Broken pavement showed where old, damaged swings and slides had been torn out and the holes had been left unpatched. One could have turned it into a parking lot without altering a thing.

There were children of all ages, from tots through late teens everywhere on the streets, sitting in doorways, and leaning against lampposts. When I talked about the idea of rebuilding the tot lot for the small children, the teenagers left no doubt in my mind that they had felt unfairly treated when, in the presence of an official from the Recreation Commission, they had been ejected from the old space. They soon told me that, reacting to this kind of treatment, they had found it satisfying to tear out the jungle gym, to break the slides and to steal the swings used by the younger ones. In response to this the Recreation Commission had given up trying to maintain the area.

The neighborhood was populated in the main by working-class Italians. Many of the children had no access to the interiors of their own houses during the day while their mothers were away working. Children were put in the charge of other families, left to themselves or in the care of some other, older, child. The only play space, possessable space, or homeplace that they could hope for was that which the city would give them. They looked for space in someone else's backyard or alley, or in the street. These children had no place to keep anything of their own, in which to hide their toys or to use them.

As often happens in such close old neighborhoods, children were noisily and actively discouraged from using vacant lots next to houses, side alleys and back yards by the abutting property owners, who feared the litter of broken glass, vandalism, and the noise.

Between us, the children and I devised a plan for the playground, whose layout was based upon safety requirements and on the necessity to separate more violent, active play areas from those offering some peace and security. The equipment was designed to be built by and for children with materials they could, with a little help, manipulate and control. Our goals were very limited and simple. Given the budget, we were restricted to using industrial surplus materials, and to scavenging what we could. The city would provide us with fencing material, with paving, water pipes and conduit, and with fill.

Within a few weeks we had accumulated on the playground stocks of railroad ties, telephone poles, cable drumheads and many truckloads full of wood chips. These were to be our raw materials; they would also to some extent dictate aesthetics.

In addition, the playground was a kind of compromise or halfway point between the athletic field amusement park and the intimate play space required at various times. The plan represented that compromise by providing the older children with such facilities as a basketball court in return for their guarantee of protection and maintenance of the playground for the younger children. It was hinted by the older children that if this were not the case they would not protect the facilities that they were not interested in. I learned quickly and gave them their due. In return, they more than kept to their bargain, throwing themselves into the work of building the whole playground with an intensity reserved only for play. There were no further problems with vandalism, and the playground began to have a life of its own.

Arrival of the first construction equipment carrying the hulk of a strong tree-trunk galvanized the whole community. The tree-trunk was placed on its side in temporary storage and within seconds after it was maneuvered into position it became the property of the playground population which had risen to about twenty-five or thirty children. The new high level of use and involvement was maintained throughout the summer. Many of the children had court records, some of them by the age of nine. I had been warned by city officials that it was impossible to do anything with or for these children, for they were hardened delinquents and would destroy anything that we gave them.

Perhaps we were all fortunate that our plan made it necessary for the children to match, by giving their effort and involvement, whatever the city and I gave on our side. In the course of the summer there never occurred an incident of theft or of willful damage to materials on the playground. The children were on the job every morning long before I arrived. Nearly every day I would find the children had torn down and completely rebuilt their little city. The first of these structures, ambitious quasi-shelters constructed of railroad ties, appeared in a shaded corner of the lot and, as I approached, one of the littler kids came running out, pleading: "Mr. Spivack, Mr. Spivack, you're not going to tear it down, are you?" That was their image of "adult authority" and of "city hall," each of which I represented to them.

As the summer progressed, this same structure, modified time after time into new forms, would reappear. I was amazed at the ease with which these kids could move the railroad ties, some of which were 17 feet long and weighed over 300 pounds. I suspected adult collusion, for I never saw them building this way in the daytime: apparently construction was a nocturnal act.

Building the playground became play. The only fights I observed were over the privilege of using a shovel or a pick, or some other tool, for there were not enough of these to go around. As the children built the space it became clear that they were building themselves as well. Pride in accomplishment, in competence, and just plain pleasure were almost always visible on the faces and in the movements of the children while they worked. Having invested themselves so obviously and so thoroughly in a community-sponsored, valued project, they also developed a sense of identification with and responsibility for, the publicly owned property. The work and the playground were theirs.

They became visible members of a child community which had a certain amount of effect on, and esteem from, the adult community. They learned to get along with older people because they worked and played with them. They had the chance in a short span of time to participate with adults in the conception, planning, and implementation of a complex piece of work which had obvious and tangible consequences in their world. They widened their repertoire of social roles and contexts within which they could experiment and search for new notions of self-identity. They became, in a very real sense, political actors whose opinions were valued, whose responsibilities were clear; citizens of a small, organized, functioning community—leaders and followers at once. They experienced a sense of community.

Since much of the work and its planning was the responsibility of the children, problems encountered during construction and planning were often unanticipated, and the children, when challenged, time and time again had problems of organization and process which required considerable resourcefulness individually and as cooperating groups in their solution. Perhaps more important, they generated the problems

"As the summer progressed, this same structure, modified time after time into new forms, would reappear." (PHOTO COURTESY MAYER SPIVACK)

"I was amazed at the ease with which these kids could move railroad ties, 17 feet long, weighing over 300 pounds." (PHOTO COURTESY MAYER SPIVACK)

"The tree trunk became the property of the playground population that had risen to about 25 or 30 children." (PHOTO COURTESY MAYER SPIVACK)

which they encountered in the course of their work on their own initiative. They were not told what to do unless they asked for advice.

Average children discovered in themselves abilities to lead and found that they had attitudes and aspirations toward leadership that might otherwise have been undeveloped. They were glorious in the eyes of younger children and therefore became natural nominees for leadership roles, although such roles were never formalized. Hero-worship patterns, however, could easily be observed.

The work-play fusion was complete. Work was played and play was worked. Builders must play on a job like this or it won't be done well. This is an easy, natural way to a good working habit or at least a good attitude toward work, where work comes to be viewed as an experiment with oneself and an exploration of one's

stocks of resourcefulness and one's limitations. Children who, for one reason or another, participated less in the building process, came to the playground every day anyway, and in the course of the summer saw their playmates scheme and plan and convert an ugly pile of raw materials into wonderful structures. They watched and they learned vicariously and they enjoyed it immensely.

By late August the land had been molded and distinct activity areas or zones had taken shape. We were within a few weeks of completion. Raw material stockpiled for so long was now being used in construction. It became apparent that we intended to use these materials in their final form without refinishing them. The children were perfectly happy with the materials and may even have thought them beautiful. Their parents and neighbors, however, considered telephone poles and railroad ties as industrial surplus, or, as one of them put it, "a bunch of junk."

This aesthetic conflict became the issue which was destined to destroy the project. I remained naïvely unaware that the neighbors were beginning to resent the fact that other areas of the city received shiny new playground equipment while their area was given used, ugly, wooden cast-offs. My original attempts to arouse substantial adult community involvement and support for the project had never been very successful. The neighborhood obviously preferred to have things done for them as was the case elsewhere. (Community action programs were at that time relatively new.) Their preconception also appeared to involve some notion of gaining, or at least not losing, status, by having the services of the city performed for them by "servants," as was the case in middle-class and upper-income areas.

Thus, without the support and involvement of the neighborhood and without feedback, we were completely taken by surprise when one Monday morning in early September the children and I appeared at the site to find the

To the neighbors this boy-built structure was a disgrace, but the children had been happy to use industrial surplus materials and scavenged supplies. Neighbors finally had the project destroyed. (PHOTO COURTESY MAYER SPIVACK)

project demolished and replaced by a perfectly flat, black, hot, top paving. We now had the equivalent of a parking lot. Later, in a conversation with a city councilor, I learned that an irritated property owner had persuaded him to "eliminate the mess" (*sic*) and that he had done so, even though previously he had been enthusiastic about the work and had gone so far as to propose to me other sites in his area which might be similarly transformed by neighborhood children.

Now, in the wisdom of retrospection, I understand how differences in aesthetics are closely tied to concerns about community status and to the relatively different value structures held by the adults of the community, their children, and myself, the "expert consultant" or technician. Had I identified these differences as conflicts early enough and effectively dealt with them, the project might not have failed so drastically.

Perhaps the lessons of failure are the more profoundly learned. If so, then the children have learned as well. For them, a positive image of City Hall and government formed through the optimistic period of their work and participation was inexplicably and insidiously shattered. A truly democratic experience was negated by the powerful gestures of one or two people who remained unidentified.

Most of the childen were acutely disappointed and were either unwilling or unable to understand the underlying reasons for the collapse of their efforts. They became uncommunicative and resentful.

Soon the city installed some shiny new fencing and playground equipment. Within days unmistakable signs of vandalism were visible. Fence posts were bent to the ground and the new paving covered with broken bottles. A new kind of junkpile had been created.

Even though the project failed, many ideas we explored concerning the spatial requirements of play behavior and the nature of play behavior itself have been an impetus to my continued thinking and research.

It is perhaps the fault of the Protestant ethic that we so habitually, as adults, separate the activities of children into play and work. For the child, however, things are not quite so clear-cut; given proper conditions, children, in the name of play, will thoroughly invest themselves in enterprises that would make many a strong man a work-shirker. However, on a visit to nearly any public playground in midsummer we are likely to encounter a meager population sitting discouragedly on swings or near the edges of the playground, leaning against a fence, or perhaps aimlessly riding bicycles around in circles. The often expensive and "aesthetically pleasing" equipment purchased, with the best intentions, by adults for children stands either unused or unusable because of vandalism.

Lately there has been much attention given to the subject of public playgrounds in urban areas. In Boston the Metropolitan District Commission has for several years been constructing its version of improved playgrounds for children. Manufacturers have sprung up nationally to add their notions of proper and beautiful play equipment for children. Annually architects, sculptors and designers are invited to enter one of several competitions for the design of better playground "sculpture."

Well intentioned as such efforts certainly are, the greater part of them miss the point. Playgrounds, if they are useful at all, must serve many purposes, only one of which is the satisfaction of a child's need to play in the conventional sense.

Children are rarely conscious of the fact of their playing, which may consist of intense learning and the satisfaction of curiosity about the natural world and the human one. It may involve testing of social roles, development of physical coordination and strength, and competition with age mates in contests of skill of various sorts. Fantasy-based play may or may not be accompanied by the physical manipulation of objects in the environment—the "working out" or "playing out" of conflicts, fears and other troublesome emotion-related material. In children's play we may see a wide range of behaviors.

Against this rather sketchy background of what children may do while playing, consider the range of settings available to an urban child in a "modern" playground. Most often playgrounds are designed to be miniature athletic fields or do-it-yourself amusement parks, in which the child is challenged only in the physical modes of his play behavior. There are bars to climb and hang on, slides to slide on and swings on which to swing. But for a child who

(PHOTO COURTESY MAYER SPIVACK)

wants to build or dig, hide, sing or tell stories and listen to them, there is no proper setting. It is true that children are capable of modifying almost any setting to their needs, but on a playground where other children are flying and kicking there is often little quiet space in which to sit tranquilly and play with a tiny toy or immerse oneself in dreams or fantasies.

Most playgrounds being built today resemble huge squirrel cages. They challenge and exhaust the child with a variety of intriguing and enjoyable muscle-testing experiences. This is satisfactory if it does not have to fill the play-space needs of the same child or children day after day throughout the year. Unfortunately this is the kind of playground so widely photographed and discussed in Sunday supplements, and most often used as a model by cities and towns. A playground at a school or in a community mental health center, or in an urban or suburban neighborhood must be capable of serving many requirements, especially if the group of children using it remains fairly constant. For the child in a dense urban area, ability of the space to provide a variety of play settings may be of superlative importance to his well-being.

When a child *makes* something, or attempts to change his environment, he becomes invested in the object and in his work on it. The act often symbolizes his power to change himself. To deprive a child of this opportunity may work unnecessary hardships on his efforts at self-realization and self-definition.

The aesthetics of the adult, and the basis for these aesthetics, appear to rest on criteria very different from the aesthetics of the child. And so adult-designed playgrounds tend to be neat, clean, flat surfaces with sculpturelike objects firmly attached to concrete or tar paving. But children like to play in the rather loosely organized vacant lots that adults seem to dislike.

Neighborhood play areas probably require the greatest setting adaptability of any designed environment anywhere. And manipulability of the environment appears to be the essential property for play behavior that is fluid, changing and unpredictable.

EPILOGUE

Introduction

IN need of some kind of perspective, we emerge now from the turbulence and anger of urban America to consider this story of one small solution to a large social problem in Japan's capital city.

The setting may sound exotic, but the comparisons are there. Certainly the average American ghetto dweller in all his misfortune has nothing on the despised and impoverished ragpickers of Tokyo. And certainly anyone familiar with the planning profession in America can only be fascinated by the Dostoevskian cast of characters who helped the ragpickers to better their lives. A ruined businessman; a wandering monk; a tubercular young lady of good family; and a somewhat mysterious promoter-intellectual— these four nonprofessionals performed for the ragpickers a function that in this country would probably be called advocacy. The story of their success is instructive and also, in a modest way, heartening.
—W. McQ.

17

Urban Poverty, Ragpickers, and the "Ants' Villa" in Tokyo

Koji Taira

The author is grateful to a number of his colleagues and students at Stanford University for reading the earlier versions of this paper and devoting a generous amount of time to the discussion of its problems and analyses. Special thanks are due to Professors M. Abramovitz, Harumi Befu, R. E. Gallman, Paul Hohenberg, Lawrence Lau, Michio Nagai, and Yasuhiko Torii. He is also indebted to the East Asian Studies Committee of Stanford University for research grants and facilities.

INTRODUCTION

POVERTY is a grave social problem in rich countries, while it is not in poor countries. Countries seem to "discover" poverty in their midst at a certain stage of their socioeconomic development. This may sound enigmatic, but the explanation for it may be found in the nature of all social problems. As Robert A. Dentler succinctly states: "a social problem is an event that is viewed as a deviation from, or a breakdown of, some social standard that groups believe must be upheld if human life, or the order of activities that maintains and gives meaning to life, is to be continued." [1] Social problems depend for their emergence upon social standards. Similarly, poverty as a social problem depends upon the standard of living which society accepts as a tolerable minimum. The minimum standard of living does not arise as a guide to social policy unless a good majority of people have attained standards of living above the minimum. Poverty therefore emerges as a social problem and, especially, as a problem in public

policy when society has achieved some measure of socioeconomic development.

The emergence of a minimum standard of living by social consensus, by its sheer logical force, divides the population into two groups: those above and those below the minimum. The same socioeconomic forces which have produced the social minimum will also have shaped the attitudes, motives, and social roles of the two groups on both sides of the minimum. These forces are the ones which underlay the historical development of today's rich countries: widespread desire for economic gains, technological progress, and efficient resource allocation (including the mobility of human resources). In an economically successful society, the acquisitive impulse and achievement motive are particularly strong. A society's standard of living emerges from the feeling of accomplishment and the constantly renewed resolve for further efforts on the part of those who have kept up with the general pace of output expansion, technological progress, and resource mobility. The minimum standard of living marks the lowest boundary of the general standard of living and, like the latter, constantly rises in pace with the general change. The poor are those who, for one reason or another fail to keep up with the rising community standard of living or who, starting with a subminimum status, fail to rise above the minimum. The poor are therefore an example of the social cost of economic progress. They are fallouts of human materials from the never-ceasing machine of economic development.[2]

Japan has experienced a century of modern economic growth involving structural shifts, innovations, and resource mobility. Poverty as a social problem must therefore have arisen at a certain stage of Japan's economic development. How and when did Japan "discover" poverty? What kind of poverty was it that Japan "discovered"? How has Japanese poverty changed over time? How does the Japanese society at large regard its poor? How do the poor regard themselves? What helps the poor climb out of poverty? These are some of the questions we would like to answer in the course of our inquiry into the evolution of urban poverty in Japanese development.

I. THE "DISCOVERY" OF URBAN POVERTY

It was an interesting coincidence in timing that Japan began to take notice of her urban poverty when she was about to start her modern economic growth in the late 1880s. The "discoverers" of urban poverty in Japan were a small group of young intellectuals. In the course of their education, these young men had read about the social consequences of industrialization in the West. They were also under the influence of the proletarian literature and literary realism that were just beginning to sway the sentiments of the reading public of Japan. The Meiji Restoration (1868) was nearly twenty years old, and Japan was evidently following the course of economic development in the way it took place in the West. This group descended into the ghettos of Japan's major cities partly to verify the social consequences of capitalist development that they had learned about through books and partly to gain a more complete picture of the type of society that was unfolding in Japan.

The poor, for their part, neither talked nor wrote about their plight for the information of the general society. Nor did the leaders, officials, and the public of Meiji Japan care much about the poor. Having emerged from centuries of feudalism only in 1868, Japan was busy trying to acquire the rules and institutions of a modern state throughout the remainder of the nineteenth century. The poor occasionally offended the eyes of the political dignitaries by straying into the main streets of the city. On such occasions they were summarily evicted by the police. So long as the poor stayed in the back alleys, however, they were on the whole left alone, and the authorities rarely bothered with them. The poor existed somewhere in silence and darkness, but Meiji Japan was too busy with the tasks of modernization and industrialization to pay serious attention to them. The shocking reports of the poverty explorers fell like so many bombshells on the dynamic but single-minded society of Meiji Japan.

We shall concentrate on Tokyo because of our greater familiarity with this city, although other cities were explored with equal intensity by the Meiji intellectuals. One of the earliest reports on Tokyo's slums appeared in a newspaper called *Chōya shimbun* in 1886. One of the motives for the social survey that led to this report was to search for explanations for an apparent increase in the number of beggars on the streets of Tokyo. Reporters were sent out into all parts of the city of Tokyo to locate the poor and to learn about their living conditions, jobs, and customs. The result was the discovery of Tokyo's three great ghettos (*sandai hinminkutsu*): i.e., Yotsuya Samegabashi to the west, Shiba Shin'-ami-cho to the south, and Shitaya Man'nen-cho to the north, all within a few miles from Tokyo Railroad Station (see Fig. 1).[3] These poverty pockets were subsequently revisited and restudied by many other individuals at different times. The best-known landmark in the history of social studies of this kind during the Meiji era was Yokoyama's work on Japan's lower-class society, published in 1898, which has stood the test of time remarkably well.[4] We owe to Yokoyama a reasonably detailed statistical description of the households, occupations, earnings, and living conditions in the three great ghettos just mentioned.

Later studies made it clear that the three poverty pockets which shocked the Meiji public were largely "traditional" poor-quarters which had their origins in the social policy of Tokugawa Japan prior to the Meiji era.[5] These were the areas where the Tokugawa government huddled the low-caste people like freed convicts, beggars, drifters, *Eta*, and *Hinin* (the last two commonly known as Japan's "untouchables"). After the Meiji government emancipated all classes of people from the feudal restrictions, the traditional poor-quarters were used by the poor in general, regardless of their social origins. The sheer size of these ghettos was astonishing. The largest of the three, Yotsuya Samegabashi, harbored more than a thousand households, or nearly 5,000 persons. Even in the smallest one, Shiba Shin'ami-cho, there were more than 500 households or more than 3,000 persons.[6] Yokoyama could hardly believe his eyes when he first confronted these poverty pockets. He had seen clusters of poor-quarters in other parts of Tokyo, containing ten, twenty, or at most several tens of poor households, but each of the three great ghettos was something that "made him rub his eyes twice before he was sure of its existence."[7]

During the early decades of the twentieth century, the poor-quarters gave way to new commercial and residential buildings. The poor who could not afford to pay rising rents moved out of the former ghetto areas to the periphery of Tokyo City and often beyond it. A final blow was dealt to these areas by the great earthquake of 1923. While the three great poverty pockets of the Meiji era had largely disappeared by 1920, field surveys undertaken in 1919–21 uncovered three new ghettos, each of which contained more than 200 poor households.[8] An investigation by the city of Tokyo in 1926 identified thirteen poverty pockets containing 1,100 households in all, less than the extent of poverty which was once packed into the largest slumland, Yotsuya Samegabashi, of the 1890s. All of them lay farther toward the city limits of Tokyo than the earlier ghettos. With the exception of Yotsuya Asahicho (marked "d" in Fig. 1), which originated in the Tokugawa period and expanded as a ghetto by absorbing the poor displaced from elsewhere, all of the ghettos of the 1920s within the city of Tokyo were products of Tokyo's urban development and Japan's modern economic growth.[9]

Factories rose inside and outside the city of Tokyo, while the population of Tokyo and its vicinity increased by natural growth and by immigration from all parts of Japan. Economic forces and urban policies made living too expensive and uncomfortable for the poor within the city limits of Tokyo. The great fire that broke out with the earthquake in 1923 wiped out all the slums east of the Imperial Palace. Care was taken, with success, not to allow the

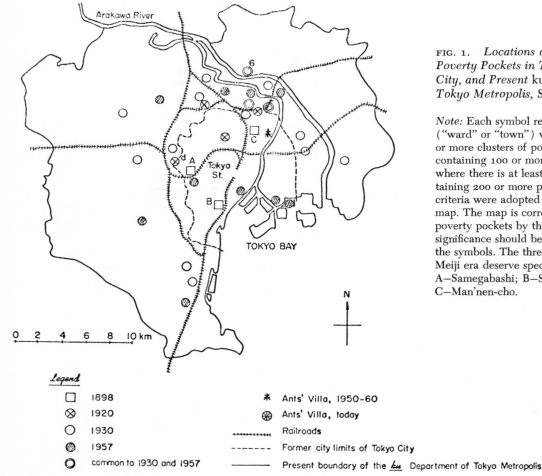

FIG. 1. *Locations of Representative Poverty Pockets in Tokyo, Former Tokyo City, and Present* ku *Department of Tokyo Metropolis, Selected Years*

Note: Each symbol represents a single *cho* ("ward" or "town") where there are three or more clusters of poor houses, each cluster containing 100 or more poor households, or where there is at least one large cluster containing 200 or more poor households. These criteria were adopted to avoid cluttering the map. The map is correct on the location of poverty pockets by this definition, but no significance should be attached to the size of the symbols. The three great ghettos of the Meiji era deserve special emphasis: A—Samegabashi; B—Shin-ami-cho; and C—Man'nen-cho.

Legend

□	1898	✳	Ants' Villa, 1950-60
⊗	1920	⊛	Ants' Villa, today
○	1930	┈┈┈	Railroads
◍	1957	-------	Former city limits of Tokyo City
◖	common to 1930 and 1957	———	Present boundary of the *ku* Department of Tokyo Metropolis

re-emergence of poverty pockets in these areas. The city of Tokyo ruthlessly pursued city planning, including zoning, street widening, restoration of more lands for parks and green areas, tighter housing regulations, area improvements, extensive public health measures, and so on. The poor had no place in a city where the standards of urban life and environment suddenly soared to such a height. Strange though it may seem from today's perspective, there were flights of the poor from the city to its outskirts in the 1920s and 1930s.

In 1930, the prefectural government of Tokyo surveyed the housing situation in the vicinity of Tokyo City and discovered more than 400 clusters of dilapidated housing units.[10] Nearly 60 percent of these poverty pockets were found in the towns immediately adjacent to the city of Tokyo. A further 25 percent were in the next ring of towns. Not only were the poverty pockets in the towns adjacent to Tokyo more numerous, but they were also larger and more densely populated than in towns and villages farther out. There were 52 poverty pockets, each of which contained more than 100 households, and 32 of them were in the towns adjacent to Tokyo. As may be seen from Fig. 1, the larger poverty pockets tended to be more concentrated in areas northwest to east of the city of Tokyo. The poor also moved south, but left the western areas open. It is into these areas that the fashionable middle-class residences spread in the next decades, especially in the 1950s and 1960s.

In 1932, the city of Tokyo expanded roughly to its present *ku* (borough) department of the metropolis of Tokyo. In 1938, the dichotomy of the city (*shi*) and prefecture (*fu*) was sublimated into a unified administration of the metropolis of Tokyo (*to*). Within the metropolis there were three geographical departments; viz., boroughs (*ku*), cities (*shi*), and counties (*gun*).[11] After a series of rearrangements, the *ku* department had by 1950 settled to its present 23 *ku*. (The whole of the *ku* department is shown in Fig. 1.) Poverty did not disappear during these years, however. Poverty pockets re-emerged in all parts of the metropolis of Tokyo after World War II, even in the midst of the old city of Tokyo, from which it had almost disappeared by 1940. In 1957, the metropolitan government found 273 clusters of poor housing units, of which 231 (85 percent) were in the central city area (*ku* department).[12] There were

exceptions, but the legacy of the poverty of the northern parts of Tokyo was visible in the distribution of the poverty pockets in the 1950s (see Fig. 1).

To put the matter in the terminology of J. K. Galbraith, we have so far traced the development of "insular poverty" in Tokyo. It is useful to add that poverty does not exist only in islands; there are instances of individual, family, or "case" poverty which arise everywhere.[13] We have discussed these latter types of poverty elsewhere.[14] For example, the poor households depending upon public assistance in Tokyo numbered about 70,000 in 1959, while the households within the islands of poverty already referred to were less than 20,000.[15] Poverty as an individual or family phenomenon is much more ubiquitous than "insular poverty."[16] From the point of view of public policy, individual or family poverty is primarily an issue for welfare administration, while insular poverty is one for housing policy. In Japan, insular poverty has been tackled by accommodating individuals or families in public housing units as they have become available. Where poverty pockets have acquired a measure of identity as communities, the policy of separate accommodations has amounted to a sort of eviction policy and as such has resulted in considerable difficulties with its "beneficiaries."

II. THE INCOMES AND OCCUPATIONS OF THE POOR

The typical living space for a poor household in Japan during the 1890s was a one-room apartment 9 feet wide and 12 feet long (*ni-ken kyu-shaku*) in a long one-story multiplex apartment house called *nagaya*. Except for size and density, the physical layout of the poor-quarters of Japan would have looked very much like a cheap motor inn with its rows of one-story multiroom buildings in America today. The 9 × 12 room contains six Japanese straw mats (*tatami*), although one *tatami*-equivalent of space (3 × 6) is allocated to the use for the vestibule, closet, and kitchen. Ordinarily, one *tatami* area would be the absolute minimum sleeping space for one person, although many poor households might have to put up with less space per capita than that.[17]

Table 1 presents data on the income of

TABLE 1.

The Incomes of the Poor in Tokyo and Related Data, Selected Years

Year (1)	Household income per month (yen) (2)	Size of household (persons) (3)	Poverty income per capita per annum (yen) (4)	(4) in 1934–36 prices (yen) (5)	Average living space per poor household (tatami) (6)	Rent per month (yen) (7)	National income per capita (yen) (8)	(4) as percent of (8) (9)
1886	4.00	4.0	12	39	5.0	0.30	18	66.7
1897	10.00	4.0	30	59	5.0	0.75	35	85.7
1912	15.43	3.6	51	68	4.5	3.00	81	63.4
1921	61.83	4.3	173	113	4.5	4.20	194	89.2
1926	49.45	3.9	152	117	6.4	6.79	218	69.7
1929	48.84	3.9	149	126	7.7	14.27	212	70.3
1957	17,432.00	3.9	53,700	174	8.4	634.00	91,200	59.0

Sources: 1886—Broad estimates from information in "Tokyofuka hinmin no shinkyo" [Truths about the Poor in Tokyo], a series of articles that appeared in the *Chōya shimbun* in 1886, reprinted in Taketoshi Nishida (ed.), *Toshi kasō shakai* [Urban Lower-Class Society] (Tokyo: Seikatsusha, 1949), pp. 263–77. 1897—Estimates from data in Gen'nosuke Yokoyama, *Nihon no kasō shakai* [Japan's Lower-Class Society] (Tokyo, 1898). 1912—Taken from Ministry of Home Affairs, *Saimin chōsa tōkeihyō tekiyō* [Statistical Abstracts on the Poor Survey] (Tokyo, 1914); the survey covered Honjo and Fukagawa in Tokyo. 1921—Taken from Ministry of Home Affairs, *Saimin chōsa tōkeihyō* [Statistics from the Poor Survey] (Tokyo, 1922). 1926—Estimated from data in Yasoo Kusama, "Daitokio no saimingai to seikatsu no taiyō" [The Poor-Quarters and Their Living Conditions in Greater Tokyo], *Nihon chiri taikei* [Compendium of Japanese Geography] (Tokyo, 1930), Vol. III, pp. 370–80; Kusama's sources were the poor surveys by the city of Tokyo. 1929—*Ibid.*, p. 372. 1957—Metropolitan Government of Tokyo, *Tokyoto chiku kankyō chōsa* [A Survey of Area Environments in Tokyo] (Tokyo, 1959).

National income, population, and prices—Kazushi Ohkawa and associates, *The Growth Rate of the Japanese Economy* (Tokyo: Kinokuniya, 1957).

Tokyo's poor for selected years over a stretch of sixty years—since the beginning of Japan's modern economic growth in the 1880s. The data illustrate how living conditions in the poverty pockets of Tokyo have improved over these years. However, a word of caution is in order about the nature of the data before we proceed. The quality of the data given varies. The household incomes and rents for 1886 and 1897 are only broad estimates based on the observations of the ghetto life by the Meiji intellectuals discussed in the preceding section of this paper. The data for the other years come from official surveys of the poor, as explained in the notes attached to Table 1. The surveys of 1912, 1921, 1926, and 1929 were sample surveys based on the definition of a poor household as one which was located in the poor-quarters, paying a monthly rent not exceeding a specified level, and whose head was engaged in unskilled and miscellaneous occupations, earning not more than a specified amount per month. The 1957 survey was an exhaustive census of poverty pockets meeting certain qualifications regarding living conditions, public safety, and housing quality. On the whole, for this purpose the poverty pocket had to be a cluster of fifty or more dwelling units of qualities markedly lower than the housing standards of the general community. Exceptions were allowed for the clusters of fewer units in the case of improvised shacks.

Table 1 suggests that the income of the poor in real terms has improved considerably over time (columns 1–5). Despite the dilapidated housing structures and generally disagreeable habitats, housing space at least has seen some improvement over time both per household and per capita (columns 3 and 6). These modest improvements were purchased by rising rents relative to household incomes before World War II (columns 2 and 7). In 1957, rent was exceptionally low relative to household income, but this was due to many unusual circumstances. Many of the dwelling units in the ghettos of 1957 were obsolete public housing units on which rents were controlled, abandoned military barracks and dormitories, bombed-out factory structures, decaying private and public buildings, improvised shacks, and additions and extensions built around them. Table 1 also suggests that, contrary to the popular myth which associates poverty with many progeny, the average size of the poor household is small (column 3).

Despite some improvement in ghetto life over

time, the poor have always remained poor relative to members of the society at large. The per capita income of the poor has always been lower than national income per capita. Since the subject of this paper is poverty in Tokyo, however, a more appropriate comparison would be with the average income in Tokyo. Unfortunately, the data for the latter are not available except for the postwar years. In 1957, personal income per capita of the residents of the metropolis of Tokyo was 70 percent above national income per capita.[18] Prior to World War II, because of the greater geographical income disparities associated with a less advanced economy, Tokyo may have enjoyed relatively greater advantages of income and amenities over the rest of Japan than it does today. In terms of income per capita, Tokyo's advantages may have been in the order of 2 to 3 times as high as the national average. With Tokyo's income at a level 2.5 times higher than national income per capita, for example, one would infer from columns 8 and 9 of Table 1 that income per head of the poor in Tokyo had fluctuated between 25 and 40 percent of average per capita income in Tokyo.[19] While there is no doubt that the real income of the poor has increased during the last several decades, it may be fair to say that the poor today are just as poor relative to the general community as eighty years ago.

The poor earn their pitiful incomes through a variety of low-paying jobs. The diversity and irregularity of these jobs, as well as the multiple job-holding common to the poor, make it extremely difficult to summarize the employment characteristics of the poor. Statistical neatness is least important in this regard. For example, the poor in 1957 can be classified cogently as follows: paid employment (subdivided into blue-collar and white-collar categories); self-employment (subdivided into craftsmen, entrepreneurs, and others); those out of the labor force; and miscellaneous, including those not elsewhere specified.[20] This classification conceals the instability of employment status, frequent job changes, unclear job demarcations, low skill levels, moonlighting, blurred differences between the occupied and unoccupied status, and other characteristics that differentiate the activities of the poor from the regular and steady employment of the nonpoor with clear job territories, working hours, and rates of remuneration. The blur of poverty-linked occupations increases as we move back in time. For the

Meiji period, the only sensible way of describing the occupations of the poor is to say that they struggled to eke out a living by whatever activities they could lay their hands on.

Among the activities of the poor during the Meiji period, there were three least remunerative occupations which were close substitutes: i.e., carrying, mud-handling, and ragpicking. The representative carrying jobs were rickshaw-pulling and hand-carting. For this reason, the number of rickshaw pullers in an area was regarded a reasonable indicator of the degree of its poverty. The handling of mud, sand, and pebbles was an activity associated with the construction industry. Finally, ragpicking was an activity of scavenging in the streets. It was clearly the least preferred form of gainful employment, and many of the poor would rather beg or steal than pick rags under severe circumstances. All the data, private and public, indicate that the earnings from ragpicking are far below those from other activities the poor are capable of.[21] Ragpicking is on the borderline between employment and vagrancy.

Closely related to, but somewhat better off than, the ragpicker is the rag buyer, who buys waste materials from households. The capital with which the rag buyer acquires waste materials is advanced to him on a daily basis by a rag dealer (*shikiriya*), who stores, classifies, and disposes of the materials obtained from rag buyers and ragpickers. Both rag buyers and ragpickers are highly dependent upon the rag dealer, who provides them with shelter for a nominal rent in the shanties improvised in his junkyard. The people to whom rag dealers sell their collections are called "processors" (*kakō gyōsha*), who are specialized by category of material and who, after proper treatment of the materials bought from the rag dealers, pass them on to factories and plants. Ragpickers, rag buyers, rag dealers, and processors among them constitute an industry which the Japanese call "regenerated resources industry" (*saisei shigen gyō*).[22] Some call it *shigen saisei gyo*—"resource regeneration industry," which, though a mere reshuffling of terms, conveys the sense of a dynamic process that characterizes this industry. It is also the preferred expression because of its favorable implication for the ragpicker as an agent of resource regeneration. One who regenerates resources may eventually regenerate oneself. This psychological dimension will be discussed in Section IV below.

Table 2 shows the size of the "resource regeneration industry" in Tokyo and its change over time. Ragpicking and rag buying as poverty-linked occupations have demonstrated a remarkable staying power. The "resource regeneration industry" expanded remarkably during the early postwar years, reaching its peak in terms of employment in 1952. Table 2 indicates that, except for 1940, rag buyers have always been more numerous than ragpickers. When employment in this industry was increasing during the early postwar years, the number of pickers increased more slowly than the number of buyers. Since 1952, pickers have been decreasing faster than buyers. This is understandable, because rag buying is somewhat more respectable than ragpicking. It may be noted that the number of rag dealers has increased in recent years. Why this has occurred is somewhat enigmatic, but it may well have been due to the increase in the productivity of ragpickers and rag buyers associated with more efficient methods of junk collection. At the centers of junk trade today, we often see bicycle-pulled carts with pneumatic tires on their wheels, small three-wheeled motor vehicles, and, in more favorable cases, trucks of varying sizes. When we recall that the ragpicker's sole means of production during the Meiji period were a bamboo basket and a long stick, we notice that the general progress of the economy and technology has touched even the lowest boundary of gainful employment, such as ragpicking.

III. THE PERSONALITY PROBLEMS OF THE POOR

Whatever the rate of change in the economy and society may be, the average person seems to possess the will and ability to keep up with it. The poor are those who fall behind the general pace of economic growth and social change. Why do they fail where the average person succeeds? This question interested the Japanese government in the closing years of the Meiji era. The official inquiries into the state and problems of the poor in 1911 and 1912 tried to illumine the issue by asking the poor to name the predominant causes for their predicament. More than twenty causes for poverty were mentioned. These can be grouped under a few major headings arranged according to the degree of in-

TABLE 2.

Employment in the "Resource Regeneration Industry" in Tokyo, Selected Years (Number of persons)

Year	Pickers	Buyers	Dealers	Processors
1896[a]	788	6,153	n.a.	n.a.
1940[b]	7,000	2,000	260	370
1947[c]	5,800	7,900	n.a.	n.a.
1952	7,300	11,800	n.a.	n.a.
1954	6,800	10,500	854	608
1960	4,800	7,200	940	1,100
1965	1,700	5,800	972	1,074

n.a.—not available.

[a] Kunijiro Tashiro (ed.), *Nihon shakai fukushi no kisoteki kenkyū* [Basic Studies on Social Welfare in Japan] (Tokyo: Doshinsha, 1965), p. 92.

[b] Metropolitan Government of Tokyo, *Saisei shigen gyōkai no enkakau* [A Short History of the Regenerated Resources Industry] (mimeographed, undated), p. 5.

[c] Data for this and ensuing years were supplied to the author from the worksheets in the Sanitation Bureau of the metropolitan government of Tokyo.

dividual responsibility for poverty that they suggest. At one extreme, there are "acts of God" over which individuals clearly have no control. At another extreme, there are personal weaknesses like debauchery, gambling, or excessive drinking for which individuals can clearly be held responsible. Table 3 presents the result of this type of grouping applied to the 1911 data.

Eliminating those who either equivocated or gave no answers, one notes that nearly 70 percent of the poor had been reduced to their current difficulties by the factors which they could not have controlled, such as "acts of God," general economic factors, aging, sickness, and death in the family. A fifth of the poor admitted that their personal deficiencies were to blame for their poverty. A tenth either mentioned causes other than those specified so far or said that they could think of no special causes for their poverty. The source unfortunately does not illustrate what these "other causes" are. One may suppose, however, that at least some of these may have suggested that they had lived in poverty as long as they could remember. Conspicuous among the causes for poverty specified in the source is the absence of any tendency on the part of the poor to blame their predicament on their parents and forebears. Perhaps a large proportion of the "miscellaneous" and "ambiguous" answers were of this nature, to the embarrassment of both the interviewees and the officials doing the interviews.[23]

The data referring to ragpickers in Table 3 present a different picture concerning the weights of various factors responsible for poverty from that of the poor in general. More than half of the ragpickers in the sample admitted that their current predicament was due to their personal weaknesses. The greater weight of personal causes for poverty among ragpickers than among the poor in general is striking indeed. It may well be that when one has fallen so low that one has to subsist on the waste in the streets, one is likely to give up any pretenses to respectability.

A recent study of ragpickers undertaken by a group of sociologists indicates much the same picture as fifty years ago. The study, which was conducted in 1959–60, was of 90 ragpickers working for two out of some 60 rag dealers in the largest center of the rag business in today's Tokyo, Motoki-cho, Adachi-ku (marked No. 6 on Fig. 1).[24] When the factors that had led these ragpickers to their present trade are grouped by the method used for Table 3, 23 out of 90 are seen to have said that World War II was responsible for their current status. No "acts of God" as such were mentioned in this study. "Economic factors" accounted for

TABLE 3.
The Distribution of the Poor and Ragpickers by Factors Responsible for Their Poverty, Male Heads of Household, Tokyo, 1911

Factors responsible for poverty	Poor as a whole		Ragpickers	
	Number	Percent	Number	Percent
"ACTS OF GOD": flood, fire, crop failure, etc.	190	7	3	3
ECONOMIC FACTORS: bankruptcy, unemployment, unstable jobs, low wages, inflation, low demand for labor.	917	35	14	13
BIOLOGICAL FACTORS: aging, illness, death in the family, death of the principal earner, large family.	713	27	26	23
PERSONAL FACTORS: no skills, no education, incompetence, laziness, debauchery, excessive drinking, gambling, speculation, debts, family breakup.	536	21	61	55
MISCELLANEOUS: "no special causes," not elsewhere classified.	251	10	7	6
TOTAL	2,607	100	111	100
NEBULOUS ANSWERS: no answers, those hard to interpret.	224		12	

Source: Ministry of Home Affairs, *Saimin chōsa tōkeihyō* [Statistics on the Poor-Survey] (Tokyo, 1912), Table 23. The report refers to the poor in selected areas of Shitaya-ku and Asakusa-ku.

the downfall of 29 ragpickers. Seven said that they were in this trade because they could do no other work because of age and sickness. Finally, 28 ragpickers attributed their predicament to personal deficiencies of all kinds. These factors were even more intensely personal than those mentioned in relation to the poor and ragpickers of 1911 in Table 3. They included family discord, quarrels with friends, broken romances, gambling, abortive attempts at quick riches, embezzlement, unidentified emotional troubles, and so on.[25]

What should we make of the fact that such high proportions of the poor and, especially, of ragpickers voluntarily admitted that their unfortunate conditions were due to their personal deficiencies and hence largely of their own making? Would anyone in his right mind confess to strangers, whether public officials or sociologists, that his poverty and hardship were caused by factors which he could very well have avoided had he tried? Pride alone would induce anyone to blame his difficulties on society in general or, at best, on forces of circumstances beyond his control, whatever the truth might have been. The plausibility of this kind of defense mechanism as a normal psychological factor is important for the interpretation of the materials presented above, for two reasons. First, to the extent that this defense mechanism was present on the part of the poor, the weight of the "personal factors" might have been greater than indicated in Table 3 and by the social survey of 1959–60 just summarized. In particular, many of the ragpickers of Motokicho, who fifteen years after World War II blamed their status on the war, may have been covering up true but embarrassing reasons. They were not the only victims of that war.

The second reason for the importance of the defense mechanism just mentioned is that there were a substantial number of the poor who did not resort to this mechanism and that the breakdown of self-defense may have been an aspect of a deeper problem of personality disorganization. The ordinary person would not easily admit that his poverty was of his own making. One who did would be a person to whom personal pride and self-esteem no longer mattered. He was willing to capitulate by conceding failure and powerlessness. He was resigned to his fate and had lost the bounce, energy, and stamina required to rise above pov-

erty and take a new lease on life. The poor who fit this characterization are literally "down and out." Especially grave from this point of view are the personality problems of ragpickers. The contempt of the general public for ragpickers has always been deep. The police have maintained close watch over ragpickers as potentially dangerous vagrants, while the public health authorities have regulated the location and standards of the rag business from a sanitary point of view. If the general community regards ragpickers as of no more value than the junk they pick, ragpickers themselves tend to accept this lowly status and social role. How to help these social failures "up and into" the ordinary world is a great social problem. The story of the "Ants' Villa" in Tokyo, to which we now turn, is one of the few examples of psychological rehabilitation, spiritual growth, and economic success among ragpickers.

IV. THE "ANTS' VILLA" IN TOKYO, A RAGPICKERS' COMMUNITY

The "Ants' Villa" is a community of 50 households located on Tract No. 8 of the reclaimed land at the waterfront of Tokyo Bay belonging to the administrative district of Koto-ku.[26] The economic activity of the community consists in recovering value from all kinds of junk—cans, glass, paper, rags, rubber, scrap metals, straw, wood, etc. Everyday life is organized on a thoroughly communal basis, beginning and ending with a group prayer in the community chapel, which is a constituent of the Catholic archdiocese of Tokyo. The work process is highly rationalized; junk is collected in large quantities from major business concerns in the central area of Tokyo, transported to the community workshops in several trucks, sorted out by teams of worker-residents, packed by machines, and delivered to the commercial processors of these materials for further rounds of industrial use. The organization of work in the community compares favorably with any efficient small-scale firm in Tokyo. The compound of the community is spacious (16,700 square meters). In addition to the chapel, workshops, and equipment just mentioned, there are four residential structures meeting reasonable standards, a house for children's recreation, a guest house, a community restaurant where the residents take their regular meals, and a store of daily necessities with adjacent facilities for between-meal snacks. The community is clean, quiet, and prosperous. Its standard of living is above the social minimum in every sense.

Fifteen years ago, however, the Ants' Villa was a totally different place. Not only was its location different, but it was "subminimum" in every sense, verging in fact upon the underworld of vagrants and criminals. The history of the Ants' Villa at its present location dates back to June, 1960, prior to which it was located at a corner of the Sumida Park on the right bank of the Sumida River (marked by an asterisk in Fig. 1). The Ants' Villa leased its present site from the metropolitan government of Tokyo for 15 million yen, payable in installments over five years. The Ants' Villa accepted these terms in 1958, when they seemed extraordinarily stiff with reference to the financial capability of ordinary workers. The annual installment, which amounted to 3 million yen, was 10 percent of the annual earnings of 100 able-bodied workers working full time at the monthly rate of 25,000 yen. During 1955–58, however, the average monthly earnings of the regular employees in Japanese manufacturing was less than 20,000 yen.[27] Moreover, the taming of the wild land, which was a refuse disposal area for Tokyo, required a considerable initial investment, to be borne entirely by the Ants' Villa. All of this meant that the Ants' Villa had to work many times as hard and as ingeniously as regular workers, and to formulate and implement a re-

settlement plan with the care and efficiency of a first-class business enterprise.

The Ants' Villa surmounted these obstacles, despite the fact that its members were ragpickers, whom one would not ordinarily expect to have regular work habits, sustained efforts, foresight, planning, saving, investment, or other qualities indispensable to an efficient enterprise. It is a fact of great importance that the ragpickers of the Ants' Villa, during their Sumida Park period (1950–60), succeeded in reforming themselves and in creating a community endowed with these qualities.

The Ants' Villa was organized as a ragpickers' cooperative by Motomu Ozawa when he took charge of fifteen unemployed ragpickers dismissed by a retiring ragdealer in 1950. Ozawa (born in 1895), who was a successful businessman before the war, was ruined by being caught in the disorders in China following Japan's defeat. When he returned to war-torn Asakusa of Tokyo after the war, he was homeless and penniless. He found a lumber yard lying idle in Sumida Park; the lumber mill had been destroyed by a typhoon. In order to accommodate himself and his fellow ragpickers, Ozawa subleased the lumber yard from a philanthropic association which had previously leased it from the metropolitan government to make lumber for housing projects for repatriates from overseas territories of Japan. In organizing the ragpickers' cooperative, Ozawa was assisted by Toru Matsui. Matsui (born in 1910) directed the Taiwan Theatrical Association during World

The symbol of Ants' Villa which means the spirit of Ants' Villa can lead the world. (PHOTO COURTESY SHINZO TSUKAMOTO)

War II and returned to Japan in 1946. Before he joined the ragpickers of the Ants' Villa, he had taken on a variety of jobs, including junk collection in the military compounds of the Allied Forces, land reclamation in a mountain region, and promotion of a movement for world government. The constitution, by-laws, and formal organizational structure of the Ants' Villa were Matsui's artifacts.[28]

Ozawa's practical leadership and Matsui's intellectual counsel would perhaps have maintained the Ants' Villa as a ragpickers' cooperative. But an efficient cooperative was still a far cry from being an effective community. In the light of the blighted outlook and shattered personality which were described in the preceding section and which applied equally to the ragpickers of the Ants' Villa, its development into an effective community seemed to be fraught with enormous difficulties. But an additional stroke of luck was in store for the Ants' Villa. Early in 1950, the person who was to become the spiritual catalyst for the community development of the Ants' Villa moved into the nearby area of Asakusa. She was Miss Satoko Kitahara, a young lady twenty years of age. The historic introduction of Miss Kitahara to the Ants' Villa was brought about through the person of Brother Zeno, a Polish Franciscan. One day in December, 1950, on his way to the Ants' Villa for his second visit, Brother Zeno coincidentally stopped at the Kitahara residence to ask for a prayer for the poor, as was his habit

Brother Zeno (PHOTO COURTESY SHINZO TSUKAMOTO)

whenever and wherever he met anyone. Miss Kitahara was impressed and followed Brother Zeno to visit the poor for whom she was asked to pray.[29]

Fate has strange ways of fulfilling itself. Born and raised in a professorial family, Satoko Kitahara (Elizabeth Mary, 1929–58) could have enjoyed the best of everything that Japan had to offer. It must have been unthinkable that she would die so young amid the junk piles of the Ants' Villa. She graduated from a pharmaceutical college in Tokyo in the spring of 1949 and then pursued religious study which led to her conversion to Catholicism. When Miss Kitahara visited the Ants' Villa in December, 1950, it was the first real contact with poverty she had ever experienced. Eight years later, in January, 1958, she died in the Ants' Villa.[30]

Owing to Matsui's public-relations activities and the sustained interest of the press in the work of Miss Kitahara, to whom they never failed to refer respectfully as a "university professor's graceful daughter" (*kyōju reijō*), the Ants' Villa attracted many homeless persons and families.[31] In effect, it was an open refugee camp. During the 1950s, the population of the Ants' Villa fluctuated around 150 persons in about 90 households.[32] Miss Kitahara's first job in the Ants' Villa was as matron of the children. They disliked school for obvious reasons: the other children would not tolerate them except as objects of scorn and contempt.[33] It was extremely difficult for the children of the Ants' Villa to improve their school records under these circumstances. Miss Kitahara worked with sympathy and understanding. She used her own home in Asakusa for teaching and entertaining the Ants' Villa children. She often accompanied them to school and worked in close cooperation with their teachers to remedy their deficiencies.

In May, 1951, Miss Kitahara decided to pick rags in the streets. From May to December, 1951, when the recurrence of her illness forced her to rest, she rose regularly at five in the morning; tramped in the streets picking rags; disposed of her collection in the Ants' Villa's accounting section early in the afternoon; made her rounds to visit the aged, sick, and infants in the Villa, dispensing medicine where necessary; and taught children at her home in the evening until 10 P.M. She also organized community recreation activities for children, with adult participation. These events and activities,

Right: Miss Satoko Kitahara (center), playing with the children of Ants' Villa. (PHOTO COURTESY SHINZO TSUKAMOTO)

Below: Toru Matsui and Miss Satoko Kitahara. (PHOTO COURTESY SHINZO TSUKAMOTO)

executed with Miss Kitahara's delightful ingenuity, ushered into the Ants' Villa those essential elements of community life: solidarity, identity, planning, expectation, and general warmth of feeling among people. Miss Kitahara took up her permanent residence within the Ants' Villa in 1952 and stayed there until she succumbed to the critical complications arising from her tuberculosis in 1958.[34]

The cultural interests of the Ants' Villa residents expanded. Some of them had begun to attend mass in the nearby Catholic Church of Asakusa by the end of 1951. The Church also sent a mission to the Ants' Villa to help the ragpickers improve their knowledge of Christianity.

Brother Zeno, who was tramping all over Japan, frequently dropped in for varying lengths of time. The task of putting these events in proper perspective usually fell upon Matsui, who, although an ordained Buddhist in lay clothing, included an extensive knowledge of the world's great religions among his intellectual accomplishments.[35] Matsui complied with the wishes of his fellow ragpickers by narrating biblical stories to them. The ragpickers, despised souls in contemporary Japan, could easily identify themselves in the biblical world. They were comforted by the stories that beggars, lepers, thieves, prostitutes, and other despicable persons were raised to a spiritual height by their simple faith in Christ.

Ozawa, chief of the Ants' Villa, was particularly impressed with the principles of the Christian way of life. Early in his career as a ragpicker, he acquired a copy of the New Testament in Japanese and had since been studying the Bible assiduously. One day in the summer of 1952, Ozawa summed up his feelings about Christianity in words which were more vivid and understandable to the ragpickers than any preaching of biblical scholars. He observed that there were considerable similarities between the Christ-Christian relations and Japan's traditional *oyabun-kobun* relations. (It is well known that in interpersonal relations within an informal group the Japanese tend to simulate a family. The group is called *ikka,* "house," where *oyabun,* "parent surrogate," presides over a number of *kobun,* "child surrogate." A well-run "house" embodies the traditional principles of a good Japanese family, emphasizing solidarity, loyalty, and survival.) Ozawa asked whether Christians were not like *kobun* in the "House of Christ." The decisive superiority of Christianity, according to Ozawa, was that the supreme *Oyabun,* Jesus, sacrificed his life to save his *kobun,* while the Japanese system was often liable to degenerate into *oyabun's* despotism at the expense of *kobun.* For this reason, Ozawa was quite willing to drink wine from Christ's glass to pledge his loyalty to him as his *kobun.* (Drinking from the same glass is a traditional Japanese vow to effect the bond of *oyabun* and *kobun.*) The ragpickers of the Ants' Villa were impressed by Ozawa's interpretation. Ten of them forthwith joined him in becoming Christ's *kobun.* Matsui was also prevailed upon to join them as their counsellor in their new spiritual venture. Thus twelve new Christians were solemnly baptized in the Catholic Church of Asakusa. This was only the beginning; in a few years' time, the Christianization of the Ants' Villa was total.

The psychological breakthrough of its resi-

dents and the development of the Ants' Villa as a genuine community with a sense of purpose and solidarity made possible the next step in its history. Although not illegal, the Ants' Villa was squatting on a public park. There was no question about the desirability of restoring its site to public use. What the Ants' Villa wanted to avoid was a purposeless eviction accompanied by a dispersion of its members. The metropolitan government had so far shown no interest in the question of community relocation; i.e., as mentioned in Section I, the public authorities were interested either in the alleviation of individual poverty or in the removal or improvement of insular poverty. The Ants' Villa patiently negotiated with the metropolitan government, emphasizing that it would be poor social policy to destroy a community which had demonstrated its moral integrity and economic efficiency. In January, 1958, the metropolitan government finally yielded to the request of the Ants' Villa, though at a price outlined at the beginning of this section. Rejoicing at the news of the definite possibility for the relocation of the Ants' Villa as a community, Miss Kitahara passed on a few days later. After two-and-a-half years of planning and preparation, the Ants' Villa moved to its present site in June, 1960.

A machine for cutting scrap iron. (PHOTO COURTESY SHINZO TSUKAMOTO)

CONCLUSION

A dynamic socioeconomic system is full of shifts and changes. Individuals and institutions must accommodate themselves to the requirements of the dynamic system with ingenuity, flexibility, and speed. The problem of poverty arises because not all individuals or institutions are capable of the required adjustments. Urbanization is an aspect of shifting resource allocation, as well as an ingredient of cultural change. Where there are shifts and changes, there are lags and gaps. Urban insular poverty is a gap between the individuals' or households' resources and the cost of housing of adequate standards. Behind this is the lag between the individuals' or households' employment capability and changes in the occupational structure of a dynamic economy.

Our review of the historical experience of Japan indicates several policy areas for minimizing the social cost of a dynamic urban industrialism. These are suggested with special effectiveness by the causes of poverty we have examined. They include: (1) vigorous housing policy and urban policy far in advance of urban growth; (2) efficient institutions of help and remedy to counteract the dislocations arising from war and "acts of God"; (3) economic policy to stabilize general economic conditions and the employment market in particular; (4) social policy to neutralize the effects of age, sickness, and family size; and (5) what might be called "psychocultural policy" to regenerate and strengthen the personality, outlook, and will-to-live of the hard-core poor.

We would like to emphasize the last policy area, for it is novel and tends to be overlooked in practice. Nations and cities have often acquired substantial experience in the other policy areas. But the "psychocultural" policy has only begun to receive some attention in recent years in connection with the antipoverty community action programs under the War on Poverty. The professions required for an effective policy of this type come under various new titles: e.g., "animateur," "encourager," "nonprofessional" social worker, etc.[36] Governmental, philanthropic, and religious organizations would maximize the effectiveness of ongoing welfare projects by a conscious reorientation of the required means and methods along this line. A new outlook is also needed on the part of the society at large toward the maximum generation of what Sorokin calls "love energy" in order to ensure the success of psychocultural policies.[37]

NOTES

1. Robert A. Dentler, *American Community Problems* (New York: McGraw-Hill, 1968), p. 5.

2. Once a viewpoint gets hold of a man, it tends to dominate him for some time. The nature of poverty roundly defined in this and preceding paragraphs emerged as a guideline for my previous contribution, "Japan," in *Low Income Groups and Methods of Dealing with Their Problems* (Paris: OECD, 1965). Professor S. M. Miller thought it "striking" but did not think that it was entirely accurate. See "Poverty in an International Context," Convener's Paper for the Working Group on Poverty, World Congress of Sociology, Evian, France, September, 1966. Nevertheless, I still feel that poverty as a relative deprivation and as something having a definable historical dimension is a useful guideline for poverty research in the context of economic development.

3. The reports in the *Chōya shimbun* are reproduced in Taketoshi Nishida (ed.), *Toshi kasō shakai* [Urban Lower-Class Society] (Tokyo: Seikatsusha, 1949); and in Kunijiro Tashiro (ed.), *Nihon shaki fukushi no kisoteki kenkyū* [Basic Studies on Social Welfare in Japan] (Tokyo: Doshinsha, 1965). With the exception of some overlapping in relation to the *Chōya shimbun* reports, these two books complement each other as compendia of historical materials on poverty and welfare in Japan.

4. Gen'nosuke Yokoyama, *Nihon no kasō shakai* [Japan's Lower-Class Society] (Tokyo, 1898), reprinted by Chūō rōdō gakuen (Central Labor Academy), Tokyo, in 1949 and the Iwanami Book Company in 1958.

5. Especially see Yasoo Kusama, "Daitokio no saimingai to seikatsu no taiyō" [The Poor-Quarters and Their Living Conditions in Greater Tokyo], in *Nihon chiri taikei* [Compendium on Japanese Geography] (Tokyo, 1930), Vol. 3, pp. 370–80.

6. Yokoyama, *op. cit.* (Iwanami version), pp. 28–29.

7. *Ibid.*, p. 22.

8. Teizo Inoue, *Hinminkutsu to shōsū dōbō* [The Islands of the Poor and Minority Brothers] (Tokyo: Ganshobo, 1923), pp. 1–34.

9. Kusama, *op. cit.*, p. 380. For an overview of Japanese urbanization, see Thomas O. Wilkinson, *The Urbanization of Japanese Labor 1868–1955* (Amherst: University of Massachusetts Press, 1965).

10. Tokyo Prefecture, Social Affairs Section, *Shūdanteki furyō jūtaku chiku jōkyō chōsa* [A Survey of Areas with Clusters of Substandard Houses] (Tokyo, 1930).

11. Each *ku* consists of many *chō*. I follow R. P. Dore's usage of "borough" for *ku* and "ward" for *chō*. See *City Life in Japan* (Berkeley: University of California Press, 1958). Many Japanese often translate *ku* as "ward."

12. Tokyo Metropolis, Living Conditions Bureau, *Tokioto chiku kankyō chōsa* [A Survey of Area Environments] (Tokyo, 1959).

13. J. K. Galbraith, *The Affluent Society* (Boston: Houghton Mifflin, 1958), Ch. 23.

14. Koji Taira, "Public Assistance in Japan," *Journal of Asian Studies*, Vol. 27 (November, 1967).

15. Tokyo Metropolis, Living Conditions Bureau, *Tomin no seikatsu* [The Living Conditions of the Metropolitan Inhabitants] (Tokyo, 1965), Ch. 8.

16. This also applies to the prewar period. Kusama points out that the "scattered" poor are much more numerous in all than the "clustered" poor. *Op. cit.*, p. 170.

17. For a useful description of housing standards in Japan, see Dore, *op. cit.*, Ch. 4.

18. *Tomin no seikatsu, op. cit.*, p. 149.

19. Data in Table 1 are too rough to warrant rigorous inferences about the cyclicity of the relative income of the poor. But a note at least that the relative position of the poor in Tokyo vis-à-vis the whole nation improved in economically good years like 1897 and 1921 and deteriorated in economically bad years like 1886, 1912, and the 1920s. Perhaps 1957 is a case apart. Interestingly enough, this cyclical pattern conforms rather closely to the general pattern of relative wages over time which we have extensively documented elsewhere. See Koji Taira, "The Dynamics of Japanese Wage Differentials

1881–1959," unpublished Ph.D. dissertation, Stanford University, 1961.

20. *Tomin no seikatsu, op. cit.*, p. 291.

21. According to Yokoyama's data, the daily earnings from nine unskilled jobs averaged 0.36 yen, while those from ragpicking averaged 0.15 yen. The 1912 official survey of the poor noted that the average monthly income of the poor was 12.77 yen, while that of ragpickers was 4.25 yen. (These sources are cited in connection with Table 1.) In 1959–60, a selected group of ragpickers earned 9,097 yen per month. For the source, see n. 24 below. In the same years, Tokyo's unskilled workers earned on the average 16,584 yen per month, as may be seen from data in *Tomin no seikatsu, op. cit.*, p. 278.

22. Tokyo Metropolis, Sanitation Bureau, *Saisei shigen gyōkai no enkaku* [A Short History of the Regenerated Resources Industry] (mimeographed, undated).

23. The 1912 survey of the poor in different parts of Tokyo (*op. cit.*) adopted a different approach to the classification of causes for poverty. The poor were first classified into those who were born poor and those who had become poor in their own generation. Twenty-eight percent of the poor in the survey fell into the first category. Those in the second category were then asked to mention causes for their poverty and were permitted to mention more than one. These causes were distributed as follows: "acts of God"—17.2 percent; economic factors —44.1 percent; biological factors—21.6 percent; personal factors—13.2 percent; and all other causes—3.9 percent. The causes mentioned averaged at 2.1 per household. There was no breakdown of the data by occupation.

24. Eiichi Isomura (ed.), *Nihon no suramu* [Slums in Japan] (Tokyo: Seishin shobo, 1962).

25. *Ibid.*, p. 29. Three ragpickers had no answers.

26. See the circled asterisk in Fig. 1. The formal title of the Ants' Villa is *Ari no kai* (Association "Ants"). This follows the usual practice of naming a social service organization, although the Ants' Villa has not yet acquired this status. It is popularly called *Ari no machi* (literally, Ants' Town). But the whole community is like one huge household, so that the residents themselves prefer to have it called Ants' Villa when a translation is necessary.

27. Japanese Government, Economic Planning Agency, *Keizai yōran* [Economic Abstract] (Tokyo, 1961), p. 232.

28. Matsui has also offered the reading public his numerous writings on the Ants' Villa, on which this section of the present paper is based. For an overall view of the Ants' Villa, see his *Ari no machi kiseki* [The Miracle of the Ants' Villa] (Tokyo: Kokudosha, 1953); *Binbo tsuiho—Ari no machi no keizaigaku* [Conquest of Poverty: Economics of the Ants' Villa] (Tokyo, Sankei shinsho, 1956); and "Ari no machi no kuraku" [Trials and Triumphs of the Ants' Villa], a series of four articles in the Sunday Editions of the *Yomiuri shimbun* (Tokyo), starting on November 13, 1966.

29. Brother Zeno (1882?–   ) came to Japan in 1930 as a missionary monk with the Knights of Mary in Nagasaki. His prewar and wartime activities were confined within Nagasaki, because of the Japanese government's control over foreigners. With the end of the war, Zeno began his famous wandering throughout Japan, helping the poor wherever he went. See Toru Matsui, *Zeno shinu hima nai—Ari no machi no shimpu jinsei henreki* [Zeno Is Too Busy to Die: Life of the "Father" of the Ants' Villa] (Tokyo: Shunjusha, 1966).

30. For a detailed description and interpretation of Miss Kitahara's life and work, see Toru Matsui, *Ari no machi no mariya—Kitahara Satoko* [Satoko Kitahara, Mary of the Ants' Villa] (Tokyo: Chiseisha, 1958, and Shunjusha, 1963).

31. The Ants' Villa by the Sumida River must have been very much like Resurrection City by the Potomac in Washington, D.C., though very much smaller and poorer than the latter.

32. The Living Conditions Bureau of the metropolitan government estimated the Ants' Villa population to be 164 persons in 69 households in August, 1951. In 1957, the same bureau put it at 150 persons in 87 households. The former figures are quoted in Matsui's 1953 book (*op. cit.*, p. 152). The latter figures appear in the 1957 survey of area environments (*op. cit.*, p. 134). Furthermore, the eviction of squatters in other parts of Tokyo sometimes swelled the population of the Ants' Villa, as can be inferred from Matsui's various books.

33. The place of ragpickers in Japanese society is not unlike that of the minority groups called *burakumin*, which is intensively discussed in George de Vos and Hiroshi Wagatsuma, *Japan's Invisible Race* (Berkeley: University of California Press, 1966), esp. Chs. 8 and 9.

34. The story given here of Miss Kitahara's work in the Ants' Villa is drawn from Matsui's book on her (*op. cit.*). A well-known theatrical troupe, *Geijutsu-za*, performed a play adapted from this book in July, 1958. In January, 1959, a famous sculptor, Misawa Hiroshi, carved a statue in honor of Miss Kitahara. In 1963, the book was translated into Korean by Mr. Su-kil Pak, head of the Federation of Young Catholic Workers of Korea, and became a spiritual stimulus for the organization of "Ants' Villas" in Seoul and Puzan under Mr. Pak's guidance.

35. As a Zen practitioner of long training, Matsui puts on a great air of casualness in his speech and writing, which nevertheless does not conceal from his audience and readers the great depth of his scholarly learning. The story of his espousal of Catholicism appears later in the text. But he sees no contradiction in this. There exists a basic unity of spiritual principles and training between Zen and Catholicism, he claims. On this point, he is of course not alone; for example, see Dom Aelred Graham, *Zen Catholicism* (New York: Harcourt, Brace and World, 1963).

36. Peter Marris and Martin Rein, *Dilemma of Social Reform: Poverty and Community Action in the United States* (New York: Atherton Press, 1967); William W. Biddle and Loureide J. Biddle, *Encouraging Community Development* (New York: Holt, Rinehart and Winston, 1967).

37. Pitirim A. Sorokin, *The Ways and Power of Love* (Boston: Beacon Press, 1954); Sorokin (ed.), *Forms and Techniques of Altruistic and Spiritual Growth: A Symposium* (Boston: Beacon Press, 1954).

50690